WIRTSCHAFTSGEOGRAPHISCHE STUDIEN
Heft 24/25

Herausgeber: Klaus ARNOLD
für die
Österreichische Gesellschaft für Wirtschaftsraumforschung
A-1090 Wien, Rossauer Lände 23, Tel. ++43-1-31336-5770

Schriftleitung: Albert HOFMAYER

Festschrift für Karl A. Sinnhuber
zum 80. Geburtstag

Themenschwerpunkt:
Ost-Mitteleuropa

Wien, Oktober 1999

SERVICE FACHVERLAG • WIEN

ISBN 3-85428-407-1

© SERVICE FACHVERLAG, Wien

Printed in Austria 1999

INHALT

Klaus ARNOLD: Geleitwort zu diesem Band III

Programm des Festkolloquiums am 15. Oktober 1999 V

Alois BRUSATTI: Leopold Scheidl und die Wirtschaftsgeographie VII

Tabula gratulatoria zum 80. Geburtstag von Karl A. Sinnhuber XI

Wigand RITTER: Karl A. Sinnhuber zum 80. Geburtstag 1

Karl A. SINNHUBER / M. W. DOW: Recollections of an Emeritus *(Interview, 1992)* 5

Karl A. SINNHUBER: Central Europe – Mitteleuropa – Europe Centrale : An Analysis of a Geographical Term *(Reprint from: 'Transactions and Papers 1954', Institute of British Geographers)* 14

Francis W. CARTER: The Geography of Foreign Direct Investment in Central-East Europe during the 1990's 40

Bolesław DOMAŃSKI: Regional Distribution and Selected Effects of Foreign Direct Investment in Polish Manufacturing in the 1990s 71

William F. STANLEY / Elke KNAPPE: Kaliningrad and the Changing Geopolitics of the Baltic 89

Peter JORDAN: Regionalisierung und Dezentralisierung in Rumänien – Möglichkeiten und Hindernisse 104

Walter MANSHARD: Aspekte der Urbanisierung, der Verkehrsentwicklung und der Umweltprobleme Japans 122

Robert POMBERGER / Christian STAUDACHER: Rock'n'Roll-Akrobatik-Dienstleistungen : eine unternehmensgeographische Analyse 130

GESELLSCHAFTSNACHRICHTEN 156

Verzeichnis der Autoren und Mitarbeiter dieses Bandes 162

Emeritus-Professor Karl A(emilian) Sinnhuber
geboren 10. 1. 1919

Aufnahmedatum: 24. Juni 1999
Ort: am Portage-Gletscher
nahe Anchorage,
Alaska

Ad multos annos!

GELEITWORT ZU DIESEM BAND

Der vorliegende Band der „Wirtschaftsgeographischen Studien" ist als Ehrung für Karl Sinnhuber gedacht, der nicht nur lange Zeit erfolgreich als Präsident der ÖGW hervorgetreten ist, sondern auch als Professor und Vorstand des Instituts für Wirtschaftsgeographie einen wesentlichen Beitrag zur Gestaltung und Entwicklung des Faches an der Wirtschaftsuniversität Wien geleistet hat. Dieser Festband soll dazu dienen, die Verdienste des Jubilars, der heuer seinen 80. Geburtstag begeht, zusammen mit einem Festkolloquium an der Stätte seiner langjährigen Wirksamkeit, der ehemaligen Hochschule für Welthandel, gebührend herauszustreichen. Dies veranlaßt uns, auch den bedeutendsten Beitrag, den Karl Sinnhuber der geographischen Wissenschaft gegeben hat, seinen grundlegenden Aufsatz über Mitteleuropa, in einem Neudruck in Erinnerung zu rufen.

Einen Rückblick auf das wissenschaftliche und berufliche Leben Karl Sinnhubers gibt Wigand Ritter in seiner Laudatio, die anläßlich des Festkolloquiums am 15. Oktober 1999 vorgetragen wird. Wir haben uns auch entschlossen, ein Interview, das Sinnhuber anläßlich des IGU-Kongresses 1992 für die Serie „Geographers on Film" gab, zu veröffentlichen. Darin blickt der Interviewte nicht nur auf seine wissenschaftliche Laufbahn und seine Lehrer und Vorbilder zurück, sondern verrät auch viel von seiner Einstellung und seinen Interessen.

Auch an einen anderen bedeutenden Vertreter der österreichischen Wirtschaftsgeographie wird in diesem Band erinnert. Prof. Brusatti, langjähriger Freund und Berufsgefährte, erinnert an Prof. Leopold Scheidl, den Gründer der ÖGW und sein Wirken an der damaligen Hochschule für Welthandel. Seines 25. Todestages wurde beim Festkolloquium auf ausdrücklichen Wunsch Sinnhubers ebenfalls gedacht.

Die wissenschaftlichen Beiträge beginnen mit Arbeiten von guten Freunden Sinnhubers über osteuropäische Themen. Zunächst führt Frank Carter anhand neuer statistischer Zahlen die Entwicklung der ausländischen Direktinvestitionen in Ostmitteleuropa vor. Bolesław Domański greift diese Thematik auf und verdeutlicht sie besonders am Beispiel von Polen. William Stanley und Elke Knappe streifen in einem kurzen Überblick die wesentlichsten Probleme der russischen Exklave Kaliningrad, wobei einige für viele überraschende Bezüge zur Biographie Karl Sinnhubers hergestellt werden. Schließlich widmet auch Peter Jordan seinen Beitrag einem osteuropäischen Thema, den Fragen der

Grenzbildung und Regionalisierung in Osteuropa am Beispiel Rumäniens. Diese Schwerpunktsetzung weist darauf hin, daß Sinnhuber es bereits lange vor der Ostliberalisierung verstanden hat, durch sein gewinnendes Wesen viele Freunde in Osteuropa zu gewinnen.

Darüber hinaus hatte er aber „die ganze Welt zum Freund", und bis heute ist die „ganze Welt sein Zuhause". Darauf soll der Beitrag von Walter Manshard hinweisen, der einige Aspekte und aktuelle Probleme Japans behandelt, eines Landes, in dem sich Sinnhuber auf mehreren Reisen aufgehalten hat und über das er neben Vorträgen auch zwei Publikationen veröffentlichte.

Schließlich kommt Christian Staudacher gemeinsam mit seinem Schüler Robert Pomberger, der über das Thema der Rock'n'Roll-Akrobatik eine vielbeachtete Dissertation schrieb, in einem gemeinsamen Aufsatz zu Wort. Sie erinnern daran, daß ein wesentlicher Teil der wissenschaftlichen Arbeit Sinnhubers der Geographie des Freizeitverhaltens und des Tourismus gewidmet war.

Nicht zuletzt muß ich Albert Hofmayer dafür danken, daß er als Schriftleiter ganz wesentlich an der Herausgabe dieses Festbandes mitgewirkt hat.

Ich wünsche dem Jubilar viel Freude mit diesem Festband und mit dem Kolloquium, das wir ihm zu Ehren gestaltet haben. Mit beidem ehren wir nicht nur einen bedeutenden österreichischen Wirtschaftsgeographen, sondern auch einen echten Freund.

Klaus Arnold

A Brief Note to English Speaking Readers

Since Karl A. Sinnhuber is as much a British geographer as he is an Austrian one, this Festschrift on the occasion of his eightieth birthday contains about half of the papers in English. Doing so, we hope to meet the wishes of his many friends throughout the English speaking world and to raise their interest in Austrian and Central-European geography.

Österreichische Gesellschaft für
Wirtschaftsraumforschung (ÖGW)

Abteilung *Angewandte Regional- und Wirtschafts-*
geographie (AWI) der Wirtschaftsuniversität Wien

Festkolloquium

zum 80. Geburtstag von

Emeritus-Professor Mag. Dr. Karl A. Sinnhuber

in memoriam

Professor Leopold Scheidl (1904 – 1974)

Freitag 15. Oktober 1999, 14 Uhr c. t.

Ort: Festsaal der ehemaligen Hochschule für Welthandel,
1190 Wien, Franz Klein-Gasse 1
(am Währinger Park)

Programm

Begrüßung durch den Präsidenten der ÖGW und den Leiter der Abteilung

Grußworte des Rektors der Wirtschaftsuniversität

Emer.-Prof. Dkfm. Dr. Wigand RITTER (Universität Erlangen – Nürnberg):
Karl A. Sinnhuber zum 80. Geburtstag (*)

Prof. Dr. mult. Frank CARTER, University of London:
„Where has all the money gone?"
The Geography of Foreign Direct Investment
in Central-East Europe during the 1990´s (*)

Kaffeepause / coffee break

Em. o.Univ.Prof. Dr. Alois BRUSATTI (Alt-Rektor der Wirtschaftsuniversität):
Gedenkworte für Leopold Scheidl (*)
Ordinarius für Wirtschaftsgeographie und Rektor der Hochschule für Welthandel, Gründer der Österr. Gesellschaft für Wirtschaftsraumforschung

Prof. Dr. Lutz HOLZNER, University of Wisconsin, Milwaukee:
Reglementierte und demokratisierte Kulturlandschaften: Zur Frage der sogenannten ‚Amerikanismen' in deutschen und österreichischen Städten

Präsentation der Festschrift

Gratulationen

Dankesworte des Jubilars

Ende des Festkolloquiums: ca. 18 Uhr

*Anschließend lädt der Jubilar zu einem Imbiß und Umtrunk ein /
Afterwards Karl A. Sinnhuber will invite all participants to refreshments.*

Anmerkung:

Die mit *(*)* gekennzeichneten Beiträge sind in der vorliegenden Festschrift abgedruckt.

Der Vortrag von Prof. L. Holzner enthält Ergebnisse eines DFG-Forschungsprojekts, die für den Druck in der Zeitschrift „Erdkunde" vorgesehen sind.

Leopold Scheidl und die Wirtschaftsgeographie

Gedenkworte zum 25. Todestag von Univ.-Prof. Dr. Leopold G. Scheidl [1]

Alois BRUSATTI (Baden bei Wien)

Gerade am heutigen Festtag sind die beiden Namen, die im Titel aufscheinen, untrennbar verbunden. Der Name Wirtschaftsgeographie ist im Lauf der Jahre unterschiedlich interpretiert worden, doch wir können feststellen, daß es Leopold Scheidl gelungen ist, das Fach Wirtschaftsgeographie neu zu definieren und ihm in einer Zeit zunehmender Internationalisierung der Wirtschaft eine neue Richtung zu geben. Wie kam es dazu?

Es ist nicht meine Aufgabe, das Leben und vor allem das Werk Leopold Scheidls in allen seinen Facetten hier vorzulegen. Das ist schon von kompetenterer Seite geschehen. Ich verweise nur auf den Beitrag von Kollegen Matznetter: "Leopold Scheidl, eine Betrachtung zum vollendeten 60. Lebensjahr", und auf die Beiträge zur Gedenkschrift, die als Festschrift zum 70. Geburtstag gedacht war. Der Lebenslauf, die großen Leistungen in Forschung und Lehre, aber auch der Mensch Leopold Scheidl wird uns in allen seinen Facetten nahe gebracht. Schon an der Universität Wien war er nicht nur darauf bedacht, ein strebsamer Student zu sein, sondern er bereiste schon damals fremde Länder, vor allem Südosteuropa und Kleinasien, wobei ihm seine hervorragenden Sprachkenntnisse eine große Hilfe waren. In dieser Zeit konnte man sich als Sohn eines durch Krieg und Krise verarmten Bürgertums kaum große Reisen gönnen, wenn nicht der junge Wissenschaftler mit viel Energie und durch Hilfe nicht leicht erwerbbarer Stipendien solche Reisen, die mehr Expeditionen glichen, durchführen wollte. Die Promotion erfolgte 1928. Das große und für das spätere Leben einschneidende Erlebnis war die Fahrt und der Aufenthalt in Japan, sowie die Möglichkeit, damals noch weitgehend unbekannte Gebiete Asiens zu durchstreifen. Solche Fahrten konnte nur einer erleben, der bewußt auf vieles verzichten mußte, auf Erleichterungen, die für den heute Reisenden Selbstverständlichkeiten sind. Diese besonderen Anstrengungen und Entbehrungen während der Ausbildungszeit haben Scheidl als Persönlichkeit nachhaltig geprägt.

---

[1] Emer. Prof. Dr. Alois Brusatti hat das hier abgedruckte Manuskript seiner Gedenkworte im voraus geschickt, doch gleichzeitig betont, daß er seinen Vortrag beim Festkolloquium am 15. Oktober 1999 frei halten wird. Herausgeber und Schriftleiter danken Altrektor Prof. Brusatti für seinen Einsatz und seine Mitwirkung sehr herzlich.

Es war damals schwierig, die Ergebnisse dieser erfolgreichen Reisen wissenschaftlich auszuwerten. Wirtschaftsnot und der Schatten des Krieges verhinderten vieles. Dennoch konnte sich Scheidl 1932 habilitieren, und eine mannigfache wissenschaftliche Tätigkeit in Deutschland war die Folge. Er hatte auch in Berlin das Glück, seine Frau zu finden, eine Verbindung, die für beide Seiten eine Bereicherung war.

Die Einberufung zur Wehrmacht und danach die Kriegsgefangenschaft hinderten ihn bei seiner wissenschaftlichen Arbeit, aber unterbrachen sie nicht. Er suchte und fand im wieder erstandenen Österreich die Möglichkeit, eine neue Existenz zu gründen. Seit Herbst 1947 war er Professor an der Handelsakademie in Graz. Gleichzeitig kehrte er an die Universität zurück und übernahm Lehraufträge am Geographischen Institut in Graz. Er war bald so bekannt, daß er zu Berufungsverhandlungen mit amerikanischen Universitäten eingeladen wurde. Ende 1953 entschied sich Scheidl aber dafür, mit seiner Familie in Österreich zu bleiben, und nahm einen Ruf an die damalige Hochschule für Welthandel an. Diese sollte für volle zwei Jahrzehnte seine Hauptwirkungsstätte werden, bis zu seinem plötzlichen Tod unmittelbar nach seiner Emeritierung im Dezember 1974.

Die Hochschule für Welthandel: Was erwartete ihn dort, und wie war dort die Stellung des Faches Geographie? Die Hochschule war 1898 als k.k. Exportakademie gegründet worden, um gut ausgebildete Fachleute für den Außenhandel der Monarchie hervorzubringen. Betriebswirtschaft, samt allen dazu gehörigen Techniken, etwas Nationalökonomie, Handelsrecht und Fremdsprachen waren die Schwerpunkte des Studiums; aber nicht weniger wichtig erschien den Gründern der Akademie die Handelsgeographie, wie dieses Fach bis in die Zwanzigerjahre heißen sollte. Es wurde ganz bewußt auf die guten Kenntnisse fremder Länder Wert gelegt, wobei der zuständige Lehrer auch Wirtschaftspolitik und Fragen der Währung behandeln mußte. Diese Teile, die eigentlich zum Fach Nationalökonomie gehörten, fielen dann nach dem Ersten Weltkrieg weg, da durch die Entwicklung der Volkswirtschaftslehre und das Aufkommen von Ideologien unterschiedlichster Art die Wirtschaftsgeographie überfordert gewesen wäre. Dafür wurde die Länderkunde besonders gepflegt und bekannte Wissenschaftler wie Robert Sieger, Franz Heiderich, Hermann Leiter, Bruno Dietrich und schließlich noch Hans Bobek prägten das Fach.

Nach dem Abgang des Letztgenannten wurde 1954 Leopold Scheidl zum Professor und Institutsvorstand berufen. Scheidl ging mit großem Schwung an diese Aufgabe heran, und seine Lehrveranstaltungen sowie auch die seiner Mitarbeiter galten als mustergültig. Die Ausbildung in den Seminaren, die Betreuung der Diplomarbeiten und Dissertationen waren vorbildlich. Als Prüfungsfach galt die Geographie, um im Jargon der damaligen Studenten zu sprechen, als schwierige Hürde, was aber auch als Zeichen der wissenschaftlichen Hochschätzung des Faches, wie auch der gesamten Hochschule, zu gelten vermag. Beliebt waren bei den Studenten die Exkursionen, die auch ins Ausland gingen, unter Überwindung der damals noch bestehenden Schwierigkeiten. Ein Anliegen Scheidls war es, Mitarbeiter für den Institutsbetrieb heranzubilden und zu eigenständigen wissenschaftlichen Arbeiten anzuregen. Eine beachtliche Anzahl von Professoren und anderen Wissenschaftlern kamen aus der Schule Scheidl.

Leopold Scheidl führte nicht nur sein Institut, er hatte auch Gelegenheit, weiterhin reisend die Welt zu durchforschen. Er hatte jetzt auch die Möglichkeit, seine wissenschaftlichen Forschungsarbeiten weiterzuführen und zu verwerten. Eine große Anzahl von Publikationen stammt aus dieser Zeit.

Scheidl wirkte nicht nur an der Hochschule, sondern wurde führend in vielen wissenschaftlichen Gesellschaften und fachlichen Gremien. Besonders engagierte sich Scheidl in den Bemühungen, ausländische Studenten besser an den österreichischen Hochschulen zu integrieren. Seine Erfahrungen führten unter anderem auch dazu, daß er Leiter der österreichischen Delegation bei Tagungen des Europarates wurde; er vertrat Österreich bei Sitzungen in Berlin, Paris und anderen Orten.

Seine erfolgreiche Tätigkeit als Institutsvorstand, aber auch in den diversen internationalen Gremien führten dazu, daß er für zwei Jahre – 1962 bis 1964 – zum Rektor der Hochschule für Welthandel gewählt wurde. Der Rektor war damals der Repräsentant der Hochschule nach außen und hatte neben sich nur das Professorenkollegium. Die Hochschule wuchs in diesen Jahren sowohl an Zahl der Hörer als auch des Lehrpersonals. Scheidl löste seine Aufgabe souverän. Aber gerade in dieser Zeit gab es erste Anzeichen des Wandels. Immer mehr wurden Reformgedanken gewälzt, sowohl in bezug auf eine Neufassung der Hochschulorganisation – Stichwort: Demokratisierung aller Lebensbereiche – wie auch eine Neufassung der Studien. Es machten sich Vorstellungen und Ideen breit, die man der später so bezeichneten Generation der Achtundsechziger zuschrieb. In diesen Jahren wurden auch neue Hochschulen gegründet – so etwa in Linz –, und die schon bestehenden Universitäten begannen Wirtschaftsfakultäten einzurichten; damit verlor die Hochschule für Welthandel ihre Monopolstellung. Es kam zu Fakultätentagen, und man suchte nach einem für alle entsprechenden Hochschulen einheitlichen Studium der Wirtschaftswissenschaften. Da auch neue Fächer, wie Soziologie oder Öffentliches Recht, in den Studienplan aufgenommen werden sollten, gab es heftige Diskussionen, auch um die Frage der Wirtschaftsgeographie innerhalb der wirtschaftswissenschaftlichen Studien. Scheidl erkannte wohl, daß er sich für eine bessere Bewertung seines Faches einsetzen mußte. Letztlich hat er aber als Rektor den Konsens der gesamten Hochschule den spezifischen Fachinteressen vorgezogen. In den folgenden Jahres als Prorektor mußte er in Vertretung des abwesenden Rektors einschreiten, als gegen ein Mitglied des Kollegiums schwerwiegende politische Angriffe erfolgten. Ohne hier auf Einzelheiten eingehen zu wollen, muß gesagt werden, daß der damalige Prorektor Scheidl diese heikle Angelegenheit mit großem Geschick geregelt hat.

So gelang es Scheidl, als Professor und als Rektor nutzbringend für alle zu wirken. Er besaß in den Kreisen von Politik und Wirtschaft hohes Ansehen und zahlreiche Freunde. Dies befähigte ihn auch, eine Tat zu setzen, der wir heute gedenken. Sein Schüler Josef Matznetter, später Ordinarius für Wirtschaftsgeographie in Frankfurt am Main, schreibt hierüber 1964 (Seite 9): "... über den engen Rahmen des Instituts ... hinausgreifend, gründete er 1962 die Österreichische Gesellschaft für Wirtschaftsraumforschung, die namentlich der lebendigen Verbindung zwischen der Wirtschaftsgeographie und dem öffentlichen Leben dienen soll und deren erster Präsident er wurde."

Leopold Scheidl hat damit dem Institut und seinen Mitarbeitern die Möglichkeit gegeben, über den engen Rahmen der Universität hinaus für die Wirtschaftspraxis in vielfältiger Weise wirksam zu werden. Diese Initiative hat sich gelohnt, wofür das heutige Festkolloquium der beste Beweis ist.

Zitierte Literatur:

Matznetter, J. (1964): Leopold G. Scheidl – eine Betrachtung zum vollendeten 60. Lebensjahr. In: Festschrift Leopold G. Scheidl zum 60. Geburtstag, I. Teil, Wien, S. 1-17 (Wiener Geographische Schriften, Band 18-23)

Winkler, E. / Lechleitner, H. (Hg.): Beiträge zur Wirtschaftsgeographie, I. und II. Teil, "Dem Andenken an Leopold G. Scheidl gewidmet von seinen Mitarbeitern und Schülern", Wien 1975/76 (Wiener Geographische Schriften, Bände 43-45 bzw. 46-48)

Die zitierten Bände enthalten ausführliche Lebensbeschreibungen, Würdigungen sowie Verzeichnisse der wissenschaftlichen Veröffentlichungen von Leopold G. Scheidl (1904–1974).

Tabula gratulatoria
für
Karl A. Sinnhuber
zum 80. Geburtstag

Vorbemerkung

Diese Liste von Gratulanten enthält sicher nicht alle Personen, die dem Jubilar gratulieren wollen. Die Unvollständigkeit hat mehrere Gründe:
Erstens hatten nur jene Personen überhaupt eine Eintragungsmöglichkeit, die von den Herausgebern dieser Festschrift angeschrieben wurden.
Zweitens war die Zeit zur Rückantwort ziemlich knapp bemessen, da die Tabula in der Festschrift mitpubliziert werden sollte und der Redaktionsschluß mit 24. September festgesetzt war, weil die Festschrift beim Festkolloquium am 15. Oktober 1999 übergeben werden sollte.
Drittens gab es ab Mitte September wiederholt technische Schwierigkeiten in der E-Mail- und Fax-Kommunikation, was teilweise mit der Übersiedlung der Redaktion zusammenhängt.
Herausgeber und Schriftleitung bitten alle, die aus dem einen oder anderen Grund nicht die Möglichkeit fanden, sich einzutragen, um Nachsicht.
Bei den Namen und Titeln der Gratulanten waren wir bemüht, größtmögliche Einheitlichkeit zwischen den sehr unterschiedlich ausführlichen Angaben herzustellen. Für die fallweise vorgenommene Weglassung von Titeln bitten wir daher um Verständnis.

Dr. Hertha Arnberger, Wien
Prof. Dr. Klaus Arnold, Wirtschaftsuniversität Wien
Prof. Fabrizio Bartaletti, Università di Genova
Prof. Dr. Berthold Bauer, Universität Wien
Hofrat Dr. Friedrich Benesch, Wien
Prof. Dr. Bruno Benthien, Greifswald
Prof. Dr. Klaus-A. Boesler, Bonn
Prof. Dr. Axel Borsdorf, Österr. Akademie d. Wiss. / Univ. Innsbruck
Rachel Bowles, University of Greenwich, London
Prof. em. Dr. Alois Brusatti, Baden bei Wien
Prof. Eric H. Brown, University College London
Prof. Dr. Dr. Frank Carter, University of London
Prof. William C. Clarke, Australian National University, Canberra
Prof. em. Terence Coppock, Dunfermline, Fife (GB)
Prof. em. Alice Coleman, London
Prof. Dr. Ivan Crkvenčić, Geografski odsjek PMF, Zagreb
Anne Daubercies, London
Dipl.-Vw. Dr. Maria Demand, Wien
Dozent Dr. Bolesław Domański, Jagiellon. Universität, Kraków

Maynard Weston Dow, Bristol, New Hampshire
Dr. Wolfgang A. Entmayr, Europ. Kommission, Brüssel
Brigadier Dr. Gerhard Fasching, Salzburg
Prof. Dr. Hans Fischer, Universität Wien
Prof. Dr. Werner Fricke, Universität Heidelberg
Dr. Franz Graul, Gutenzell - Hürbel (BRD)
D.I. Dr. Heinrich Grienauer, Waldbronn - Etzenrot (BRD)
Ursula Grienauer, Waldbronn - Etzenrot (BRD)
Gen.-Dir. a.D. Dkfm. Johann Grünn, Baden bei Wien
Prof. em. Chauncy D. Harris, University of Chicago
Prof. Dr. Dhimiter Haxhimihali, University of Tirana
Dr. Tatjana Haxhimihali, „People to People Albania", Tirana
Prof. em. Frederick M. Helleiner, Trent University (Canada)
Prof. Dr. Staffan Helmfrid, Stockholm University
Prof. em. Dr. Helmut Heuberger, Salzburg
Prof. em. John Yoshio Higa, Naha, Okinawa (Japan)
Dr. Albert Hofmayer, Wirtschaftsuniversität Wien
Prof. em. Dr. Burkhard Hofmeister, Bad Reichenhall
Prof. Lutz Holzner, University of Wisconsin, Milwaukee
Prof. em. Dr. Helmut Jäger, Gerbrunn bei Würzburg
Dozent Dr. Peter Jordan, Österr. Ost- und Südosteuropa-Institut, Wien
Prof. Dkfm. Dr. Felix Jülg, Wirtschaftsuniversität Wien
Dozent Dr. Hermann Kohl, Linz
Bürgermeister Johann Kothmayr, Gschwandt (Oberösterreich)
Prof. em. Dr. Václav Král, Prag
Prof. em. Dr. H. J. Kramm, Potsdam
Prof. Dr. Ingrid Kretschmer, Universität Wien
Senator mult. Präsident Prof. Dkfm. Dr. Alfred Lehr, Wien
Prof. Dr. Herwig Lechleitner, Wien
Walter Leitner, Landesrat a. D., Salzburg
Hofrat DDr. Hans Lentner, Villach
Prof. em. Dr. Karl Lenz, Berlin
Prof. Dr. Teofil Lijewski, Inst. of Geography & Spatial Organization, Warszawa
Prof. em. David Lowenthal, Harrow, Middlesex (GB)
Prof. em. Dr. Dr.h.c. Walter Manshard, Bad Krozingen (Freiburg i. Br.)
Prof. Dr. Dieter Manske, Altenthann (Regensburg)
Kommerzialrat Dkfm. Dr. Hans Martinek, Wien
Silvia Mayer, Gablitz bei Wien
Prof. em. William R. Mead, Aston Clinton, Buckinghamshire (GB)
Prof. Dr. Nasip Meçaj, Geographic Studies Center, Tirana
Prof. Dr. Horst Mensching, Hamburg / Wien
Dipl.-Geogr. Gerlinde Neumeyer, Leipzig

Dr. Günter Nevosad, Fachhochschule „Unternehmensführung", Wien
William Packard, Australian National University, Canberra
Prof. Dr. Zlatko Pepeonik, Universität Zagreb
Mag. Dr. Marianne Phillips, Colchester, Essex (GB)
Prof. Hugh Prince, University College London
Dr. Sheila Prince, London
Direktor Dr. Günther Ramusch, Oberbank AG, Linz
Ernst und Johanna Resch, Sturt, South Australia
Prof. em. Dr. Hans Richter, Leipzig
Prof. em. Dkfm. Dr. Wigand Ritter, Nürnberg
Prof. em. Dr. Karl Ruppert, München
Prof. Dr. Michael Sauberer, Universität Klagenfurt
Prof. Dr. Martin Seger, Universität Klagenfurt
Prof. Dr. Shigeru Shirasaka, St. Paul's University, Niiza-shi (Japan)
Dr. Karl Schappelwein, Österr. Ost- und Südosteuropa-Institut, Wien
Prof. Dr. Robert Sinclair, Wayne State University, Detroit
Dkfm. Dr. Stefan Skowronek, Wien
Prof. Dr. Konrad Spindler, Universität Innsbruck
Prof. Dr. Christoph Stadel, Universität Salzburg
Prof. William Stanley, University of South Carolina, Columbia
Prof. Dr. Christian Staudacher, Wirtschaftsuniversität Wien
Mag. Ing. Arwed Stehlik, Österr. Gesundheitsministerium, Wien
Dr. Malvine Stenzel, Salzburg
Prof. em. Dr. Karl Stiglbauer, Wien
Dr. Tadeusz Stryjakiewicz, Adam Mickiewicz Univ., Poznań
Prof. Dr. Jan Szupryczyński, Polish Academy of Sciences, Toruń
Prof. em. David Thomas, Wenvoe, Cardiff
Marie-Luise und Wolf Tietze, Helmstedt
Margarete Torreilles, Bourg des Comptes (Frankreich)
Prof. Dr. Elmar Vonbank, Bregenz
Prof. R. Gerard Ward, Australian National University, Canberra
Prof. em. Dr. Ernst Weigt, Nürnberg
Dr. Manfred Weißmann, VÖWA Oberösterreich, Linz
Rudolf Wendorff, Gütersloh
Prof. em. Dr. Erhart Winkler, Wien
Eugen Wirth, Erlangen
Prof. em. Michael Wise, London
Prof. Dr. Klaus Wolf, J.W.Goethe-Universität, Frankfurt am Main
Prof. Dr. Junji Yamamura, Chiba University (Japan)
Dr. Schapour Zafarpour, Wirtschaftsuniversität Wien
Mag. Angelika Zimmermann, Graz
Prof. Dr. Friedrich Zimmermann, Universität Graz

XIV

Karl A. Sinnhuber zum 80. Geburtstag [1]

Wigand RITTER (Nürnberg)

Karl Sinnhuber hat es geschafft, sein achtzigstes Lebensjahr in voller Gesundheit zu vollenden. Dies allein schon rechtfertigt unsere Glückwünsche, denn es ist für Hochschullehrer nach der Emeritierung gar nicht mehr so einfach, bis dahin am Leben zu bleiben.

Was sagt man zu diesem Geburtstag? Eine Laudatio für einen Achtziger hat sinnvoll nicht mehr den gleichen Inhalt wie zu einem früheren Zeitpunkt. Bei einem Sechziger wollen noch alle Fachkollegen wissen, was macht er, was wird er vielleicht noch forschen und schreiben? Beim Siebziger ist die Zeit des Weihrauchstreuens gekommen. Das wissenschaftliche Werk ist nach menschlichem Ermessen nun abgeschlossen und der Jubilar kein Konkurrent mehr. Nun beim 80. Geburtstag stellt sich schon die Frage, was bleibt von dem Menschen, was hat von seinem Werk Bestand?

Daß nun von Karl Sinnhuber etwas bleibt, beweist uns bereits diese Feier. Wenn sich 13 Jahre nach der Emeritierung eines akademischen Lehrers Gäste von weither, sogar aus England und Amerika in seinem Namen versammeln, so heißt dies ja, daß Persönlichkeit und Werk des Jubilars wirksam sind.

Lassen Sie mich mit der Persönlichkeit beginnen und meine Worte ganz unkonventionell mit einem Sprung in ein Schwimmbecken einleiten:

Ort: Port Camargue;
Zeit: September 1981;
Anlaß: Feierliches Festessen zum Abschluß der Tagung der IGU-Arbeitsgruppe Freizeit und Tourismus. Die Tische waren rund um besagtes Becken gruppiert worden. Es ist heiß und das Wasser lockt.
Die versammelten Honoratioren und Forscher aus Frankreich, England, Österreich und einem Dutzend anderer kleiner Länder sind aber viel zu gesittet und vornehm. Bis dann Sinnhuber den Bann bricht, ohne auf Dessert und Mokka zu waren. Wir anderen können ihm begeistert folgen.

Damit jemand solches tun kann, braucht er eine robuste Seele und ein festes Selbstvertrauen. Diese zwei Eigenschaften hat unser Jubilar sicherlich. Die schwierige Frage für mich ist nur, woher?

Sinnhubers vor 10 Jahren publizierter Lebenslauf nennt Salzburg als Geburtsort, wogegen ich immer Oberndorf an der Salzach im Gedächtnis hatte. Wie dem auch sei, er stammt aus jenem kulturhistorisch bemerkenswerten Winkel zwischen Bayern und Österreich, über welchen Altötting den himmli-

---
[1] Vorbereiteter Text der Laudatio beim Festkolloquium in der ehemaligen Hochschule für Welthandel in Wien am 15. Oktober 1999.

schen Segen lenkt, das die eigentliche Mitte Bayerns und seiner Kolonisationsgebiete darstellt. Das Regnum Bavariae wieder war einst die Mitte Europas.

Als Kind dieser Region erläuterte Sinnhuber uns einmal den fundamentalen Unterschied zwischen den Bräustübl-Salzburgern und den Kaffeehaus-Salzburgern und ließ keinen Zweifel, wohin sein Herz gehörte. In Sinnhuber sehe ich einen Menschen dieses Landes. Sie sind keine Weltverbesserer, aber auch nicht autoritätsgläubig. Dafür haben sie zu lange unter dem Krummstab gelebt. Dennoch ist er wie sie ein guter Christ. Er ist allen Menschen gegenüber offen und herzlich, hilfreich, wo es notwendig ist, und fair in seinem Verhalten. Machtstreben und Neid habe ich an ihm nie bemerkt. Den Wiener Nationalsport, die „Haxlbeißerei" und das Spinnen von Intrigen brauchte er nicht. Ich habe von ihm niemals ein abfälliges Wort über andere gehört, und man konnte ihm immer Freund sein. So gibt es denn auch ein Sinnhubersches Freundschaftsnetzwerk von globaler Dimension, welches von Österreich über Westeuropa nach den USA und Japan reicht. So erklärt sich auch sein überaus vielfältiges soziales und kollegiales Engagement an der Wirtschaftsuniversität Wien, zumeist in ehrenamtlichen Funktionen.

Aus dieser Haltung wohl ist sein Lebensweg zu erklären, über den ich eigentlich wenig weiß. Es hätte auch nichts genützt, wenn man mir rechtzeitig alle schriftlichen Unterlagen zugesandt hätte, denn das Wichtige steht ja doch nie drin! Wie ist Sinnhuber zur Geographie gekommen, die offenbar nicht seine erste Wahl war? Warum ging gerade er nach England, das kurz zuvor noch Feindesland war? Dank welcher Umstände konnte er dort in seinem Fach und an der Universität so rasch Fuß fassen? Wann und wo hat er die Sprache gelernt; so gut gelernt, daß ihn seine Fachkollegen in England als „fellow" anerkannten? Dies steht nicht in den Lebensläufen, die anläßlich früherer Geburtstage erschienen sind. Dies wären aber die interessanten Punkte, natürlich samt den Irrungen, Scheidewegen und fallweisen Rückschlägen, die das Leben so mit sich bringt.

In England und während einer langen Tätigkeit in Guildford in Surrey gehörte es zu seinen Anliegen, den Briten einige Kernaspekte der deutschen Geographie näherzubringen. Diese wurden damals generell mißverstanden und hatten wenig Ansehen, was so kurz nach dem Kriege nicht weiter verwunderlich war. Ich will mich dabei auf seine Schrift: „Mitteleuropa – Central Europe – an analysis of a geographical term" beschränken, weil sie wichtig ist – und auch weil ich offen bekennen muß, daß ich in meiner sommerlichen Einsiedlerklause gar keine Möglichkeit gehabt hätte, mir alle seine Schriften zu beschaffen. Diese Abhandlung wurde 1954 geschrieben und entspricht zeitlich und sachlich einer Habilitationsschrift.

Wenn aber Sinnhuber Verständnis für deutsche Positionen schaffen wollte, so wurde er darin gründlich mißverstanden. Immer wieder werden seine Befunde in englischen und amerikanischen Publikationen zwar ausführlich zitiert, aber sie dienen als Beleg für die faktische Unmöglichkeit, unter Geographen eine einheitliche Meinung bezüglich der Abgrenzung einer geographischen Region zu finden. Andersherum aber haben diese Autoren damit durchaus den Kernpunkt der wissenschaftlichen Kritik am Mitteleuropabegriff gefunden. Denn wenn selbst die Fachleute eine Region nicht eindeutig definieren können, wie kann diese dann eine geographische Einheit sein? Und ist sie das nicht, was berechtigt dann dazu, sie mit einem Namen zu belegen und ihr einen Erklärungswert beizumessen, von welchem dann wieder praktische und politische Folgerungen hergeleitet werden? Dabei hatten sich die vielen Autoren von Mitteleuropakonzepten auf einem sicheren wissenschaftlichen Pfad gewähnt. Ihre Analysen der Natur- und Kulturlandschaft ergaben statische geographische Elemente, deren räumliche Addition und letztliche Synthese die Regionsbegriffe bringen müßte. So hatte sich dies wohl schon Carl Ritter 150 Jahre früher vorgestellt. Man sah in Landschaftselementen, Haus-, Flur- und Siedlungsformen dauerhafte kulturspezifische Gegebenheiten, für deren Wurzeln man sogar die Urgeschichte bemühte.

In England glaubte man dies alles nicht so recht. Sinnhuber mußte daher breiter ausholen, und gerade dies macht seine Schrift heute noch lesenswert. Europa als zunächst topographischer Begriff hat natürlich eine geometrische Mitte, die nur ganz woanders liegt, als man vermuten möchte. Auch festgemacht an physisch-geographischen Momenten ergibt sich eine Mitte, die etwas exzentrisch zwischen Böhmen und dem Alpenraum liegt. Nicht weit von Altötting, aber weit von den historischen Schwerpunkten des Kontinents. Mit Europa als historisch-politischem Konzept sind Geographen nie so recht zurande gekommen, sodaß ihre Überlegungen immer wieder in die Gleichsetzung ihres Mitteleuropa mit den Gebieten deutscher Kultur und deutschen Kultureinflusses einmündeten. Dem Anschein nach wurde dies auch noch durch die vierte Untersuchungsebene, die kulturgeographische Synthese gestützt.

In seinen Überlegungen ist Sinnhuber daher offener. Er zitiert Hassinger mit dessen Feststellung, daß sich der Mitteleuropabegriff ostwärts im Zuge der allmählichen Expansion Europa ausgeweitet habe, und führt in prozeßorientierter Sicht die damals einsetzende Umgestaltung im Osten nach sozialistischen Modellvorstellungen an. Ein Landschafts- und Bevölkerungswandel, der Mitteleuropa grundsätzlich in Frage stellte. Offen bleibt dabei, warum sich Mitteleuropa nur nach Osten ausgeweitet haben sollte und nicht auch nach Westen, Norden und Süden. Gab es eine graduelle Ausweitung Europas, dann müßten ja auch dort die Anzeichen einer Mitteleuropäisierung zu finden sein. Folgt man gar den neueren Überlegungen, welche die Vereinigung Europas aufwirft, so muß man eigentlich die „Lothringer Achse" bzw. die „Blaue Banane" als die Mitte Europas deklarieren. Von hier aus gab es tatsächlich eine Expansion Europas in alle Himmelsrichtungen bis weit nach Übersee, und gleichzeitig erhalten viele historische und politische Entwicklungen in Europa einen verständlichen Sinn. Aber diese Mitte Europas war niemals deutsch allein. Franzosen, Italiener und viele andere Völker haben daran ihren Teil.

Die Mitteleuropafrage ist in der Geographie nicht ausdiskutiert. Sinnhubers Beitrag wird noch weiter aktuell bleiben und sicher noch oftmals zitiert werden. Leider eben auch nur partiell verstanden. Daher komme ich zu einem letzten Problemkreis. In der Geographie wie in vielen anderen Wissenschaften ergibt sich ein Ausufern der Forschung in vielerlei angewandte und praktische Fragen, die aber nicht so begriffen werden. Man sieht sie nicht als Techniken sondern als Grundlagenforschung. Über dieser Fülle läßt man Basisfragen unbeantwortet in einem diffusen Diskussionsstand liegen. Boshaft gesagt „ist die Geographie nicht geographisch genug". Ich zähle dazu auch das Mitteleuropa- bzw. Ostmitteleuropaproblem.

Es ist dies aufs engste mit der notorischen Schwierigkeit verbunden, ein echtes geographisches Objekt zu finden. Nachdem sich die Vorstellungen von Ländern (Staaten) und Landschaften als Kernstücke zu brüchig erwiesen hatten, weil sie sich theoretisch nicht recht fassen ließen, hat man in meiner Generation Modelle, Theorien und Forschungsansätze massenweise im Supermarkt der Nachbardisziplinen in Selbstbedienung eingekauft. Das wäre ja noch nicht schlecht, doch kommt dazu ein ausgeprägter Unwille, diese Theorien kreativ auf geographische Situationen anzuwenden und dafür spezifisch weiterzuentwickeln.

Tatsächlich hat nichts in unserer Umwelt sonderlich lange Bestand. Viele Erscheinungen entstehen als Innovationen, die später vielleicht eine Zeit lang strukturbestimmend sind, später dann wieder rückgebaut werden oder ihren Sinnbezug wechseln. Die geographische Substanz, in deren Matrix wir sie beobachten, enthält solche Dinge in ganz unterschiedlichen Altersformen, Ausprägungen und systematischen Bezügen. Keine dieser Erscheinungen ist „gerade" gewachsen, so daß sie ihrer theoretischen Idealform entsprechen könnte, ebenso wie niemals eine Eiche im Wald der idealen Eiche entsprechen kann. Ein Berg ist nicht nur ein Berg im morphologischen Sinn, was der Flieger Sinnhuber sehr wohl weiß. Keine Stadt ist idealtypisch Zentraler Ort im Christaller'schen Sinne. So liefern die gängigen Theorien zwar intellektuell ansprechende Modelle, aber keine rechte Erklärung der Realität. Sie sind auch selten aus dieser zwingend herzuleiten. Diese Realität aber, wir sollten sie mit Lautensach „geographische Substanz" nennen, einst als Zustand von Dauer verstanden, heute eher als wandelbares Systemgefüge, bleibt das Objekt der Geographie.

Karl Sinnhuber hat einst auf den Schultern seiner Vorgänger die Metapher Mitteleuropa als vermeintliche Entität zum Untersuchungsgegenstand gemacht. Er ist ihr gegenüber letztlich skeptisch geblieben. Gerade diese Skepsis hat zum nachhaltigen Erfolg seiner Arbeit, zu ihrem Überleben beigetragen. Wir hätten heute allen Grund, diese Frage mit dem inzwischen gewonnenen Rüstzeug von Innovationstheorie, Wissen um räumliche Entwicklungsprozesse und um Systemstrukturen wieder anzugehen. Sinnhuber hatte solche Instrumente noch gar nicht zur Verfügung. Geschieht dies aber, lieber Kollege Sinnhuber, dann werden sich auch zu Deinem einhundertsten Geburtstag noch Geographen in Deinem Namen versammeln.

Recollections of an Emeritus

Karl A. SINNHUBER, interviewed by Maynard Weston DOW

In August 1992, during the 27th Congress of the International Geographical Union in Washington D.C., Professor Maynard Weston Dow of Plymouth State College, New Hampshire, USA, interviewed Professor Karl A. Sinnhuber for his series **Geographers on Film**. *What follows is an edited version of the interview.* [1]

Dow: *Here with us today is Karl Sinnhuber of the University of Economics and Business Administration, Vienna, Austria, Emeritus Professor I might add. What is your academic background?*

SINNHUBER: My academic background started with studying at the University of Berlin where I read prehistoric archaeology and anthropology, but my studies were then interrupted because of the war. I started in 1937 and in 1939 I was called up and served in the war as a pilot and could only continue my studies in 1945, but by then I was back in Austria and I continued at Innsbruck University.

And what did you study at Innsbruck?

At Innsbruck initially I thought there was no point going on with archaeology, I wouldn't get a job. I thought I would have to be a school teacher and geography had always interested me so I took up geography, but when I came to the first lectures of my professor there, Hans Kinzl, I became converted to geography.

What can you tell about Hans Kinzl?

Hans Kinzl was a marvellous person, a marvellous teacher and I think in Austria, at least, he was the last universalist in geography. He was able to inspire students in all aspects of geography. Some pupils did their *Habilitation* (a postdoctoral qualification necessary to become a university professor) in physi-

---

[1] Note by M. W. Dow: Geographers on Film (GOF) began in August 1970. Participants speak for the record that samples of the geographical experience are retained. The GOF series includes 274 film and videotape interviews of the thought and reflection of 249 geographers, plus 211 additional holdings, which feature distinctive themes and embody 96 supplemental geographers. 53 of the GOF films/videos are multiple interviews of 25 selected individuals (e.g. Richard Hartshorne, 1972, 1978, 1979, 1986A, 1986B). The complete 238 hours of GOF have been converted to the readily accessible VHS (NTSC) format and are available for rental. For more information concerning GOF please consult the following:
M. W. Dow, Geographers on Film, 44 Towne Road, Bristol, NH, USA 03222; Telephone (603) 744-8846; E-Mail: MWD@mail.plymouth.edu; Website: http://oz.plymouth.edu/~mwd.

cal geography, others in social geography, human geography and regional geography in which his special subject was Peru.

As a young man what did you specialise in under him?

Under him I did not then really specialise in anything but the first lecture course I had was cultural geography and he talked about the *Urlandschaft*, so I thought this is not so far away from prehistoric archaeology. That also helped me to go into geography.

Are there any graduate students that were with you at that time whom you might mention?

Yes, there was Leidlmair, he was professor in Karlsruhe and Bonn then succeeded Kinzl in Innsbruck; Heuberger who is a Himalayan researcher and became professor in Munich and later in Salzburg; Troger who was professor of social geography and regional geography in Vienna; Fliri, also professor at Innsbruck, who made his mark in climatology; Müller who is still active as professor in Salzburg. Altogether there were about a dozen of those immediate post-war students who became professors in Austria.

Well now, you spent twenty-five years in Britain. Will you tell us a bit about your years in Britain and how you happened to go there?

After I concluded my studies with an M.Phil. in geography and a D.Phil. in prehistoric archaeology, which I had continued with simultaneously to complete it, I did a year of school teaching in Austria. Then I saw a circular from the education ministry asking who would be interested in going to Britain for a year as an exchange teacher so I applied even though I did not teach English, arguing that a geographer must see the world. I was successful and was sent to Glasgow. It was not my choice but was very fortunate because Professor Stephens at the university there knew Kinzl and he particularly knew Kinzl's teacher, Sölch, and so I immediately established a good contact with him and the department introduced for me a postgraduate course in social geography, which I completed with a diploma after a year.

You met Sölch? Are you familiar with Hartshorne who translated much of Hettner for his 'Nature of geography'. That was probably in the late thirties, that's how I recognise the name.

I never met him personally. He was in England about 1949 and I wanted to meet him, but shortly afterwards he died, so I was very sorry. In a sense, academically, I am a grandson of Sölch.

You are a grandson, all right. And how about Southampton; was that your first job?

While I was in Glasgow, I was supposed to return to Austria after a year, but I applied for any academic job that was going anywhere. I would have applied on the moon because I didn't want to go back to school teaching. I was invited to come to Southampton just for a year, and I lectured there on whatever I had to, regional geography, mainly of the German speaking lands, and economic geography. Amongst my final year students was James Bird who later became professor in Southampton but in between was Reader (associate professor) in London and I think I gave him the idea for his „Any port" because I also lectured there on Johann Heinrich von Thünen who at that time geographers in England seemed not to have heard of.

Nobody had heard of him. Now what about Christaller, do you think they had heard of him?

Christaller was a little known but not much appreciated.

I may come back to him in a moment. Where else were you in Britain?

During this one year I went to the annual meeting of the Institute of British Geographers in Oxford. I met Professor Darby and he kindly inquired what was my special interest. I had never heard of him and said what are your special interests and he didn't bat an eyelid. Anyway, there was suddenly a vacancy on his staff because someone had died and he invited me to join his staff at University College London and I stayed there for fifteen years.

You did?

And of course I taught mainly historical geography of the German lands because of my background in archaeology and German.

Did you ever work together in seminar, with Darby?

I advised him on a number of occasions and translated papers for him and so on as he didn't know German.

I first became familiar with your work through two articles you did for the 'Scottish Geographical Magazine' in 1959, Humboldt and Ritter. What is the origin of those papers?

I was at a meeting of the British Association for the Advancement of Science, and Professor Miller, who was then the editor of the *Scottish Geographical Magazine*, suggested I should do these articles. So I agreed and then really worked hard and did a lot of reading and got thoroughly interested and wrote those two papers and have continued from that time to have an interest in the history of geographical thought and have lectured on it. My last teaching post was in New Zealand after I became Emeritus and I also lectured there on Ritter and Humboldt and Ratzel and Hettner and so on.

You have? Well look, tell us about your opinions on the relationship between physical and general geography, speaking of Humboldt and Ritter.

There is, in my opinion unfortunately, now a tendency to break them completely apart, and I agree if you really want to advance the body of knowledge you have to specialise in the one or the other, but to train a geographer to be a real geographer both are necessary. I mean I am always very happy that with Kinzl I learnt about glaciers and know some geomorphology. I am not a geomorphologist but when I am in a landscape I can understand it and it makes sense to me.

That is one of our contributions within the social sciences, would you agree, that we see both sides better than, for instance, the anthropologist?

Yes, I am completely with you there.

How would you assess the work of Humboldt?

Of course, Humboldt was the last great universalist, much more than a geographer. I should say, in a sense, a person like Goethe. He was just an absolutely fantastic man.

The last Renaissance Man perhaps?

Yes, I mean, Ritter was more of a geographer, but Humboldt was probably a greater person.

How would you describe Ritter's contribution, what was his main theme?

I don't agree with his teleological view that the earth is there to educate human beings to some kind of destination, but he was a meticulous scholar in using sources and then pulling all the threads together to give a comprehensive account of the „personality" of a region.

Would he be the father of regional geography in this sense?

The father of, I should say, a scholarly regional geography.

Is he very difficult to read in German, by the way?

Not very. But one thing that puts people off, of course, is that his books are very voluminous so I don't say I have read everything, but I have read quite a bit of it, especially special papers, not so much his work on Asia. Of course he never completed what he set out to do.

And now, what about the contributions of Ratzel?

I think Ratzel is also very important but he was quite a bit misunderstood. He is not the „arch determinist". Kinzl always said you mustn't take short cuts, for example "it's hot therefore people have black skin", and so on. It's much more complicated, and I think Ratzel was very careful in establishing relationships between physical, environmental and human geography, but subsequently some people just simplified it too much. That's how he got this reputation as many people heard of him, learned of him, only indirectly, but were not able to read him in the original.

Is he difficult to read?

No, as he started off as a journalist, he is easy to read if you are familiar with German.

You know, Carl Sauer in his later years spent a lot of time studying Ratzel's writings.

I am very happy that I met Sauer, personally.

You did, where?

In Heidelberg. With Pfeiffer, who once worked with him in California.

Well, now let's go back to von Thünen for a moment. You say you introduced him to British geography?

Kinzl suggested I should do something on von Thünen for my thesis in Glasgow and I fortunately got the original edition of von Thünen's *Der Isolierte Staat* from Glasgow University library where I read it and was absolutely fascinated. I first wanted to do this thesis on von Thünen but then I thought "no, I must spend much more time over this", so I did one on the *Urlandschaft* as put forward by Gradmann. I continued work on von Thünen but whoever I talked to in Britain said this is not geography, completely unimportant. But I must have talked about it and I gave some special lectures on von Thünen, and Brian Berry was one of my students and maybe I kindled some thoughts in him by introducing him to von Thünen.

I suspect you did.

But unfortunately, though I had collected a lot of material, I never had the time to publish it. But I advised Peter Hall in his von Thünen translation and Michael Chisholm on the book which deals with agricultural location.

For the record, I believe the date of von Thünen's book is what, 1828?

Yes, 1828 for Volume I and 1850 for Volume II.

Now, do you see any contemporary application for von Thünen?

Oh yes, *Der Isolierte Staat* is an idea which doesn't date. If one takes it literally it doesn't apply and, of course, many people took it literally. But if you take just the idea it is timeless.

Which brings us to Christaller – there's a jump there of about 100 years. What can you tell us about Christaller?

First of all, I have met him in Bonn, personally. He was a very unassuming man. Concerning his work there is a similarity with that of von Thünen. His concept of a system of central places is also timeless. Many geographers had said that, since one cannot find his hexagonal pattern of central places in actual nature, it was geometry, not geography, and thus of no use. However, this theory is a heuristic principle. By reference to the model one can investigate for what reasons the actual pattern deviates.

Well, think of all that's come from it. What about Loesch? Well, Loesch had quite an influence on American geographers.

I also read Loesch.

Did you have your students become involved in things of this nature?

Not very much because one is tied to a syllabus and in England you can't really do what you want. In Austria you are much freer to do that.

Well, look, speaking of Austria, how is geography considered as a discipline? Is it respected?

Oh, it's a respected discipline and also a discipline which many students take up because in all the grammar schools in Austria, that is the schools which prepare you for university, geography is a compulsory subject and so there are jobs for the teachers. In these schools it's mixed with economics so the geography teachers also have to teach something on economics and marketing.

I see, but there's the physical side as well?

The physical side is not neglected; they do teach physical geography as well.

As a university discipline how is it accepted?

There is a new university in Linz which didn't have geography when courses began. It was on the plan and the professor in Vienna whom eventually I succeeded, Scheidl, said „That will be a job for you", but unfortunately for lack of money a chair was not created there. All other Austrian universities have geography chairs and geography departments.

Are they large compared with, say, political sciences, history or economics?

About the same. I mean, Salzburg is pretty large, Vienna is very large, there are about 30 staff.

What do you consider your main field of geographical interest?

It has changed somewhat in the course of time. I started off with historical geography and then came into economic geography and rather uniquely I was asked to come to the University of Surrey, in Guildford, a new university, to teach in German economic geography of Germany to the students who specialised in German. I stayed there for seven years, until 1974, when I was appointed to the chair in Vienna.

What about your interest in historical geography; you had this before you met Darby?

The interest was there, yes, because of my background of archaeology and *Urlandschaft* and development of the landscape. Darby then encouraged me to develop it. So I did for fifteen years while I was at University College London.

Who were some of your colleagues in the faculty at that time?

Bill Mead, Terry Coppock, Eric Brown, and of my students of those times, Ron Cook, who became Professor of Geography at UC, Brian Berry I have already mentioned, James Bird joined the staff for a time before he left to become professor in Southampton.

You have an interest in regional geography; is there any continued relevance in this or is it by the board?

I would never say regional geography could ever be by the board, even though some people say „How terrible, regional geography", because there is an inherent curiosity in a human being to know about his environment both nearby and further away so you have to tell them about it. But I believe you shouldn't teach a course on an area where you haven't actually been for some time and learned about it from personal experience. I haven never given a course on a country where I haven't been. I have been to many countries.

What about the concept of a world regional course? Do you have such things in Europe, where you try to give the students all the world in a semester or two?

I think it is a valid idea, but I don't think one single person could do it. I certainly would not dare do it, but I think for the students it would be a good thing to have. But teaching would have to be co-operative, done by people who really know the areas.

So perhaps use a team. All right, now you say that it's relevant because we need to know about the other places.

We need to know about the other places for practical purposes. I was at the University of Economics and then my students became business men and women selling, buying, all over the world. This university was started as an „Export Academy" to support the purely practical side but I think knowing about the world is also important in liberal education to understand other regions, other people, to break down prejudices, misconceptions. That's also an important contribution to be made by geography.

To know the other fellow as it were, is that correct, and break down the prejudices?

Yes.

What about your activities with the IGU?

The first IGU conference I attended, apart from the London one in 1964 when I was at University College, was in Delhi, the next one was in Montreal. I was then at the foundation meeting of the study group which became the Commission on Tourism and Recreation of which my Austrian colleague, though he taught at Frankfurt, Matznetter, was the chairman. I was active in this and a few years later organised a symposium of the still a study group in Birmingham. I was by then in Austria; it was a bit difficult to organise from Austria but I think it was successful. I continued in the commission. Shortly after moving to Austria I became the secretary of the Austrian National Committee for the IGU and then became its president. As the conference was a joint venture of Austria, France, Germany, Italy and Switzerland I became a vice-president of the organising committee for the Paris meeting in 1984.

Have you been able to continue your interest in recreation and tourism throughout the years? You say you started in Montreal organising this group.

I am involved. I have not mentioned that in Austria I also studied physical education as one of my subjects, and having been a pilot in the war, I took up gliding again. My presidential address in Birmingham was about recreation in the mountains but I concentrated on glider flying in the mountains. And I am a skier, and I go sailing and hiking and so on.

You continue to glide, do you?

Yes, I continue to glide, despite my advanced age, and I enjoy it. [2]

This is terribly philosophical but what do you figure about the role of geography in the world today?

I think I come back again to what I said. It's important to break down barriers and geography can play a contribution there: barriers of prejudice, of misconception.

How are we doing this as a discipline, do you think, are we effective?

You cannot be 100% effective, but it would be much worse without geography.

Be much worse?

I think so.

How do you see your important contributions to the field?

I saw myself in a kind of bridge position between German geography and British geography. For fifteen years or so I translated the summaries into English for *Erdkunde* for Troll whom I knew very well indeed. I published in English, I published in German. I lectured on Germany in England, I lectured about Britain in German; that is one very practical contribution, and I wrote a little book

---

[2] This is still true in 1999, also for skiing. *[editor's note]*

about *Germany, its geography and growth*, which I believe became quite well known. Of my scholarly papers, the one that I hear from colleagues they consider the most important, was the one on the concept of *Mitteleuropa*, which in a way was originally prompted by Harriet Wanklyn who once wrote „*Mitteleuropa*, this concept of German geography has gone", and Kinzl had quoted it. That was one thing and then Dickinson in *The German Lebensraum* said something about *Mitteleuropa* which I disagreed with and that started me off and I wrote this paper. Before it was published by the Institute of British Geographers I had read the paper with the title *Central Europe – Mitteleuropa – l'Europe Centrale, analysis of a geographical term*, in 1953 and I was told later that it was discussed in seminars in London and elsewhere.

I am not familiar with that paper but I know of Partsch or maybe Naumann, there were two books I think written maybe in 1904, 1913.

I read Partsch's volume on *Mitteleuropa* and I quoted how it was edited by Mackinder. Partsch was commissioned by Mackinder and in fact the first edition was in English and only later it came out in German.

Well now, let's look at the situation today and talk about Middle Europe. What do you think about your paper, was it right on or not?

Yes, there was recently a symposium in Vienna on *Mitteleuropa*. It's become rather fashionable again. The organiser to whom I sent a copy of my paper after the symposium said, "what a pity you didn't send it before, it's the best thing I have read about *Mitteleuropa*". So it seems to be relevant.

Did you include Yugoslavia as part of Mitteleuropa?

Oh yes. I followed Hassinger. Have you heard of Hassinger?

No, I haven't.

Hassinger was an Austrian geographer. He wrote a paper on *Mitteleuropa* in 1915 and he considered the south-eastern part going into Romania as an evolving *Mitteleuropa*; a region in the process of becoming *Mitteleuropa*. Northern Yugoslavia definitely is part of it and the rest is on the way towards it.

Now, is your paper referred to again do you suppose in seminars?

I've been away from Britain for so long I can't tell, but as Peter Haggett included it as an example of how to define a region I suppose it is not forgotten.

Not forgotten. Well thank you very much for being with us today, I appreciate that you have taken the time to join us.

It was a great pleasure and a great honour to be asked.

Vorbemerkung zum folgenden Beitrag / Note by the Editor

Bei der "Regional Conference" der IGU in Prag 1994, deren zentrales Thema "Central Europe" war, wurde der am Ende des Interviews mit Dow erwähnte Aufsatz Sinnhubers in der Eröffnungsansprache und in zahlreichen anderen Beiträgen erwähnt, insbesondere im "key paper" von F. W. Carter (School of Slavonic and East European Studies of London University).

Der Band **Central Europe after the Fall of the Iron Curtain** (Peter Lang, Frankfurt/Main, Berlin, Bern, New York, 1996) **Wiener Osteuropa Studien**, vol. 4, der den Beitrag von Carter und weitere für den Kongreß in Prag oder danach verfaßte Beiträge enthält, beginnt mit den Worten:

During the IGU Regional Conference in Prague in 1994, which had Central Europe as its theme, Sinnhuber's paper on 'Mitteleuropa' was mentioned in the opening address and a number of times in other papers, notably in the key paper given by Dr. F. W. Carter of the School of Slavonic and East European Studies of London University.

The volume **Central Europe after the Fall of the Iron Curtain** (Peter Lang, Frankfurt/Main, Berlin, Bern, New York, 1996) **Wiener Osteuropa Studien**, vol. 4, which contains F. W. Carter's key paper and other papers read at the Congress or prepared later begins:

„This book is dedicated to Karl Sinnhuber
whose work inspired us to reconsider
the meaning of Central Europe."
The Editors: Francis W. Carter, Peter Jordan, Violette Rey.

Da der Band der **Transactions and Papers of the Institute of British Geographers 1954**, der Sinnhubers Mitteleuropa-Aufsatz enthält, seit langem vergriffen ist, dachten wir, daß das anhaltende Interesse daran ein guter Grund wäre, den Aufsatz in der Festschrift zu seinem 80. Geburtstag neu abzudrucken.

Die Genehmigung zum Wiederabdruck erteilte die Royal Geographical Society (with the Institute of British Geographers) London mit Brief vom 27.1.1998, wofür wir an dieser Stelle sehr herzlich danken.

Since the volume of the **Transactions and Papers of the Institute of British Geographers 1954** which contains Sinnhuber's paper on 'Mitteleuropa' has long been out of print we thought that the continuing interest in it was a good reason to reprint it in the Festschrift on the occasion of his 80th birthday.

The permission for reprinting was given by the Royal Geographical Society (with the Institute of British Geographers), London, with a letter from 27 Jan. 1998, which is gratefully acknowledged by the editor.

CENTRAL EUROPE — MITTELEUROPA — EUROPE CENTRALE

AN ANALYSIS OF A GEOGRAPHICAL TERM

By KARL A. SINNHUBER, D. PHIL.
(*University College, University of London*)

It is by no means the first time that the evasive term Central Europe or its equivalents in other languages has been made the basis of a discussion by a geographer. Looking at English writings alone the paper by Hilda Ormsby of almost twenty years ago and R. E. Dickinson's *The German Lebensraum* are well known. A similar theme was taken up by H. Cord Meyer in 1946.[1] Considering the attention this topic has already received, is it not unnecessary or futile to struggle again with this well-worn problem of clarifying the meaning of Central Europe or its synonyms? There appear to be two reasons, however, for making yet another attempt.

Firstly, the authors mentioned purposely based their respective treatments of the subject almost exclusively on German publications, since their aim was to explain to the 'English' reader what was understood by this term among German geographers and other German writers.[2] In the course of this paper I hope to contribute to that aim by adding some new points and correcting a few statements in the papers mentioned, but the major aim is different. By extending the literature considered beyond the German sphere, an attempt will be made to arrive at more general conclusions.

Secondly, in view of the great changes in the political boundaries and cultural landscape of Europe which have taken place during the recent past, we may need to modify our ideas as to the extent of Central Europe. But we can reach a decision only when we have re-examined the ways in which the term has been used previously.

It is unfortunate that many geographical terms either lack or come to lack precise meaning and consequently give rise to misunderstanding of geography or even to its ill repute among scholars of other subjects. One extreme case in this category is the term Central Europe (Middle Europe, *l'Europe centrale*, *Zentraleuropa*, *Mitteleuropa*, *l'Europa centrale*, etc.).[3] Perusing the literature either devoted to a discussion of the term or giving some attention to it one cannot help but be left with a feeling of absolute confusion. Since this is so

---

[1] For full bibliographical details of these and other publications, and those quoted several times, see the bibliography on pages 37-9. References to these are given by quoting the name of the author, and where appropriate the year of publication, followed by the page reference.

[2] 'German' is to be understood here as to mean 'of German mother tongue'.

[3] An indication of the present ambiguity of its meaning is the statement under the entry 'Central Europe' in *Webster's geographical dictionary* (1949), 211, where this term is called 'indefinite and occasional'.

would it not be better to cease using this term altogether? This step was indeed taken by a number of geographers, though not necessarily for that reason. Many others will, however, agree with P. M. Roxby who wrote (1926, 378) that Central Europe is a real entity, a major region with a definite personality;[4] and thus the term becomes indispensable.

Before showing by selected examples the great variation in definitions of Central Europe, it seems appropriate to quote some authors who denied its existence altogether or stated that it ceased to exist at a certain time. The Austrian scholar, Erwin Hanslik, stated emphatically during the First World War that Central Europe was only a phantom of the imagination and that along a line from Trieste via Vienna, Prague, Breslau to Königsberg, the east began without any transition.[5] Using a somewhat more westerly boundary roughly following the Elbe river, a similar principal division into east and west was used by Sir Halford Mackinder shortly after the First World War in his *Democratic ideals and reality* and in his concept again there was no space for a Central Europe.[6] Similarly the French historian, Joseph Aulneau, wrote in the inter-war period that Central Europe was no entity and existed only in the minds of the conquerors and writers.[7] As an example of those authorities who are of the opinion that Central Europe *no longer* exists, the statement of H. G. Steers may be quoted: ' "Mitteleuropa", that first principle of German geographical thought, has gone....'[8]

Among those who do believe in the existence of Central Europe we find that the conflict of opinions is even greater than is usually appreciated. An indication of this is shown in Figure 1 where the boundary lines of maps of various types and of major series of topographic maps, all bearing the name 'Central Europe' in this or another form, are indicated by different symbols. For obvious reasons

[4] Cf. also E. DE MARTONNE (1930, 3): 'Ainsi l'Europe centrale n'est pas un mot'.

[5] 'Es gibt kein "Mitteleuropa" als natürliche und kulturelle Wirklichkeit. Bei Triest, Wien, Brünn, Prag, Oderberg, Breslau, Posen und Königsberg hört der Westen auf, setzt der Osten ohne jeden Übergang ein.' (1917, 94).

[6] Map 'The real Europe' (1919, 154). His 'heartland' (1919, Figure 24) is based on a world-wide concept and might be called 'Middle Eurasia'. W. G. East stated 'Sir Halford Mackinder too found reason to distinguish a middle or transitional area in Europe, fronting the inland Black and Baltic seas, between the maritime Europe to the west and south and the purely continental area which stretches east of the Volga' (1948, 40). I have been unable to trace a publication by Sir Halford Mackinder which makes this clear distinction and I do not think that his 'inner or marginal crescent' (1904, 435), which again is part of a world-wide concept, should be interpreted in the sense of constituting a Central Europe. In fact the only clear indication that he at one time recognized the existence of a Central Europe seems to be the fact of his being the editor of the series *The regions of the world* which includes the volume *Central Europe* by Joseph Partsch. It is difficult to estimate now how much credit for this particular concept of Central Europe should go to the editor and how much to the author, but in the first instance it seems largely to be due to Sir Halford Mackinder as is indicated by the following remark by Partsch in the preface: '... he [the editor] and I were agreed that, in order to secure the unity of the whole work, the plan and division of the material must be settled by the editor for the guidance of his fellow workers' (1903, ix).

[7] 'Où commence et où finit l'Europe centrale?... Elle n'est en effet ni un Etat ni un assemblage d'Etats. Elle n'a vécu que dans l'imagination des conquérants où des écrivains' (1926, 8).

[8] (1948, 28); and on p. 31, 'Since Central Europe as conceived by modern geographers has gone....'

a map will usually depict a somewhat greater area than its title suggests, but it nevertheless conveys an idea, especially in comparison with other maps, of the

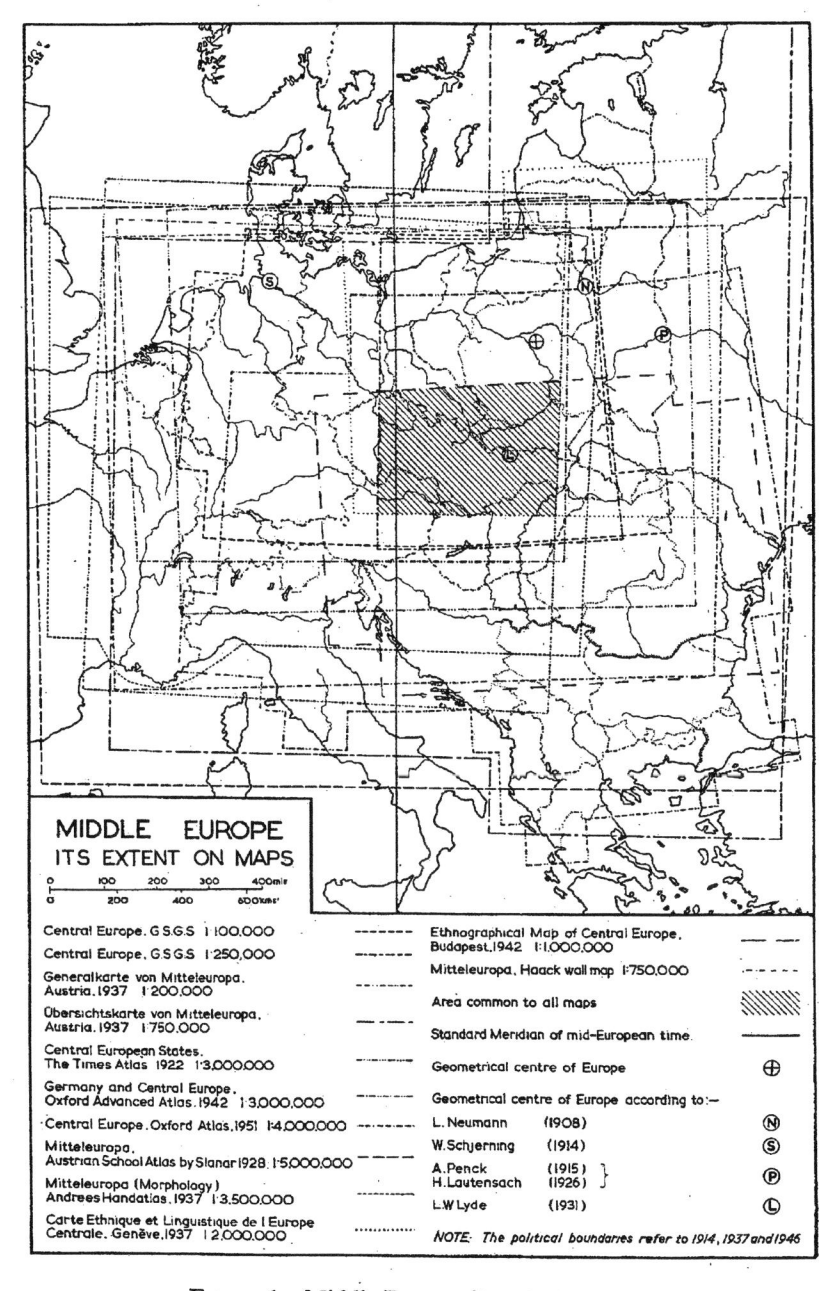

FIGURE 1—Middle Europe: its extent on maps.
The areas covered by, and the area common to, twelve maps and map series all bearing the name Central Europe (or the equivalent in French and German), and their location with respect to the geometrical centre of Europe and the standard meridian of mid-European time.

approximate extent envisaged for the area to which its title refers. Little agreement exists, and the area common to all maps, indicated by shading, is extremely small; it includes the greater part of Czechoslovakia and extends into Austria, Germany, Hungary and Poland. Two more things are indicated on the map, which by their very names, should bear a close relationship to Central Europe: the geometrical centre of Europe and the standard meridian of so-called Central European Time. One would expect that there would be agreement at least as regards the geometrical centre of Europe, since this is a question that is to be solved by measuring, but this is not the case.[9] Accepting the conventional eastern boundaries of Europe, the geometrical centre, marked on Figure 1 by a crossed circle, is near Warsaw. Other places which have been stated as the geometrical centres of Europe are Grodno; the mouth of the Elbe river; the Rokitno swamps; and the Tatra mountains.[10] Even if we accept these locations as alternatives, save for the last one, all are situated outside the common area. This applies to an even greater degree when we consider their location in relation to the area common to a selected number of definitions as shown in Figure 2. I suggest that the term 'Middle Europe' should be used in preference to 'Central Europe, since the latter inevitably creates a misleading impression about the location of the centre of Europe and thus about the space relationships within Europe.[11] For this reason, but also considering the political and cultural disintegration since 1939, it seems that the case for using *central* because it means more than geometrical centrality, as Roxby wrote (1926, 379), is no longer valid. Similarly, since the standard meridian of Central European Time (15° east of Greenwich) is far to the west of the centre of Europe, and further since we are faced with a time *belt* reaching the extremities of the Continent north and south, whereas the word *central* implies a compact area approximately equidistant from all margins, I suggest that the term mid-European Time (used for instance in the *Encyclopaedia Britannica*[12]) is to be preferred.

[9] In a strict mathematical sense an irregular surface does not possess a centre. In *Webster's new international dictionary* (London, 1943), 434, 'centre' is defined as 'orig. the point round which a circle is described; . . . a point at the average distance from the exterior points of a body or figure'. Applied to any large part of the earth's surface this may best be interpreted as that point which serves as the centre of the circle which can be drawn on the globe round the area in question touching as many points of its periphery as possible.

[10] *Grodno*: crossing point of the lines from Gibraltar to the North Cape and from Cape da Roca to the Urals [sic] (L. NEUMANN, 1908, 447); *Mouth of the Elbe*: equidistant from the entrance of the White Sea, the southernmost point of Greece, Cape Tarifa, and the north-western point of Iceland (W. SCHJERNING, 1914, 67); *Rokitno swamps*: the longest diagonals that can be drawn across Europe cross there, and nearby are also the mid-points of these diagonals. The point of Europe equidistant from the boundary meridians and parallels, which could be used as an alternative centre, is near the source of the Memel (Nyeman) (A. PENCK, 1915, 16; also H. LAUTENSACH, 1926, 17); L. W. LYDE (1931, 1), simply states: 'Even the *Tatra* mass, the geometrical centre of Europe, is within 300 miles of three seas.'

[11] Even such an experienced geographer as J. F. Unstead, who stated that 'Central Europe may be thought as lying directly across the centre of Europe', was misled (1927, 51). *Webster's new international dictionary* contains the entry Mid-Europe (1943, 1556) but not Central Europe.

[12] Fourteenth edn. (1929-32), vol. 22, 224. Section *Time, standard*, by Sir Arthur Stanley Eddington.

CENTRAL EUROPE — MITTELEUROPA — EUROPE CENTRALE 19

The divergence of opinion as to the extent of Middle Europe becomes even greater when we compare the actual *definitions* given by various authors. A map showing the boundaries of an author's particular notion is only in a few cases provided, and thus in Figure 2 I have, in the other instances, attempted to plot these boundaries on the basis of the respective texts. This map aims to give

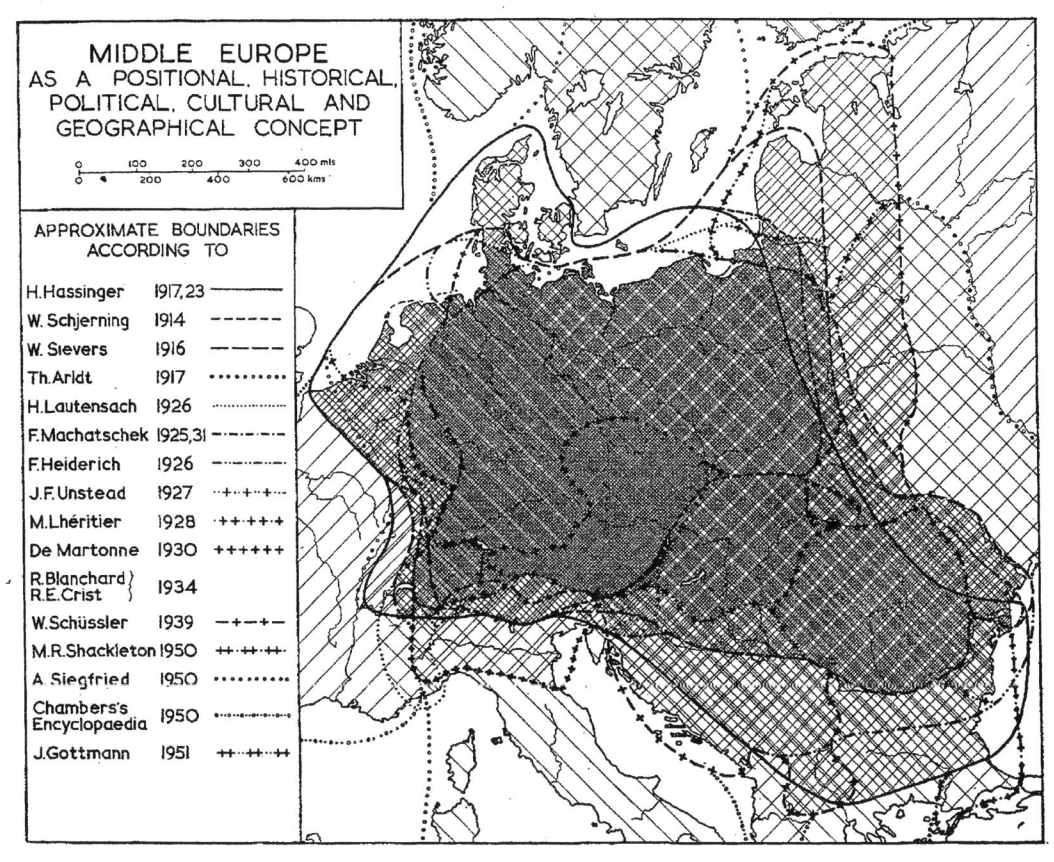

FIGURE 2—Middle Europe as a positional, historical, political, cultural and geographical concept: a graded assessment of the degree of coincidence existing between sixteen definitions of Middle Europe.
The shading density is directly proportional to the number of authorities who included a given area within Middle Europe. The various patterns are only the accidental result of the process of superimposition. For an explanation of the R. Blanchard and R. E. Crist boundary, see footnote 13.

a visual impression by graded shading of how frequently parts of Europe are included within Middle Europe: it is, in fact, sixteen maps superimposed.[13]

[13] Although in most cases it would be possible to follow on the map the boundaries of the area conceived as Middle Europe by one of the selected authors, the map aims at something different. The plotting of the boundaries was only a necessary step in the construction of the map. In cases where boundaries coincided, however, only one could be marked; in the case of Blanchard – Crist no separate symbol appears, since there is a complete coincidence with sections of boundaries of other definitions. The individual maps are based on the following sources: H. HASSINGER (1917, 478) (map); W. SCHJERNING (1914, 67); W. SIEVERS, 1916, taken from H. Hassinger (1917, 467-8); TH.

Each of these 'maps' gives one author's concept of Middle Europe, and in each case the area thus named is shaded in the same degree of density. The disposition of the lines of shading of each successive 'map' is chosen in such a way that they fall into a gap left by the previous one. The degrees of shading density, which by this process increase in an arithmetical progression, are therefore in a direct relationship to the number of authors who include a certain part within Middle Europe; the various patterns, however, are only accidental results of this process of superimposition. As can be seen, the areas in some cases included within Middle Europe extend surprisingly enough beyond the part of Europe shown on this map, and the only part of the continent which has never been included is the Iberian Peninsula. On the other hand, the area which all these authors agree belongs to Middle Europe is no more than Austria and Bohemia-Moravia.

The definitions used here are of a wide range and include strictly speaking non-geographical ones. It is often difficult to classify definitions in order to arrange them into groups, but I believe that such a grouping is the key that will disentangle the terminological knot and lead to the desired clarification. The classification I have attempted is fourfold:

(i) Middle Europe as a topographical term ('topographical' here used in its original meaning, indicating the position of an area).
(ii) Middle Europe as a physical region, based on a single physical criterion or a number of them.
(iii) Middle Europe, a concept with an historical or political bias.
(iv) Middle Europe as a geographical region delimited by means of both physical nature and cultural elements.

Middle Europe as a Topographical Term

Considering the history of modern geography and the area conceived, it is not surprising that the term appears to have been first used in its German form *Mitteleuropa*.[14] To my knowledge it appears for the first time in 1808 in a

---

[14] H. Cord Meyer rightly criticized the statement, which he incorrectly attributed to Hilda Ormsby, that it was first used by Mendelssohn in 1836. He quotes (179, footnote 4) as the first geographical use of the term *Petermanns Geographische Mitteilungen*, 7 (1861). There, in a report on new geographical literature, it appears as the title of three different railway maps, two of which, however, are quoted as already in their fourth and fifth editions respectively.

ARLDT (1917, 1-2). Arldt states that on geographical grounds Italy should be included, but on political grounds excluded, and on two maps (6, 9) he gives a number of alternatives for the western and eastern boundaries of Middle Europe. H. LAUTENSACH (1926, 6) (map); F. MACHATSCHEK (1925, 3-4, and 1931, 39-41) (map); F. HEIDERICH (1926, 3); J. F. UNSTEAD (1927, 50); M. LHÉRITIER (1928, 51); E. DE MARTONNE (1930, 2-3); R. BLANCHARD-R. E. CRIST (1934, 211); W. SCHÜSSLER (1939, 8); M. R. SHACKLETON (1950, 240-3); A. SIEGFRIED (1950, 17-20); K. RISHBETH, section Europe, anthropology, *Chambers's encyclopaedia* (London, 1950), vol. 5, 443; J. GOTTMANN (1951, 334). Not plotted on this map but interesting in this context is F. Braun's concept of Middle Europe; according to him the centre of the region is at Cologne and the region stretches for about a thousand kilometres in all directions, thus even including England. Cf. 'Europa als Erdteil', in *Das Erdbild der Gegenwart*, ed. W. Gerbing (Leipzig, 1926), 8.

publication by August Zeune of Berlin.[15] He defined *Mitteleuropa* as comprising *Karpatenland* (the lower Danube basin), *Hercinialand* (the traditional German lands including the entire Rhine basin) and *Sevennenland* (France). Although he made attempts in a later publication to justify his subdivisions of Europe as *Naturabtheilungen* (1820, 93-6), it is in fact only location which is the common denominator, the situation between the northern and southern European peninsulas and islands, forming a median west-east strip through what L. W. Lyde in 1931 termed 'Peninsular Europe'. For that reason, it seems justifiable to assign Zeune's use of the term to the first of the four groups in question. Also, merely based on location, the term *Mitteleuropa* was used by Hassel in 1819 in a comprehensive German geographical reference work to denote a median strip across Europe, this time in a north-south direction and included the German states, Austria-Hungary, Switzerland and the Italian peninsula.[16] Quoting a non-German author, the French geographer Denaix in 1833 used *l'Europe centrale* very much as Zeune had done to describe a west-east strip from the Pyrenees to the rivers Vistula and Tisza.[17] Later the use of the term in a purely topographical sense gave way to other concepts using the same term but attaching to it a specific content as a common denominator. Nevertheless it may still be found used in this original way now and then; for instance by Kathleen Rishbeth in *Chambers's encyclopaedia* (vol. 5 (1950), 443) where it denotes the *entire* part of Europe between its northern and southern islands and peninsulas and thus even includes Russia.

One might think a term doing no more than indicating location would be quite valueless to the geographer, but another aspect should also be considered. Just *because* of the absence of further implications which makes it independent of political events and historical changes, it may be useful as a term of reference to any middle part of Europe and as the name for a map or a series of topographical maps covering such a part. Since its limits may therefore legitimately vary a great deal, it is suggested that the term should not be used as a proper name, and 'middle' in this case should be spelt with a small initial letter thus forming an equivalent to the German *mittleres Europa*. Alternatively mid-Europe or median-Europe could be used. In cases of doubt, it should be referred to by its full name: middle Europe in a topographical sense.

[15] A. ZEUNE, *Gea. Versuch einer wissenschaftlichen Erdbeschreibung* (Berlin, 1808). Quoted from E. MEYNEN (1935, 84).

[16] A. C. GASPARI, G. HASSEL and J. G. F. CANNABICH, *Vollständiges Handbuch der neuesten Erdbeschreibung* (Weimar, 1819), I, viii; II, 38. Since this is the third though absolutely rewritten edition of this work an attempt was made to check whether this term had been used already in the earlier editions, the first, published in three parts in 1797, 1799 and 1801, and the second, 1802, both of which were never completed. When eventually copies of these earlier editions were traced, it was found that the term does not appear in any of them. The general plan of the work, as set out in the preface of the second edition, suggests that the term *Deutschland* was used in place of what was later referred to as *Mitteleuropa*, since it is stated by Gaspari that the first and second volumes were to contain the general introduction as well as *Deutschland*, the third volume, western and southern, and the fourth volume, northern and eastern Europe. (For a discussion of the term *Deutschland*, see p. 22.)

[17] M. A. DENAIX, *Étude de géographie naturelle sur l'Europe centrale*. Quoted from M. Lhéritier (1928, 44, footnote 2).

Middle Europe as a Physical Region

Similarly beyond historical changes is Middle Europe as a physical region.[18] Once the criteria are agreed upon, the extent of the area to which they apply can be found quite objectively by observation, measuring and plotting the results on a map. Surprisingly this concept is almost as old as the former since it resulted from August Zeune's *Naturabtheilungen* already mentioned, and especially from Carl Ritter's ideas on *Naturgebiete*, for the delimitation of which he considered relief to be the most important criterion.[19] Thus in a German geographical text-book of 1839, *Mitteleuropa* was defined as a region formed by the Alps, together with the mountain systems and lowlands attached to them.[20] This concept covered much the same area as found by Zeune. This notion, which included France within Middle Europe, prevailed until the 1870s and even later. It was, for instance, used by Friedrich Ratzel who, at the end of the century, called it 'Middle Europe in its widest sense',[21] and later still in 1904 by Wilhelm Götz in his book *Historische Geographie* which forms part 19 of the collection *Die Erdkunde*. He divided *Mitteleuropa* into three parts, Gaul-France, the Alpine regions and *Deutschland*, and stated (p. 223) that on account of space relations France is also part of *Mitteleuropa* since only a small section of that country is linked to the Mediterranean shores. Usually, however, by that time this term had come to be used for a smaller area, one which previously had commonly been called *Deutschland*, as the latter term was being applied more and more to the German Empire in spite of its official name, *Das Deutsche Reich*. Although *Deutschland* had obviously referred to an ethnical[22] and historical quality, when replaced by *Mitteleuropa* this region was nevertheless defined on the basis of physical criteria. A number of definitions of this kind could be given,[23] but one stands out, the paper by Albrecht Penck.[24]

[18] Since there is no general agreement as to whether the use of the word 'natural' should be limited to regions defined exclusively on a physical basis, as suggested by Unstead, or whether it should be used to describe the larger synthetic entities which are based on both physical and human criteria as advanced by Roxby, this term had better be avoided (cf. ROXBY, 1926, 381). The corresponding German term to physical region is *Naturraum*.

[19] *Die Erdkunde in ihrem Verhältnis zur Natur und zur Geschichte des Menschen* (Berlin, 1817).

[20] C. E. MEINECKE, *Lehrbuch der Geographie für die oberen Classen höherer Lehranstalten* (Prenzlau, 1839).

[21] 'Between the Alps and the North and Baltic Seas, between the Atlantic Ocean and the Black Sea, lies a part of Europe to which Alps, Carpathians and Balkans, vast lowlands, and rivers like the Rhine and Danube give a similarity to the major landforms, a region whose climate is of a similar type and whose plant cover from one end to the other spreads the same carpet of forests, meadows, heathlands, bogs and pastures. This is Middle Europe in its widest sense. ... To this Middle Europe belong all neighbours of Germany except Russia ... That part of the Balkan Peninsula situated towards the Danube is also drawn into its embrace by this mighty river' (1898, 7-8).

[22] *deutsch* from *diutisc*, later *diutisch* 'of the people' (popularis), cf. J. and W. GRIMM, *Deutsches Wörterbuch* (Leipzig, 1860), vol. 2, 1043.

[23] For references, cf. H. HASSINGER (1917, 450-1).

[24] 1887, 91-113. It is only fair to add that this is not the only and final definition of Middle Europe by A. Penck as is sometimes implied. Later he revised it to include the lower Danube basin and wrote: 'Durch zwanzig Jahre in Wien lebend, habe ich mehr und mehr empfunden, dass ich vor dreissig Jahren Mitteleuropa viel zu enge Grenzen gesetzt und seine Südostgrenze gerade dorthin verlegt habe, wo die geographische Gliederung Europas eine Stelle vorzeichnet, um die sich durch Jahrhunderte Länder kristallisiert haben' (1915, 17).

Since *Deutschland* as contrasted to *Deutsches Reich* has been mentioned, a few words should be said regarding it. *Deutschland* is a very vague term; little agreement existed among German writers about the area that it was meant to cover and it has often been deliberately misused. It is, however, too great a generalization when Hilda Ormsby writes that 'To the pre-war writers the term "Deutschland" signified the German administrative state...' and that the application of this term for a larger area independent of political boundaries was a 'deliberate movement to establish this new use of the term...' (1935, 340, 342). This movement, which no doubt existed, aimed to use the term in its original meaning which had persisted through the centuries since its first appearance in the eleventh century in the form *Diutischemi lande*.[25] Dickinson stated correctly (1943, 32-3) that *Deutschland* 'has been used for centuries to designate the wider area of the German-speaking peoples, and of alien peoples who in the past have been greatly influenced by German culture' and H. Cord Meyer admitted (1946, 179) that up to 1871 '*Deutschland* was an accepted ethnic-geographic term...'[26] It is truly a historical irony that the first political unit ever to bear this name as its *official* title is the Federal German Republic, the *Bundesrepublik Deutschland* which does not even cover the entire area of what remained of the German state after the Second World War.

Although for the reason outlined above Middle Europe was mostly interpreted at the turn of the century in a narrow sense among German geographers, a work was published that made a well-argued case for a wider concept of Middle Europe. This was Joseph Partsch's *Central Europe* which appeared in its English edition in 1903 and one year later in the unabridged German original. At first much criticized for this wider interpretation, not only abroad but also in Germany,[27] it eventually brought again wide recognition of a Middle Europe extending beyond the boundaries of the area formerly called *Deutschland*. Since Partsch, to indicate the area dealt with, enclosed a map showing a group of states, it is not always fully appreciated that his criterion for delimiting this region was the physical nature, in particular relief.[28] His famous sentence where he sums up the character of Middle Europe proves this point: 'The triad of Alps, hills and plain is the governing chord of the symphony of the Middle European landscape. Where one of these notes ceases to sound Middle Europe ends.'[29]

In later years the delimitation of regions and thus of Middle Europe was done more and more on the basis of both physical and cultural elements, but nevertheless some geographers retained the principle of delimiting exclusively by the former. In Figure 3 four others are plotted, besides Penck's and

---

[25] For reference cf. E. MEYNEN (1935, 6 and 135).
[26] The whole question of the origin and later uses of the term was discussed fully by Emil Meynen in his well-documented book, *Deutschland und Deutsches Reich*.
[27] G. G. CHISHOLM (1904, 242-4); A. KIRCHHOFF (1905, 28-9); TH. FISCHER (1905, 48-53).
[28] The boundaries of the region are plotted in Figure 3 on the basis of the text (1903, 1-3).
[29] Quoted in my own translation from the German edition (p. 4) since in the English edition (p. 2) much of the original flavour is lost.

Partsch's concepts already mentioned. As is brought out by the shading, which is done by using the same cartographic technique as in Figure 2, the common area is much more extensive than on the previous map where different types of definitions were represented, and consists of Germany within its 1937 boundaries, Austria, Switzerland and Bohemia-Moravia. Alfred Hettner stated his

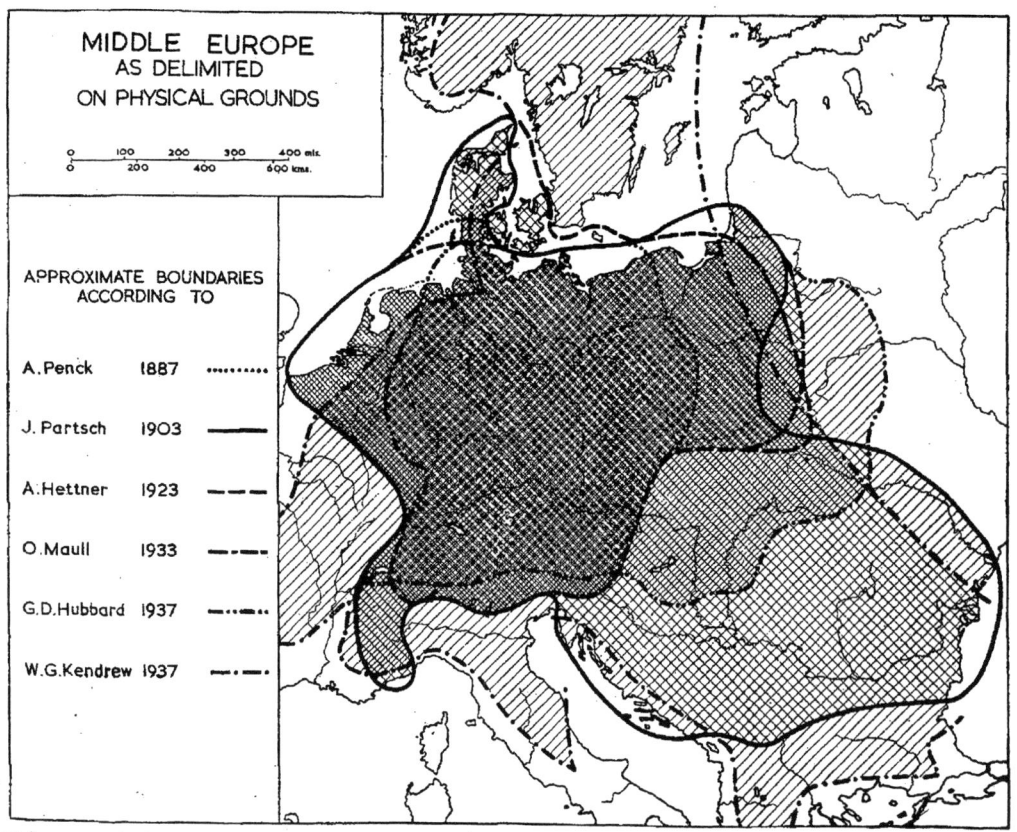

FIGURE 3—Middle Europe as delimited on physical grounds: the amount of agreement existing about the concept of Middle Europe as a physical region.
The shading density is directly proportional to the number of authorities who included a given area within Middle Europe. The various patterns are only the accidental result of the process of superimposition.

definition first in 1907 and retained it in the later editions of his book (1932, 136). His major point of disagreement with Partsch is over the south-eastern part which he added to the Balkan Peninsula, naming the whole region Southeastern Europe though he did not go back to the earlier narrow definitions of Middle Europe but stated that *Mitteleuropa* and *Deutschland* should not be equated (1923, 132). In contrast to Hettner who held that cultural criteria are unsuitable for delimitation of regions in geography (1908, 106; 1927, 296), Otto Maull recognized them as important for that purpose but employed them only at what one might call the 'lower part of the scale' of the regional hierarchy. Middle Europe, as a region to be placed approximately in the middle of the scale, was delimited exclusively on the basis of physical criteria whereas the next smaller region *Deutschland* is distinguished from Middle Europe by its distinct cultural properties, and characterized by a cultural landscape of German character (1933, 8). This Middle Europe is almost the same as Hettner's except for Denmark which is excluded on account of the different space relationships.[30] The remaining definitions indicated on this map are based on a single physical criterion, climate. W. G. Kendrew's definition aims to be only a climatic division of Europe and not a generally applicable region.[31] G. D. Hubbard, on the other hand, uses climate as the criterion to delimit the major regions of Europe but then groups a number of states together which fit best into the regions thus established (1937, 4; map). I am not aware of a British publication where the subdivision of Europe into major regions is based solely on physical factors, though the following remark of W. G. East (1948, 40) pointed in this direction: 'Central or Middle Europe remains and must remain as a permanent fact because it rests on the physical structure of the continent....'[32]

Summing up this section we may say that the concept of Middle Europe as a physical region is very useful because of its objective basis and its permanency, although many geographers would agree that it is not our ultimate aim when we wish to establish a subdivision of Europe into its major regions. But again I wish to point out that we should make ourselves quite clear and, whenever we use Middle Europe in this particular sense, give it its full name: 'Middle Europe as a physical region.'

When we turn to concepts of Middle Europe with an historical and political bias or as a geographical region, we enter much more difficult ground by introducing human elements that are liable to quick changes. Any definition given must, therefore, be related to a certain time so that many definitions, though different, may nevertheless be correct. Furthermore, here we enter the field of the humanities where the subjective element inevitably plays a greater part. The fundamental problem is that the very definition of Europe as a continent is only possible by taking the human factor into account and that, therefore, its eastern boundary has been subject to changes during history.[33] Thus we may conclude that Middle Europe, historically and geographically an area with certain cultural qualities, is not fixed in space, and once it had come

---

[30] Basis for plotting the boundaries (MAULL, 1933, 3-5).

[31] This map can be found in all editions of his book *The climates of the continents* (1922 and 1927, 211; 1937 and 1941, 241; 1953, 312). This map, with some alterations, was reproduced by L. D. STAMP, *Europe and the Mediterranean* (1932, 26), and this in turn with further alterations reproduced by N. G. J. POUNDS in *An historical and political geography of Europe* (1947, 18).

[32] Cf. WILHELM BRÜNGER (1951) who attempted a geomorphological classification of Europe in Eastern, Middle and Western Europe without, however, making this the basis of the geographical regions of Europe.

[33] For a short discussion of the concept of Europe as a continent and its changing eastern boundary, cf. O. MAULL (1951, 667-8). Ibid., 670, he states: ' "Europa" ist eben kein geographischer Begriff, der sich in die Reihe der Erdteilbegriffe einfügen liesse.'

into being it tended to expand and move eastward parallel with the gradual eastward expansion of Europe.

Middle Europe as an Historical and Political Region

The first question which presents itself is: 'At what moment in the history of Europe did Middle Europe emerge?' This question has been answered in various ways. Oskar Kossmann in his book, *Warum ist Europa so?*, where he interprets European history on a basis of time and space, came to the following conclusion: back in prehistory, when, in the general movement of civilization from the Near East via Greece and Rome, the first rays of this advance began to penetrate to the northern parts of Europe, there was one section which on account of its physical nature was particularly favoured to become the nucleus of a separate development. This was the Cimbrian region, the Danish islands and peninsulas, and they did in fact become the cradle of the Teutonic peoples and of Middle Europe. Far enough removed from the Mediterranean world, which first advanced into the continent through the Ligurian gate, and sheltered from the forces of the steppe coming from the east, it was possible that here enough energy could concentrate which eventually resulted in expansion, for various reasons, in the only possible direction, namely south. It interposed a separate Middle European world between east and west, bringing about the principal tripartition of the great northern slope of the European continent into a Celto-Roman, a Teutonic and a Slav section. The western boundary of this middle part was determined by Caesar's defence line which dammed the Teutonic flood and forced it to fill the space east of the Rhine between the northern seas and the Alps. Its eastern boundary, which persisted through the early Middle Ages, was in turn determined by the defence line from the mouth of the Elbe to the Bohemian Forest, which offered itself to the Teutonic tribes against the forces thrusting from the east (1950, 89 and 110).

The French historian, Michel Lhéritier, gave a different answer to this question in his *Régions historiques* (1928, 46). He is of the opinion that in the Middle Ages there was no space for a Middle Europe since the area meant by it was the eastern march of the continent as expressed by the name of Austria — *Österreich*, i.e. the eastern march. It emerged in history from the sixteenth century onwards as a result of the growth of Austria and the advance of German civilization to the countries which are now meant by it, although the name used then was not Middle Europe but Germany. Towards the end of the eighteenth century, Emperor Joseph II was the first to attempt its political organization, but still the name Middle Europe was not used. The concept of Middle Europe as such appears at the time of the Austro-Prussian antagonism in the middle of the nineteenth century and when the question arose as to whether Austria with its different components would be able to survive. Significant is an article in the official *Wiener Zeitung* in 1849 expressing the opinion that, in a politico-economic union of Middle Europe, Austria would inevitably become the centre of gravity on account of its central position. Exponents of this idea of Middle

Europe during the nineteenth century were the German economist, List, the Austrian Minister of Commerce, Bruck, and the German writer, Paul de Lagarde.

Nevertheless, the problem remained an academic one until the First World War brought about an economic unification of the Middle Powers. It was then possible to see how it might work in peace time, and the idea of Middle Europe as a politico-economic unit was revived. Many writings on this theme were published;[34] the most important one is undoubtedly Friedrich Naumann's *Mitteleuropa* (1915). It was soon translated into English and French, and thus became fairly well known elsewhere, though it seems that in many cases it was not studied very thoroughly. Although Naumann only expressed his private opinion, which even within Germany and Austria-Hungary received much criticism,[35] outside Germany it was often taken to be official German policy. It was interpreted as 'the German aim for domination of the middle part of the Continent' and the very word *Mitteleuropa* in English and French usage often came to mean that. It is true that Naumann envisaged a Middle Europe which should be German at its core and that German should be its *lingua franca* (1915, 101), but this, looking at the area he had in mind, was only natural. He spoke bitterly of the tendencies of Germanization (73-5) and anti-Semitism (70-1; 114) and the creation that he wished to result from the war experiences was not a new state organized on German lines, not even a federal state, but a federation of sovereign countries that joined voluntarily as equal partners on the basis of mutual treaties for their common interest (232).[36] Only two matters were to be dealt with by a common authority; economic planning and defence (249). Thus, by increasing production and producing more cheaply as a large enterprise, the living standard of the masses could be raised (118-19), and by having trenches round this group of states and a common defence force ready, further war could be averted (257).[37] Of this book G. G. Chisholm wrote a valuable review,[38] and in the same year further elaborated the subject: '... one may even find in Naumann's book much that is consonant with the proposals that have been put forward for the formation of a League of Nations' (1917(b), 129). Of present-day experience one might add 'much that is consonant with the idea of a Little Europe'.

[34] A number of these publications are quoted by H. HASSINGER (1917, 438-9) and H. CORD MEYER (1946, 185-7).

[35] Cf. *Rheinisch Westfälische Zeitung* (November 27th, 1915). 'To sacrifice the individuality of Prusso-Germany to the idea of a fictitious Middle Europe would mean to cut away the ground from underneath our feet.' Quoted from M. LHÉRITIER (1928, 47, footnote 2). A summary of the reactions in Hungary is given by Tamás Lengyel *A világháború idején felmerült középeurópatervek és a magyar közvélemény* (The *Mitteleuropa* schemes of the Great War and the Magyarian public opinion) published in *Az Ország Utja* 4 (1940), No. 7 (July). In German translation (duplicated) by the *Publikationsstelle Wien* (1940), No. 98.

[36] Not as stated by R. E. DICKINSON (1943, 24): 'There would thus be formed a federal state under German tutelage....'

[37] Cf. also p. 263, '*Mitteleuropa ist Kriegsfurcht*'.

[38] He wrote about Naumann's book: '... it is written throughout in the heat, not of passion, but of imaginative thought based on wide and intimate knowledge' (1917(a), 83).

The end of the war did not bring a political order like the one conceived by Naumann but the creation of a number of smaller states. As regards them Lhéritier made the statement: 'Le Mitteleuropa est mort, mais l'Europe centrale n'en existe pas moins . . .' (1928, 47). To him *l'Europe centrale* consisted essentially of the successor states of the Austro-Hungarian Empire: Austria, Czechoslovakia and Hungary. His definition, or a modified form of it, came to be widely accepted not so much in Austria but in the other Danube states and also in France and England, where the term Central Europe can still be found used in this sense.[39] In Germany this definition was never accepted. The whole region from Finland to Greece, of which Lhéritier's *l'Europe centrale* forms the continental part, was termed *Zwischeneuropa*.[40] This was a narrowing down of a term originally coined by Albrecht Penck in 1915 (Figure 4). Dividing Europe under the principle of nearness to the open sea and the 'maritime' attitude of its peoples, he established three major regions — *Vordereuropa*, *Zwischeneuropa* and *Hintereuropa*.[41] His idea was that common space relationships would lead the peoples together and that a closely united *Zwischeneuropa* would provide for Europe a strong backbone. He continued: 'Once a strong *Zwischeneuropa* is established then it will no longer be Utopian to speak of the United States of Europe' (1915, 40). Coming back to Lhéritier's concept, though it is a political one, it has also a well-argued geographical basis. He stated: *Europe centrale* is the continental part of a zone of greatest diversity as regards language, cultural influences and religion, which stretches from the North Cape to Cyrenaica and Egypt (1928, 49-50); 'its *raison d'être* is to be a crossroad, a bridge, a turn-plate' (50). *Europe centrale* appears as a synthesis of Europe, and each state again as a synthesis of a synthesis, a little *Europe centrale* and at the same time a whole Europe in miniature (52). The geographical criticism which must be added is one of comparative scale. Although he thought that this *Europe centrale* could be gradually extended, its size is too small to be put side by side with the other major regions of Europe.

Situated between the two powers of Russia and Germany, this *Europe centrale* did not last very long.[42] Hitler Germany, reviving the idea of Middle

---

[39] As an example cf. *The Times* in the leading article 'Europeans in exile' (January 21st, 1952). Generally, however, it has become more and more customary in the press to refer to all countries behind the 'Iron Curtain' as Eastern Europe. Cf. the article 'Eastern Europe' in the *Manchester Guardian* (May 7th, 1953).

[40] Indicative of this is a wall map with this title by H. Haack, published by Justus Perthes, Gotha, which covers the following area: from the Vener Lake and the mouth of the Oder river in the west, to a line just east of the Volkhov river, Kiev and the Danube delta in the east. In the north it just includes Helsinki and Leningrad, in the south it goes a little beyond the southernmost part of the Danube.

[41] The map appears in this publication on the cover and as Figure 3 in the text. It is reproduced in H. LAUTENSACH (1926, Figure 44, 191). It is extremely difficult to render these terms into English. Since Europe is a word of Greek origin, a combination with the appropriate Greek prefixes *pro, meso, meta*, which are also used in biology for denoting a sequence of sections, would recommend itself on linguistic grounds. The resulting terms would thus be Pro-Europe, Meso-Europe and Meta-Europe.

[42] Doubts about its lasting powers were expressed by the Austrian historian, H. STEINACKER, in his paper 'Österreich-Ungarn und Osteuropa' in *Historische Zeitschrift*, 128 (1923), 377-414, especially 413-14.

Europe as a political concept, now not in Naumann's sense but as propagated by the exponents of geopolitics in the sense of a German-ruled political unit,[43] for a time seemed near to putting it into effect. The *Anschluss*, the annexation of Bohemia-Moravia and attempts to establish political control in the other states of Danubian Middle Europe were contributing causes of war. But,

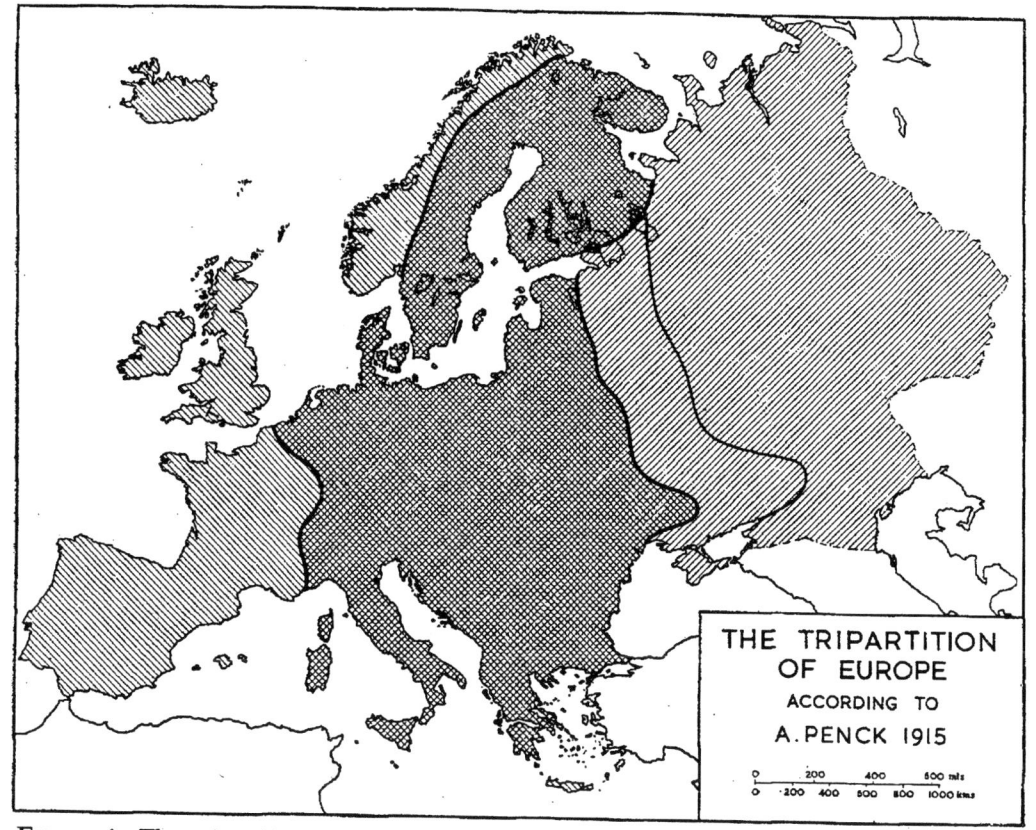

FIGURE 4—The tripartition of Europe on the basis of space relationships into *Vordereuropa*, *Zwischeneuropa* and *Hintereuropa* as suggested by Albrecht Penck in 1915. The zone between Karelia and the Asov Sea he termed the 'Varangian Fringe'.

although liberation of these states was one of the aims the Allied armies fought for, the outcome of the war did not bring the re-emergence of this *Europe centrale*. In 1945, unlike 1920, there was only one power as its neighbour; the states concerned were unable to preserve their independence and soon became Soviet Satellite Europe. Besides Finland and Yugoslavia, which are rather marginally situated, the only state left of these political concepts of *Mitteleuropa*, *Zwischeneuropa* and *Europe centrale* alike is Austria, its further existence depending on an understanding between West and East. Will it on account of its particularly advantageous geographical location once again function as a core round which a *Europe centrale* may develop?

[43] As an example, see KARL HAUSHOFER (1937).

Middle Europe as a Geographical Region

With the beginning of the twentieth century increasing weight came to be attributed to human geographic criteria for regional classification. Although there were some forerunners who attempted a definition of Middle Europe on the basis of both physical *and* cultural elements, as F. Heiderich (1909, 263-4)

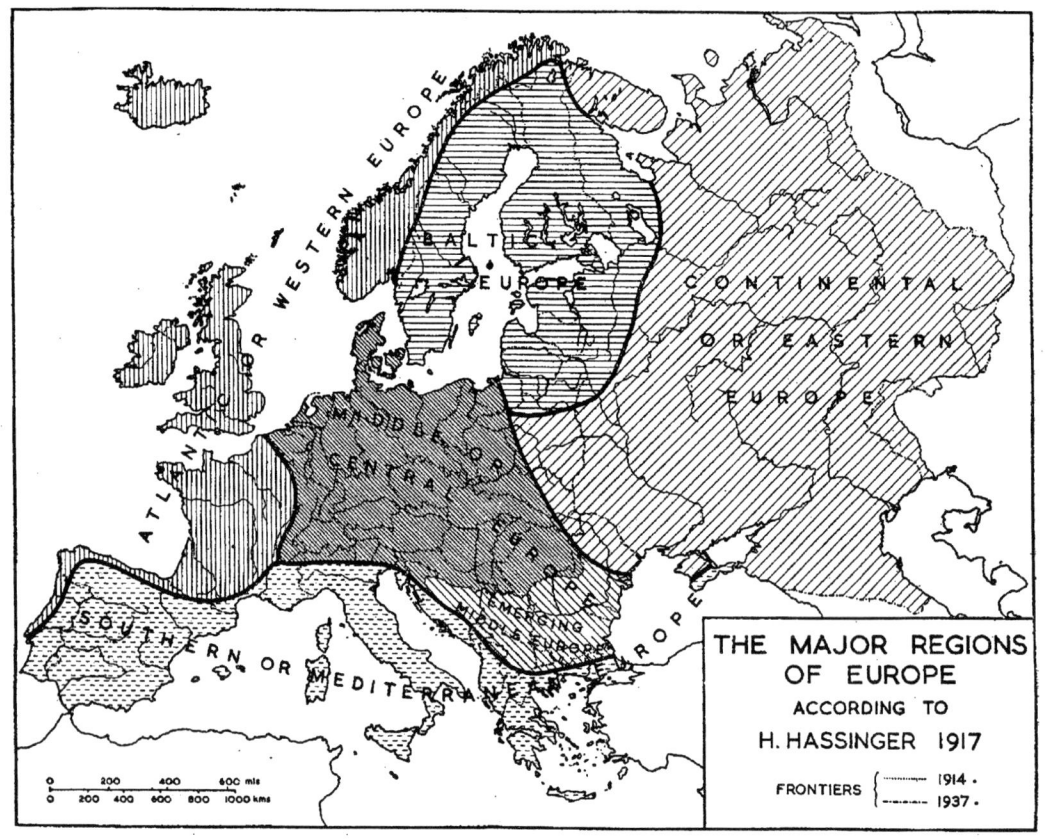

FIGURE 5—The major regions of Europe according to Hugo Hassinger, delimited on the basis of landscape character.

and G. Braun (1916, 1), I think that it is no overstatement to say that one paper stands foremost and had the greatest influence on the further development of the geographical concept of Middle Europe: Hugo Hassinger's essay, *Das geographische Wesen Mitteleuropas*, published in 1917. H. Cord Meyer called it one of the milestones in the development of the *Mitteleuropa* idea (1946, 188), and Dickinson also paid tribute to its importance as 'a masterly essay' (1943, 25). Hassinger's map has been redrawn without alteration, apart from the translation of the names and the additions of the 1937 frontiers (Figure 5).[44] Being misled by the term *Naturgebiet* it has been said that Hassinger based his

[44] The map is to be found on p. 478 of Hassinger's paper. It was reproduced by R. E. Dickinson (1943, Figure 2, 25), but as a rough sketch only.

definition only on physical facts[45] but he used the term *Naturgebiet*, which he took from Carl Ritter, in the same sense as Roxby used the term 'natural region'. Since in his opinion all geographical factors find their expression in the landscape, *the character of the landscape* is the criterion on which he based his delimitation of Middle Europe.[46] We are facing three groups of geographical factors, the physical which are relatively permanent, the human which are changing and in turn result in changes within the third group, the space relationships. Paying due regard to these changes, Hassinger termed an eastern part of the region *werdendes, heranreifendes Mitteleuropa* (emerging, maturing Middle Europe), (477, 483).

It is impossible to give a short summary of Hassinger's characterization of Middle Europe which does justice to this essay; only a few major points can be mentioned. Middle Europe, situated between the monotonous vast mass of the continent in the east and the maritime west with its indented coastline and many islands, is neither as monotonous as the former nor as diversified as the latter. Though not reaching the open ocean it has access to tributary seas in the north and south; thus maritime influences are considerable, though weaker than in Western Europe. Climate and vegetation, population and economy, and finally the entire cultural and political life owe much to this distinct geographical location. Middle Europe's potential strength lies in its nodality at the crossing of the north-south and east-west lines of communication.

In variety of structure and geology Middle Europe takes first place among the European regions. The mountains, provided with frequent passes, are separated by lowlands: thus crossing in any direction is not difficult. The diverse soils and rocks are an important prerequisite to its economic wealth, its fertility, its industry, and its highly developed division of labour and social structure. Since the rivers drain to the north-west on one hand and to the south-east on the other, a first glance at the drainage pattern might lead to the erroneous conclusion that it consists of two independent parts with their peoples standing back to back to each other, the western ones looking out to the ocean, the eastern ones looking towards the continental interior. 'Middle Europe indeed has a head like Janus looking out to west and east, but it most certainly has only *one* body. Its two halves that seemingly tend to separate are closely linked by nature through their common lines of communications.' Just because the two halves are differently endowed with natural wealth — minerals in the north-west, fertile soils and a favourable climate in the south-east — they are inter-

---

[45] 'Since he bases his ideas on natural or physical facts, these are used to define his regions...' R. E. DICKINSON (1943, 26). But Hassinger had stated quite clearly (473) 'The physical and the human as expressions of the local endowment of areas on the earth's surface are so closely interwoven in the landscape that the geographer must not take one out in order to make it the criterion of consideration, judgment and classification of the whole'. Not only did Hassinger deplore the use of a selected criterion or group of criteria as unsuitable for establishing major regions but he also stated that the independent use of all criteria is impossible since the courses of their boundaries differ so greatly (471).

[46] '... the landscape (*Landschaftsbild*) as the product of the interacting and mutually interrelated geographical factors...' (472).

dependent and more closely linked. Culturally it is the German influence which has acted on the space for centuries, giving unity to the whole. Nevertheless, its cultural and ethnographic diversity is very great. Whereas national states are the natural form of political organization in other parts of Europe where a nation could expand into physically simpler areas, Middle Europe is by its very nature destined to be a 'mediator Europe', culturally and politically (477-88). This briefly is, according to Hassinger, the character of Middle Europe and this region stretches as far as we find this character represented. As he states, its boundaries are therefore zones rather than lines and it is only for practical considerations, such as mapping, that certain natural features which are visible in the landscape have to be selected for a demarcation of its boundaries.

It can justly be said that no other geographer paid as much attention to this particular problem and contributed as much to it as Hassinger in this and subsequent publications, as for instance in the introductory chapter of his book, *Die Tschechoslowakei*.[47] This statement is by no means derogatory towards other valuable contributions like those made by Roxby, de Martonne, Dickinson and more recently André Siegfried, Jean Gottmann and G. Hoffmann. But, with the exception of Dickinson's book, it was not a central theme to those authors as it was to Hassinger, who, born in Vienna, and occupying the chair of human geography at Vienna University for almost twenty years, was quite naturally concerned with the problem of *Mitteleuropa*.

Conclusion

Taking up a basic principle expressed by Hassinger in his paper (476) that 'boundaries of regions are therefore [since the landscape changes continuously through human action] not stable but changeable and mobile in the course of history, and classifications into geographical regions are thus always only of value for the present...', it might appear to be logical to conclude with an attempt to answer the question put at the beginning — to what extent the concept of Middle Europe as a geographical region needs to be revised in order to be applicable to the present day? I was tempted to do this but refrained for two reasons. Firstly, this question is rather outside the scope of the paper, and space would not permit a reasoned presentation. Secondly, since so many important facts like the future of Germany and Austria are still undecided, and so much is still in a state of flux, it would be too soon to give any definition of Middle Europe as a geographical region today which would be of more than ephemeral validity. Nevertheless, it seems appropriate to indicate the general direction which the development of Middle Europe has taken since Hassinger's paper was published in 1917.

As a reaction against the over-emphasis once given in geography to states, their capitals, and similar subject matter, political boundaries came to be

---

[47] For some of his other contributions in this field, see the bibliography. Cf. also the obituary of H. Hassinger by H. BOBEK in *Petermanns Geographische Mitteilungen*, 97 (1953), 36-9, with a selective bibliography.

considered as outside the scope of regional geography.⁴⁸ During recent decades the pendulum has swung back and it has been shown in many examples, as for instance in Hassinger's inaugural lecture in Vienna in 1931, that the state is one of the most powerful cultural factors and that its boundaries, though in varying degree, act as differentiating forces upon the cultural landscape.⁴⁹ Changes of state boundaries are always succeeded by landscape changes, which may occur rapidly or gradually and may or may not be striking, depending on circumstances. As regards Middle Europe as a whole, the frontier changes after the First World War made no modification of the boundaries of Middle Europe necessary. On the contrary, within the new states, where areas of more advanced civilization were linked with more backward ones farther east, the process of integration of the 'emerging Middle Europe' to parts of equal standing was accelerated. The consequences of the Second World War are quite different. Since 1939, when various groups of ethnic Germans began to make their way into the *Reich*, we have witnessed a continuous disintegration of Middle Europe as a geographical region. Together with the retreating German armies on the eastern and south-eastern front went many thousands of German settlers, leaving the land that their forefathers had cultivated. In 1939 approximately ten million German nationals lived in the lost eastern provinces, and about eleven million ethnic Germans in the states of eastern and south-eastern Middle Europe. Out of this total of over twenty million Germans, about thirteen million arrived eventually in Potsdam Germany, and almost 400,000 found a refuge in Austria.⁵⁰ We are here not concerned with this greatest folk migration in history as such, but with its effects on the cultural landscape and thus on Middle Europe as a geographical region. Nevertheless, the actual figures of this population movement give an indication of the degree of the landscape changes and Figures 6 and 7 are intended to serve this purpose. The expulsion of the Germans created a population vacuum which so far has only partially been filled, on the whole by peoples taken mainly from the eastern parts of the states affected and thus of a considerably lower standard of civilization. In some cases people were even taken from Asia so that we now find an appreciable number of Mongols work-

---

⁴⁸ Cf. H. HETTNER (1927, 295).

⁴⁹ Earlier, but not dealt with in such a systematic way as by Hassinger, the geographical importance of the political factors was emphasized by L. W. LYDE: 'It is almost always the political control that gives the dominant note in the most important areas; and, as the method of treating such areas should in each case, as far as possible, be appropriate to the dominant note, the political unit cannot be made subordinate without more being lost than is gained' (1913, iv).

⁵⁰ There is already an extensive literature on the refugee problem. For examples in English see CHAUNCY D. HARRIS and G. WÜLKER, 'The refugee problem of Germany', *Economic Geography*, 29 (1953), 10-25 and the relevant chapters in J. VERNANT, *The refugee in the post-war world* (1953). Important is the publication containing the nine maps by W. ESSEN (1952), of which No. 1 and No. 7 were used for the preparation of Figures 6 and 7, supplemented with statistical data published in the *Geographisches Taschenbuch* (1950), 147-54, and in the case of South Tyrol by the paper by F. DÖRRENHAUS (1953), 191. An official work on the expulsion of the Germans, of which the first volume has appeared, is being prepared by the Federal German Government (*Dokumentation der Vertreibung der Deutschen aus Ost-Mitteleuropa bearbeitet von Theodor Schieder, herausgegeben vom Bundesministerium für Vertriebene*, Band I [1953]. (cf. *The Times*, September 17th, 1953).

ing in the industrial region of Upper Silesia.[51] In these areas where the new settlers shape the landscape in a way congenial to them, a very different cultural landscape is emerging, especially in the rural parts and in those towns where war destruction was greatest. Apart from this it is already the dichotomy of low density of rural population within these areas and increased population density

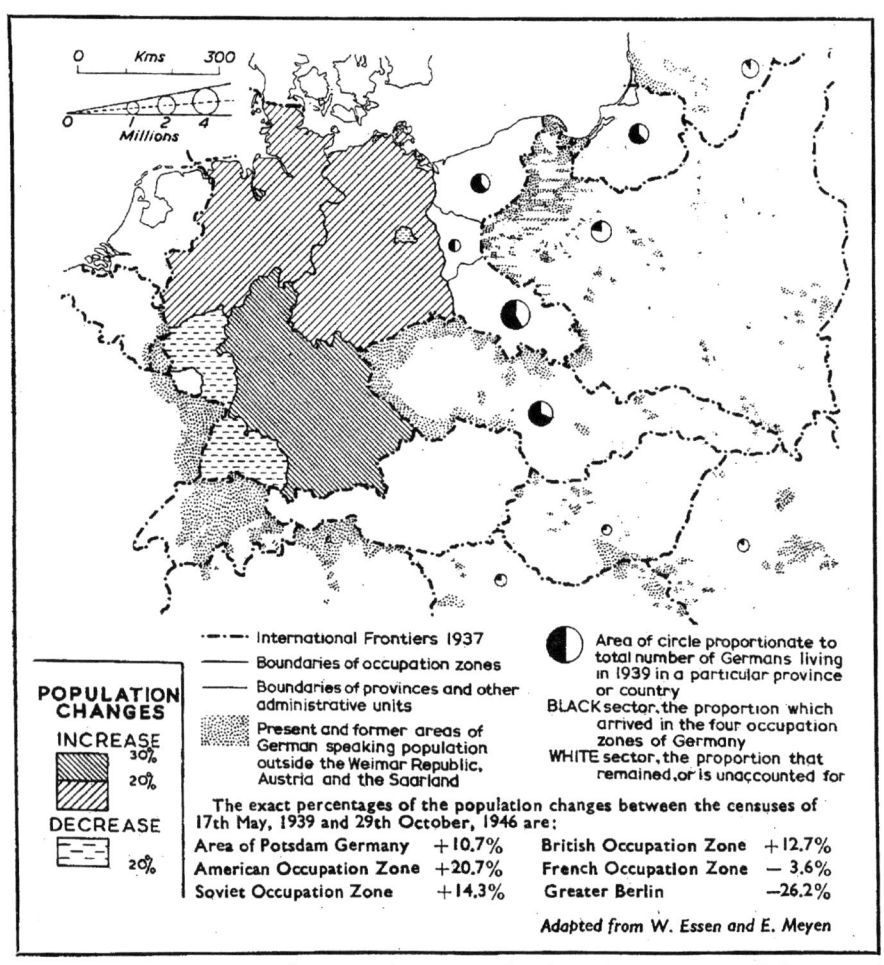

FIGURE 6—The German *Lebensraum*, its contraction from 1939 to 1946 and the overall effect of the westward migration of German nationals (*Reichsdeutsche*) and ethnic Germans (*Volksdeutsche*) on the population distribution of each occupation zone.

within the 'two Germanies' which make for differentiation of the landscape east and west of the Oder-Neisse line and the Czech-German frontier. On the one hand, farms and villages have been deserted and forest is springing up on untilled fields: it is estimated that in the lost provinces alone three million acres

[51] E. LENDL (1951, 39); *The Times* (April 1st, 1954). H. G. VON ESEBECK in 'Vertriebene Deutsche und Exilpolen', *Aussenpolitik*, 5 (1954), 20-7, states that the total population in the lost provinces now administered by Poland amounts to five million people at the most, as far as can be gathered from official statistics.

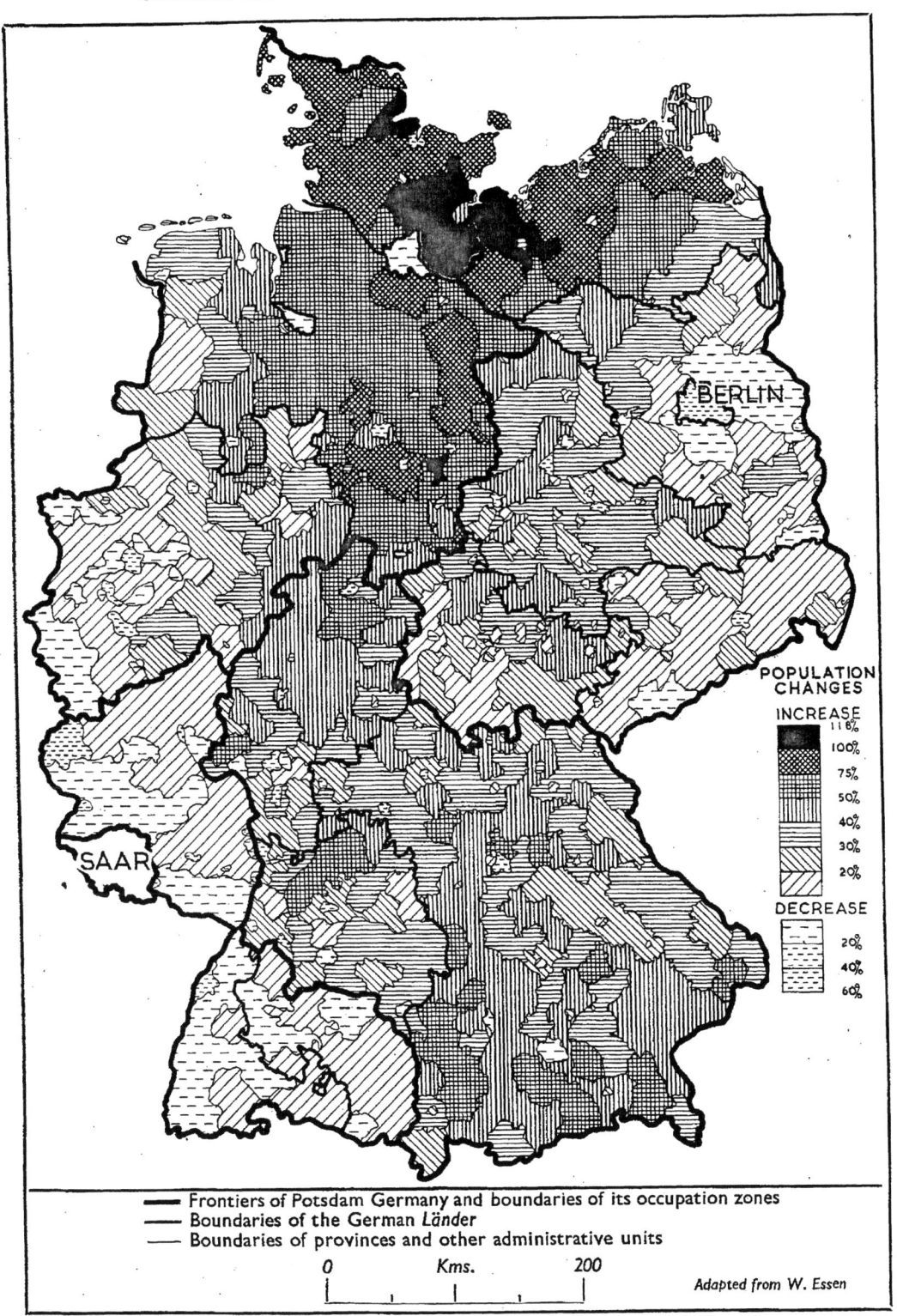

CENTRAL EUROPE — MITTELEUROPA — EUROPE CENTRALE 35

FIGURE 7—The effect of the influx of refugees and expellees on the population distribution of Potsdam Germany.

of farming land have reverted to waste[52] and it was officially stated that in Czechoslovakia 250 of the former German villages have not been resettled.[53] On the other hand there are population increases in parts of over 100 per cent, with a consequent increase in the number of dwellings and intensity of land use. This contrast is emphasized by the difference in ideology which brings with it a certain economic attitude and policy and thus again gives the landscape behind the 'Iron Curtain' a new and different imprint. One need only point at the effect that the land reform has had on the field and settlement pattern where formerly large estates, with huge fields under the same crop, were subdivided into small holdings, though this is only a first stage.[54] Despite the failures experienced so far, as long as the ideology remains the same, it is only a matter of time until the second stage will come and those newly-created farms, together with the original peasant holdings with their often minute field parcels, will be superseded by *sovkhoz* and *kolkhoz* (state and co-operative) farms giving the rural landscape yet another appearance. This influence of ideology can even be felt in the Soviet zone of Germany, which, as the events in June 1953 showed, cannot be considered a proper Soviet satellite like the other states within the Russian sphere. A particularly striking example of this is found in Berlin and attention has been drawn to it in a number of publications.[55] One sentence in *The Times* of April 11th, 1952, brings this out particularly clearly: 'The prospect is that two distinct faces of Berlin would emerge from a prolonged division of the city. Just as the west has its *Clay Allee* and the east its *Stalin Allee* so there is a marked difference in architectural forms which somehow contrives to transmute the ideological conflict into stone.'[56]

In spite of the various changes taking place which give the Soviet zone of Germany certain east European imprints, one cannot separate this area from Middle Europe if this region is to be retained at all. On the one hand, seen on a European scale, Middle Europe would then be too small to be considered a major region in its own right. On the other hand, there is at least not yet sufficient cause for such a major separation. Although Communist-ruled, the traditional cultural landscape has not altered as greatly as some instances might suggest, and the landscape of the Soviet zone is still much more akin to Western Germany than it is to Russia, the East European state *par excellence*. Similarly, but to a lesser degree, what has been said about the Soviet Zone of Germany applies also to the marches still farther east, over which German cultural influence once extended, for many traces pointing to that heritage are still visible.

[52] TERENCE PRITTIE (1953, 207).

[53] E. LENDL (1951, 45). For a more detailed discussion of the population changes in north-west Bohemia see the paper by A. HAMMERSCHMIDT where, in two maps and a table of the population figures for ten towns, he compares the population distribution of 1949 with that of 1930.

[54] Cf. A. E. MOODIE (1954).

[55] Articles in *The Times*, the *Manchester Guardian*, and a paper by P. SCHÖLLER in *Erdkunde*. For details cf. bibliography.

[56] Only a few examples of the recent geographical changes within Middle Europe as conceived by Hassinger can be given here. The topic has been dealt with more fully by E. LENDL, *Dozent* at the University of Vienna.

For how long these traces will be retained is difficult to gauge, but to change the character of a landscape completely is always a process to be measured at least in decades rather than years.

It is possible to use the 'vague' term Middle Europe in a clear and unmistakeable manner provided we express precisely which kind of Middle Europe we mean. 'Middle Europe as a topographical term' and 'Middle Europe in a physical sense' remain unchanged by historical events. 'Middle Europe in a political sense' depends on the political situation at a given time, and at least for the moment has ceased to exist. 'Middle Europe as a geographical region' is *still* with us, though smaller, but still a geographical entity worthy of being studied not as a mere group of states, but as a geographical subject of more lasting character: a geographical region.

BIBLIOGRAPHY

TH. ARLDT, *Die Völker Mitteleuropas* (Leipzig, 1917).
J. AULNEAU, *Histoire de l'Europe centrale* (Paris, 1926).
R. BLANCHARD and R. E. CRIST, *A geography of Europe* (London, 1934).
G. BRAUN, *Deutschland*, Band I (Berlin, 1916).
G. BRAUN, Mitteleuropa und seine Grenzmarken, *Wissenschaft und Bildung*, No. 141 (Leipzig, 1917).
W. BRÜNGER, 'Gedanken zur morphologischen Gliederung Europas in ostwestlicher Richtung', *Petermanns Geographische Mitteilungen*, 95 (1951), 31-4.
G. G. CHISHOLM, Review of J. Partsch's 'Central Europe', *Geographical Journal*, 23 (1904), 242-4.
G. G. CHISHOLM, (a) Review of F. Naumann's 'Mitteleuropa', *Scottish Geographical Magazine*, 33 (1917)(a), 83-8.
G. G. CHISHOLM, (b) 'Central Europe as an economic unit', *Geographical Teacher*, 9 (1917)(b), 122-33.
E. DE MARTONNE, 'La notion d'Europe centrale', introduction in *Géographie Universelle*, tome IV, première partie (Paris, 1930), 1-3.
R. E. DICKINSON, *The German Lebensraum* (Harmondsworth and New York, 1943).
F. DÖRRENHAUS, 'Deutsche und Italiener in Südtirol', *Erdkunde*, 7 (1953), 185-216.
W. G. EAST, Remarks in the discussion after Mrs. J. A. Steers' paper, 'The middle people', *Geographical Journal*, 112 (1948), 40-1.
W. ESSEN, 'Herkunftsgebiete, Wanderungswege und heutige Verteilung der deutschen Heimatvertriebenen im Vierzonen-Deutschland' (9 maps) in *Europa und die deutschen Flüchtlinge*, ed. Institut zur Förderung öffentlicher Angelegenheiten e.V. (Frankfurt/Main, 1952).
I. ESSENWEIN-ROTHE, 'Heimatvertriebene in Österreich', *Zeitschrift für Geopolitik*, 24 (1953), 307-16.
TH. FISCHER, Review of J. Partsch's 'Mitteleuropa', *Zeitschrift der Gesellschaft für Erdkunde zu Berlin* (1905), 48-53.
J. GOTTMANN, *A geography of Europe* (New York, 1951).
A. HAMMERSCHMIDT, 'Wandlungen der Bevölkerungsverteilung in Nordwestböhmen seit dem zweiten Weltkrieg', *Berichte zur Deutschen Landeskunde*, 12 (1954), 233-8, with two maps.
E. HANSLIK, Österreich, *Schriften des Instituts für Kulturforschung*, Band III (Wien, 1917).
H. HASSINGER, 'Das geographische Wesen Mitteleuropas, nebst einigen grundsätzlichen Bemerkungen über die geographischen Naturgebiete Europas und ihre Begrenzung', *Mitteilungen der Geographischen Gesellschaft Wien*, 60 (1917), 437-93.
H. HASSINGER, 'Mitteleuropa', Ewald Banse, *Lexikon der Geographie* (Braunschweig, 1923), Band II, 124-7.
H. HASSINGER, 'Weltage und Wesen des östlichen Mitteleuropa' being section II in *Die Tschechoslowakei* (Wien, 1925), 26-41.
H. HASSINGER, 'Der Staat als Landschaftsgestalter', *Zeitschrift für Geopolitik*, 9 (1932), 117-22 and 182-7.
H. HASSINGER, 'Eine französische Länderkunde von Mitteleuropa' (Review of E. de Martonne's *Europe Centrale*), *Petermanns Geographische Mitteilungen*, 78 (1932), 13.

H. Hassinger, 'Mitteleuropa, Donaueuropa, Südosteuropa', *Volkstum im Südosten* (1941), 173-6.
H. Hassinger, Österreichs Wesen und Schicksal, verwurzelt in seiner geographischen Lage, *Wiener Geographische Studien*, No. 20 (Wien, 1949).
K. Haushofer, 'Mitteleuropa und die Welt', *Zeitschrift für Geopolitik*, 14 (1937), 1-4 (4 maps).
F. Heiderich, Mitteleuropa in *Geographie des Welthandels*, Band I, Pt. 1 (1st edn., Frankfurt/Main, 1909; 4th edn., Wien, 1926).
A. Hettner, *Grundzüge der Länderkunde*, Band I, Europa (1st edn., 1907, 2nd edn., 1923, 5th edn., 1932, Leipzig and Berlin).
A. Hettner, 'Die geographische Einteilung der Erdoberfläche', *Geographische Zeitschrift*, 14 (1908), 1-13, 94-110 and 137-50.
A. Hettner, *Die Geographie, ihre Geschichte, ihr Wesen und ihre Methoden* (Breslau, 1927).
G. W. Hoffman, Section 'Central Europe' in *A geography of Europe* (London, 1953), 325-438.
G. D. Hubbard, *The geography of Europe* (London and New York, 1937).
A. Kirchhoff, Review of J. Partsch's *Mitteleuropa*, *Petermanns Geographische Mitteilungen*, 51 (1905), Literaturbericht No. 65, 28-9.
E. O. Kossmann, *Warum ist Europa so? Eine Deutung aus Raum und Zeit* (Zürich, 1950).
H. Lautensach, *Länderkunde. Ein Handbuch zum Stieler* (Gotha, 1926).
E. Lendl, Die mitteleuropäische Kulturlandschaft im Umbruch der Gegenwart, *Schriften des Instituts für Kultur und Sozialforschung e.V. in München*, No. 2 (Marburg, 1951).
M. Lhéritier, 'Régions historiques', *Revue de Synthèse Historique*, 45 (1928), 43-67.
L. W. Lyde, *The continent of Europe* (London, 1913; 2nd edn., London, 1924).
L. W. Lyde, *Peninsular Europe* (London, 1931).
F. Machatschek, Länderkunde von Mitteleuropa, *Enzyklopädie der Erdkunde* (Leipzig and Wien, 1925).
F. Machatschek, Mitteleuropa, *E. von Seydlitz'sche Geographie, Hundertjahr Ausgabe*, Band II Europa (ohne Deutschland) (Breslau, 1931), 39-68.
H. J. Mackinder, 'The geographical pivot of history', *Geographical Journal*, 23 (1904), 421-37.
H. J. Mackinder, *Democratic ideals and reality: a study in the politics of reconstruction* (London, 1919; republished 1944).
O. Maull, 'Deutschland', vol. in *Allgemeine Länderkunde*, founded by W. Sievers (Leipzig, 1933).
O. Maull, 'Europa–nicht Erdteil, sondern Aufgabe', *Zeitschrift für Geopolitik*, 22 (1951), 666-70.
H. Cord Meyer, 'Mitteleuropa in German political geography', *Annals of the Association of American Geographers*, 36 (1946), 178-94.
E. Meynen, *Deutschland und Deutsches Reich* (Leipzig, 1935).
A. E. Moodie, 'Agrarian reform in East Central Europe', *Yearbook of World Affairs*, 8 (1954), 242-56.
F. Naumann, *Mitteleuropa* (Berlin, 1915).
F. Naumann, *Central Europe* (translated by C. M. Meredith, with an introduction by W. J. Ashley) (London, 1916).
L. Neumann, Länder und Staatenkunde von Europa, in *Scobels Geographisches Handbuch* (5th edn., Leipzig, 1908).
H. Ormsby, 'The definition of Mitteleuropa and its relation to the conception of Deutschland in the writings of modern German geographers', *Scottish Geographical Magazine*, 51 (1935), 337-47.
J. Partsch, Central Europe (translated by Clementina Black), vol. in *The regions of the world*, ed. H. J. Mackinder (London, 1903).
J. Partsch, *Mitteleuropa* (Gotha, 1904).
A. Penck, Physikalische Skizze von Mitteleuropa, in *Unser Wissen von der Erde*, ed. A. Kirchhoff, Band II, 91-113 (Prag, 1887).
A. Penck, Politisch-geographische Lehren des Krieges, *Meereskunde*, 9 (1915), Heft 10.
T. Prittie, 'Germany's lost provinces', *Listener* (February 5th, 1953), 207 and 225.
F. Ratzel, *Deutschland. Einführung in die Heimatkunde* (1st edn., Leipzig, 1898).
P. Reilly, 'Social realism of Stalinallee', *Manchester Guardian* (May 4th, 1953).
P. M. Roxby, 'The theory of natural regions', *Geographical Teacher*, 13 (1925-26), 376-82.
W. Schjerning, Europa, in *Illustrierte Länderkunde*, ed. E. Banse (Braunschweig, 1914).
P. Schöller, 'Stadtgeographische Probleme des geteilten Berlin', *Erdkunde*, 7 (1953), 1-11 (English summary).
M. Schüssler, *Mitteleuropa als Wirklichkeit und Schicksal* (2nd edn., Köln, 1939).
A. R. Shackleton, *Europe, a regional geography* (4th edn., London, 1950).
W. Siegfried, *Switzerland* (English edition, London, 1950), 13-21.

W. Sievers, *Die geographischen Grenzen Mitteleuropas*, Akademische Rede zur Jahresfeier der grossherzoglichen Hessischen Ludwigs-Universität (Giessen, 1916).
H. G. Steers (Mrs. J. A. Steers), 'The middle people: resettlement in Czechoslovakia', *Geographical Journal*, 112 (1948), 28-40.
J. F. Unstead, *Europe of today* (London, 1927).
F. A. Voigt, 'Berlin today. A city of contrasts', *Manchester Guardian*, May 6th, 1953 (illustrations of Communist architecture).
A. Zeune, *Erdansichten oder Abriss einer Geschichte der Erdkunde* (2nd edn., Berlin, 1820).
'Berlin clearing house', *The Times* (April 11th, 1952).
'The two Berlins. A city of contrasts and artificial frontiers', *The Times* (May 4th, 1953) (illustration of Stalin Allee).
'Germany's tragic east. Polish settlers' invasion of Silesia', *The Times* (April 1st, 1954).

The Geography of Foreign Direct Investment in Central-East Europe during the 1990's

Francis W. CARTER (London)

Abstract

The collapse of communism in 1989 left the countries of the former Eastern Bloc trying to find their own way towards capitalism. At the time there was great hope, but the transition has proved to be somewhat problematic. Certain geographical factors have been significant in this transitional period and their role should not be ignored in any restructuring assessment of Central-East European economies, namely in Poland, the Czech and Slovak Republics and Hungary. Amongst these critical geographical factors is the role played by foreign direct investment (FDI) and its impact since 1990 on various regions of the above individual countries. All this has depended on how much FDI was forthcoming, its origin and relative importance for the separate branches of each country's economy. The question remains however, which of each country's regions have been the winners/losers in the scramble to secure some of this investment and why?

Key words: C-E Europe, FDI, origin, sector, regional impact.

Geographische Struktur der Ausländischen Direktinvestitionen in Ost-Mitteleuropa in den 1990-er Jahren

Kurzfassung

Nach dem Zusammenbruch des Kommunismus im Jahr 1989 mußten die Staaten des früheren Ostblocks versuchen, ihren eigenen Weg in Richtung Kapitalismus zu finden. Damals hegte man große Erwartungen, der Übergang erweist sich aber als einigermaßen problematisch. In der Übergangsperiode sind gewisse geographische Faktoren von Bedeutung, deren Wirkung man bei einer Bewertung der Restrukturierung der ostmitteleuropäischen Volkswirtschaften – Polen, Tschechische und Slowakische Republik, Ungarn – nicht übersehen sollte. Einer dieser entscheidenden geographischen Faktoren ist die Rolle, die Ausländische Direktinvestitionen (FDI) spielen, und deren Auswirkung auf die verschiedenen Regionen der genannten Länder seit 1990. Dies hängt ab von der Menge der einlangenden FDI, ihrer Herkunft und ihrer relativen Wichtigkeit für die einzelnen Branchen in jedem Land. Die Frage lautet: Welche Regionen der einzelnen Länder sind bei dieser Jagd nach Investitionen die Gewinner, welche die Verlierer, und was sind die Gründe dafür?

Introduction

The decade of change that has begun to transform the societies of Central and East Europe from rigid communist systems into freer and more dynamic Western communities has affected all aspects of life. Amongst others it has influenced public discourse, values, ideas and not least attitudes towards the economy. The transformation is not finished, nor can it ever be in a constantly developing society. In this situation the role of the economy has changed from political and ideological control to a process of adapting to new external influences and the need to adjust to the challenges of a rapidly evolving world (Pollert, 1999).

The collapse of communism in 1989 left the countries of the former Eastern Bloc trying to find their own way towards capitalism. At the time there was great optimism, but the transition has proved to be an intricate process. Clearly, in the early years there was 'a dramatic and pronounced fall in output ... [with] plummeting industrial production, sharply rising unemployment, falling wages and soaring inflation' (Alcroft & Morewood, 1995) which occurred in all the countries of Central-East Europe to a greater or lesser extent. Certain geographical factors have been significant in this transitional period and their role should be not be ignored in any restructuring assessment of the changing Central-East European economies, namely in Poland, the Czech and Slovak Republics, and Hungary.

Amongst these critical geographical factors are the part played by transport, so crucial in the development and performance of any country; telecommunications, in an era of globalisation, when a country's failure to possess reliable networks will prove a major disadvantage; and the role of foreign direct investment (FDI). The latter depends on how much there is, its origin and relative importance to which branches of the economy (Cantwell, 1999). Transport, telecommunications and FDI are all linked in many ways and have potentially large roles to play in the regional development of the transition economies. This paper will concentrate on one of these factors, namely FDI, and its impact on various regions of individual Central-East European countries since 1990. Geographical studies of this kind on the whole region of Eastern Europe are said to be 'rare', while FDI is 'difficult to assess very accurately' (Pavlinek, 1998; Hamilton, 1995).

It is therefore important to consider the spatial impact of FDI, to give it another dimension from that of the economist or political analyst. This implies some knowledge of the differential effects Western investment has had on regions within individual countries and how it has transformed the economic and social fabric of the area (Murphy, 1992). The spatial implications of FDI on regional development in Europe have been studied by geographers (e.g. Amin et al, 1994; Amin & Thrift, 1995), while specific aspects of this phenomenon in individual former Eastern bloc countries has elicited interest (e.g. Murphy, 1992; Michalak, 1993, 1995; Sadler & Swain, 1994; Buckwalter, 1995; van Hastenberg, 1996a; Smith, 1996; Bradshaw, 1997; Grabher, 1997; Pavlinek, 1998; Williams, Baláž & Zajac, 1998). There is obviously a need for more analysis of FDI in Central-East Europe at the regional level, but this has been hindered in the past by difficulties in obtaining suitable evidence and on occasions the secrecy surrounding share-dealing in the interests of foreign investors (Pavlinek, 1998).

During the 1990's considerable progress has been made in attracting FDI to the whole region (Table 1).

Table 1.
Central and Eastern Europe: Total Inflows of FDI, 1990–1997 (US$ bn)

World Region	1990	%	1995	%	1996	%	1997	%
Developed countries	176	81.10	212	61.63	196	56.32	239	58.30
Developing countries	40	18.44	120	34.88	138	39.66	152	37.07
Central and East Europe	1	0.46	12	3.49	14	4.02	19	4.63
TOTAL	217	100	344	100	348	100	410	100

Source: United Nations Conference on Trade and Development (UNCTAD), (1998), *World Investment Report 1998*, New York, p.361-635.

Although they were still below 5% of the world total in 1997, clear progress had been made in attracting foreign funding. It could perhaps have been higher but for problems that arose in these fledgling market economies. Stabilization of their macroeconomies did create difficulties in the Central-East European countries. While FDI stimulated foreign capital inflows, greatly needed for further economic development, these states gradually realized that the various forms of FDI capital inflow had become a mixed blessing (Gács, Holzmann & Wyzan, 1999; Lankes & Stern, 1998). For instance, FDI began to threaten their recently achieved macroeconomic balance. It proved difficult for some of them to continue attracting foreign capital while at the same time reducing the adverse effects of FDI on inflation, the exchange rate and current account, as well as trying to accommodate any disruptions arising from possible capital flow reductions. Moreover, the increased role of FDI had implications for the environment, which has not received much attention. To attract FDI a country may deliberately fail to impose strict environmental restrictions, but foreign direct investors can insist on them. The onus could then fall on the host-country's government to provide the right anti-pollution incentives through encouraging the transmission of pollution abatement technologies (Carter & Turnock, 1996). With these negative aspects in mind it is nevertheless hoped to portray in this paper a specific regional perspective on the role being played by FDI in the newly emerging countries of Central-East Europe (Figs. 1a + 1b).

Central-East European States; Regional Impact of FDI

In a recent survey of locational and incentive factors affecting FDI in Eastern Europe, 'geographical location' scored highly amongst western respondents about the Central-East European countries (Pye, 1997). Geographical location was defined in the questionnaire as the proximity to potential export markets in-

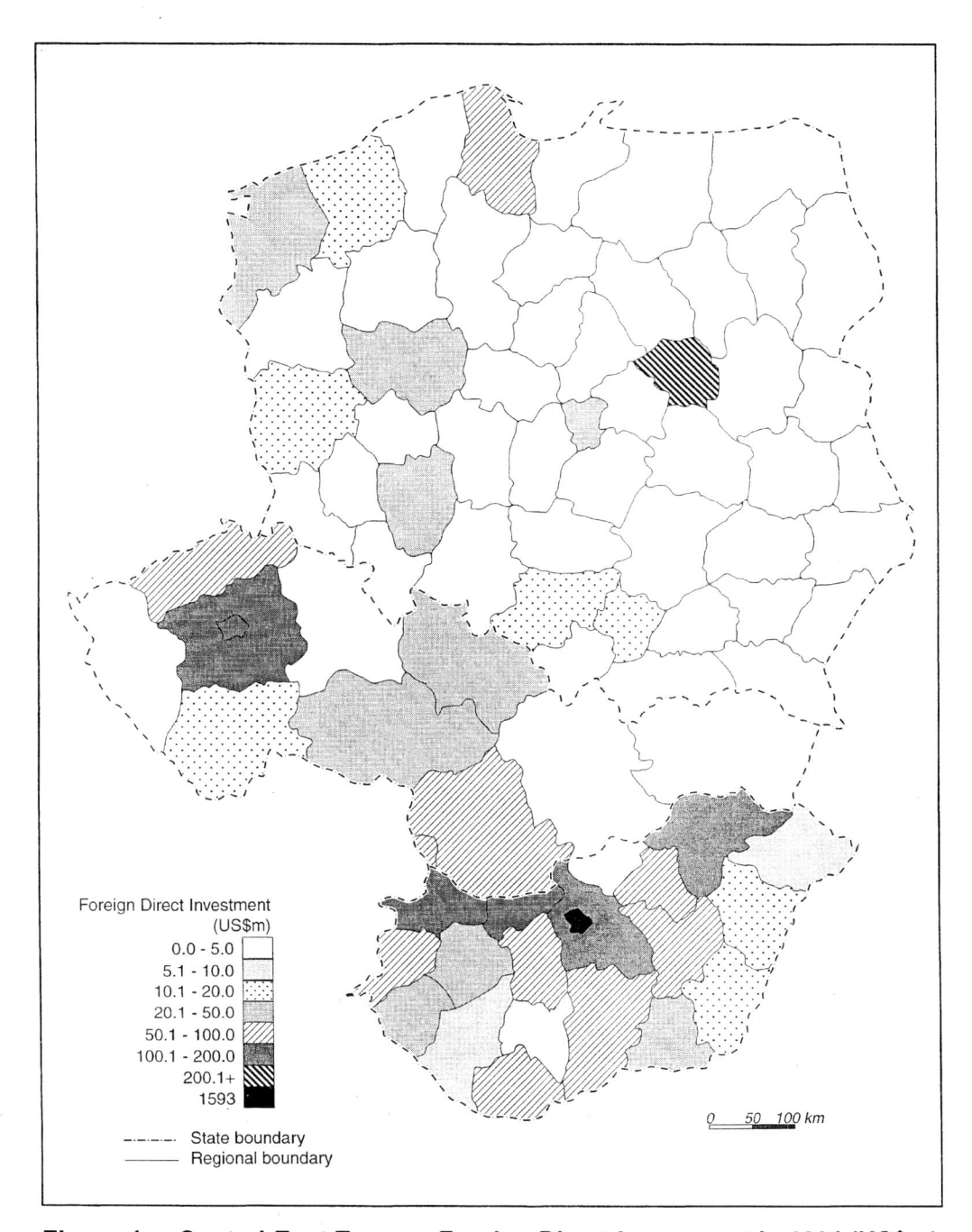

Figure 1a. Central-East Europe: Foreign Direct Investment in 1991 (US$m)
Source: W. Dziemianowicz, 1993.

cluding to buyers and/or suppliers, the western investor's desire to be active in every country of the region, and the host country's overall geographical location (Tarzi, 1999). Survey respondents gave a list of the major advantages that the ideal FDI location should offer; the dominant factor was market forces followed, almost on an equal footing by strategic economic position and investment climate. In relation to market forces, mention was frequently made to growth potential and market share/capture of the local market; the strategic position often alluded to first mover advantages, the significance of customers/clients, and the necessity to profit from international markets; investment climate mainly related to a country's overall stability, evidence of former historical trade links, and general government attitude to FDI.

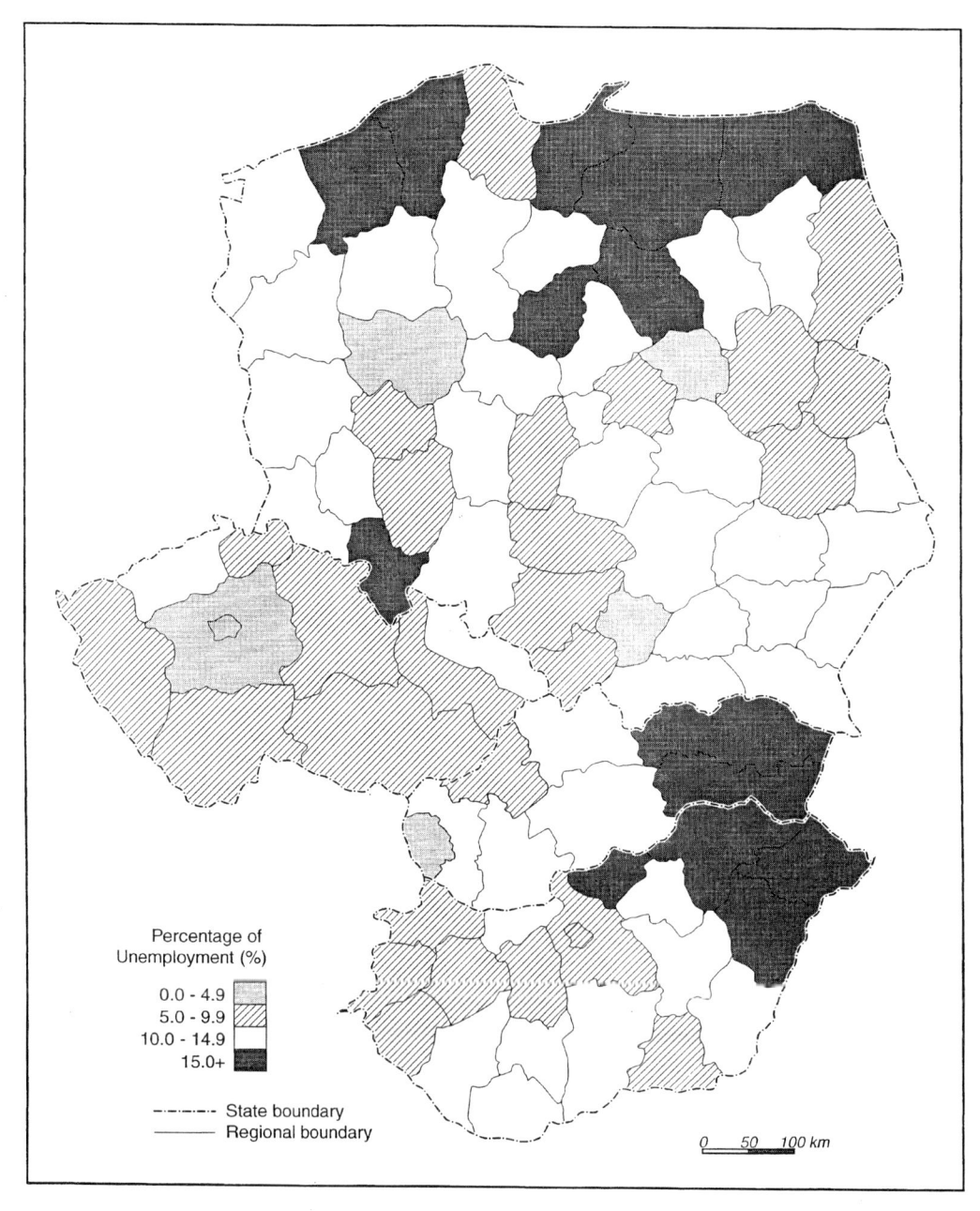

Figure 1b. Central-East Europe: Percentage Unemployment in 1997
Source: Český Republika, S.Ú., Praha, 1998; J. Musíl - personal communication.

a) Czech Republic

The regional consequences of FDI in the Czech Republic were rather limited in the very early 1990s. Prior to communism the Czech Republic had always been part of west European markets; for example, Prague is farther west geographically than Vienna. Even so, in the former Czechoslovakia, the Czech Republic attracted only 10% of the FDI flowing into Central-East Europe during 1990-1991; some would argue this poor showing was one of the reasons Slovakia pushed for independence believing (erroneously) that alone they might attract more FDI (Pavlinek, 1995).

By 1992, German capital predominated in two Czech regions (kraj), predictably Central Bohemia containing 48% and Prague 44.1% (Dubská, 1992). Most FDI went into the transport sector, followed by the food processing, service and construction industries (Dziemianowicz, 1993). The former capital of Czechoslovakia and its surrounding region attracted most FDI; For Prague, the critical factor was its capital city functions, including the location of political institutions like that for economic restructuring (Murphy, 1992). Even before the 'Velvet Divorce' of January 1993 (Wolf, 1998), nearly $1bn of FDI had flowed into the former Czechoslovakia, with Germany accounting for two-thirds of this investment. German industrial giants (Volkswagen, Siemens and Mercedes-Benz) led this charge, soon to be followed by smaller companies. In the Czech Republic, foreign investors were attracted by its long business tradition; the province of Bohemia had been the industrial heartland of the Austro-Hungarian empire. Other factors included its engineering skills, low wages, and proximity/access to east European markets. An example of such activity was Volkswagen's purchase in 1991 of 31% shares and management control of Skoda in Mladá Boleslav (northern Bohemia), with an investment of DM 600m by 1992, and a further DM 1bn in 1993. From a Czechoslovak viewpoint, the country needed FDI to achieve western efficiency levels and greater prosperity.

By 1995 there was a FDI boom in the country; investment inflows totalled US$ 2.3 bn, nearly half of the overall (US$ 5bn) since 1990. The privatisation in 1995 of SPT Telecom provided over half the annual intake, a quarter (27%) coming from PTT Telecom Netherlands and the Swiss PTT. The improved situation was also due to the introduction of transborder export-based/employment-intensive industries e.g. electronics, attracted by lower wage costs and reasonably productivity employees (Uhlíř, 1995, 1997), but which were territorially disembedded in the local milieu or capitalism without capitalists (Grabher, 1994). By 1995 many small transborder companies were concentrated along the Austrian/German border in the Czech regions of Western and Southern Bohemia. Fewer larger firms located along the Czech-German frontier zone but did include Siemens, which established factories in Stříbro (1993) and later Plzeň, drawn there mainly by cheaper unskilled female labour utilised for making BMW car parts.

In the Czech Republic prior to 1997 foreign capital, wholly or partly from joint ventures, had proved a major growth beneficiary. From a sectoral viewpoint, most foreign investment went into transport and communications (19.5%), followed by consumer goods/tobacco industries (14.6%) and transport equipment (13.3%). Neighbouring Germany provided over a quarter (27.9%) of the FDI total and was unquestionably the Czech Republic's major partner. It also helped the country infiltrate into the wider European economy through economic diffusion. FDI created links between the Czech Republic and more successful west European border countries; in turn, Germany's financial decisions were influenced by the Czech Republic's favourable geographical / geopolitical location (Anon, 1997b).

During the first half of 1997 most FDI went into banking and insurance but, by the end of that year, an increasing number of smaller foreign firms were entering the consumer goods industry, trade and services. Also in 1997 there was considerable activity in the power industry. Western power engineering giants directly invested in some of the country's power generating companies; these included Brno District Heating Plant Co., the North Moravian and Central Bohemian Power Engineering Works, Prague Power Engineering Co., and that city's Gas Works. Only in the last quarter of 1997 did a British investor provide FDI, namely for the Opatovice power station. Some new green-field sites attracted FDI including places such as Kouřim, Pohořelice, Prague suburbs and Vyškov. Surprisingly, the currency crisis of 1997, which resulted in a collapse of domestic demand, did not deter FDI during the year; it remained at the same level (circa US$ 850m) as in 1996 (Pisková, 1998).

By 1997, the regional breakdown of Czech FDI revealed a clearer west-east division in the country than the early 1990s (Table 2).

Table 2. Czech Republic: Private enterprises/corporations, and foreign control, by region in 1997

Admin. Region	Total Private	of which foreign control	%
Prague	56,302	15,242	27.07
C. Bohemia	14,225	3,035	21.34
S. Bohemia	10,385	2,771	26.68
W. Bohemia	13,853	5,469	39.48
N. Bohemia	18,566	4,081	21.98
E. Bohemia	17,326	2,132	12.31
N. Moravia	34,894	5,568	15.96
S. Moravia	22,106	2,872	12.99
Total Bohemia	130,657	32,730	25.05
Total Moravia	57,000	8,440	14.81

Source: Česká národní banka; Č.S.Ú, *Aktuality*.

Clearly in Bohemia, there was a marked west-east decrease in the number of foreign companies, while in Moravia there presence was higher in the southern region with its proximity to Austria an EU member state; regionally Northern Moravia and East Bohemia had the least foreign companies and farthest in distance and influence from the EU border. More significantly Bohemia had a quarter of the foreign controlled firms, whereas Moravia had only a seventh. Earlier FDI predominance by Prague and the Central Bohemian region were lost to the western borderland (Fig. 2a). This reflected German entrepreneurial anticipation of early EU membership by the Czech Republic.

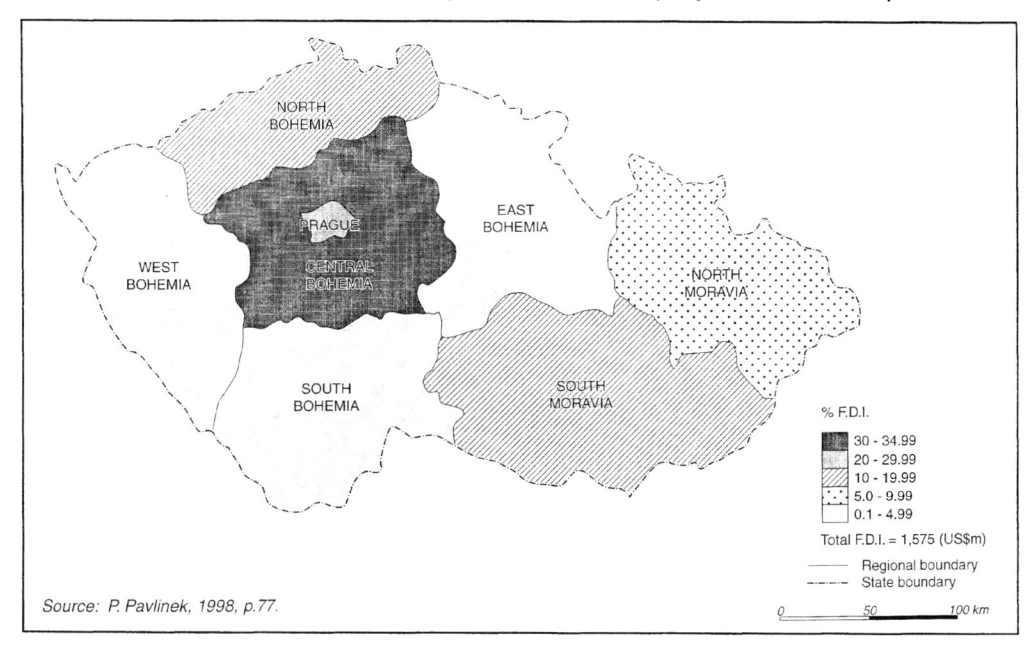

Figure 2a. Czech Republic: Percentage of Foreign Direct Investment, 1992, by Region

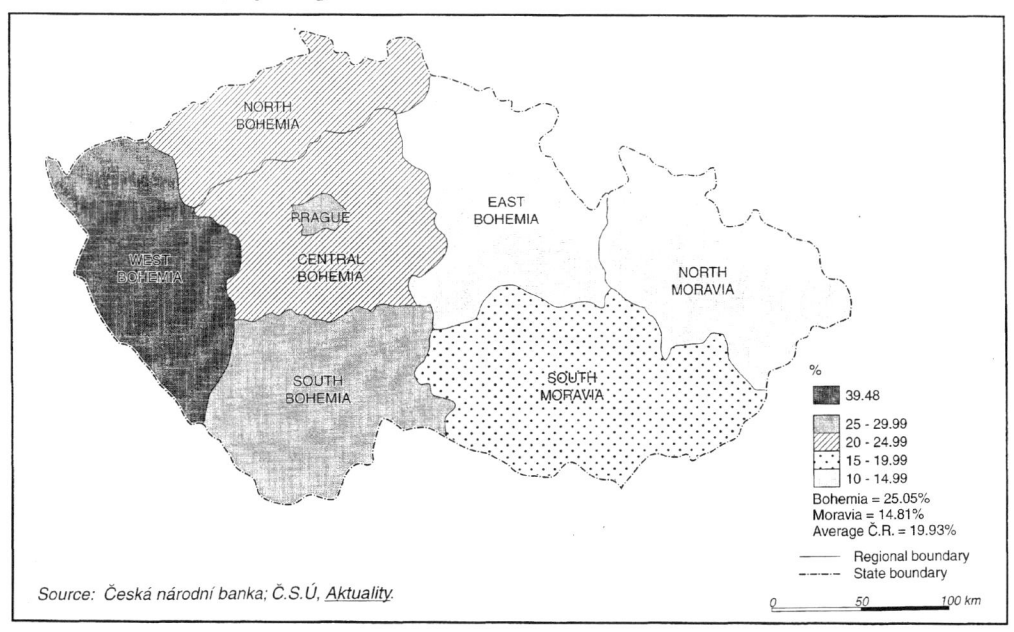

Figure 2b. Czech Republic: Private Enterprises/Corporations under Foreign Control by Region in 1997

Nevertheless, it has to be admitted that the Czech Republic's manufacturing industry has continually remained overstaffed. Also the voucher-system was previously regarded by Czech market propaganda as in the vanguard of popular capitalism. More recently it has been ironically identified as the chief hurdle against restructuring Czech industry, so vital if the reform process is to endure (Andor & Summers, 1998). Remarkably, foreign investors continued to provided a much needed economic boost, in spite of such set-backs set around a persistently limp economy. For instance, FDI manufacturers have created employment in 56 of the country's 77 administrative districts (okres), at an average rate of six new jobs per hour net. Equally imposing is the impact of indirect employment; in both manufacturing and services sectors, foreign investors support an estimated 10,0000 Czech-based suppliers providing employment for a phenomenal half a million people, or a tenth of the labour force. Besides direct employment, foreign manufacturers indirectly provide salaries for nearly a third of the workforce in Czech manufacturing. Estimates suggest that by December 2001, major foreign manufacturing companies will have seen a rise in number from 800 to 1,000 firms; more than 320,000 workers will be directly employed while, indirectly, supplier links will secure a further 600,000 employment places. A recent poll by the CzechInvest Institute revealed that nearly a third of FDI firms wanted to enlarge their number of local suppliers. This may be enhanced by the funding of a new three year programme costing US$ 117m, to identify such potential stockists and would help generate the trickle-down impact of FDI (EIU, 1999a).

In spite of such encouraging signs, the west-east tendency was also reflected in the regional unemployment pattern for 1997, but in mirror-image form (Table 3) (Fig. 2b).

Table 3. Czech Republic: Unemployment 1995–98 (% of labour force)

Region	1995	1996	1997	1998
Prague	1.8	3.8	2.7	2.3
C. Bohemia	3.4	3.0	3.9	6.0
S. Bohemia	2.1	2.7	4.1	5.6
W. Bohemia	2.8	2.8	5.1	6.4
N. Bohemia	6.0	7.0	9.9	11.4
E. Bohemia	2.7	3.2	4.2	6.3
N. Moravia	4.7	5.7	8.2	11.0
S. Moravia	2.9	3.1	4.4	7.7
Total Č.R.	3.4	3.8	5.4	7.1

Source: *Statistická Ročenka Česká Republiky '98* (Č.S.Ú), Prague 1998, p.312; Č.S.Ú, *Aktuality*; E.I.U. Country Report (4th Quarter), 1998, p.23.

Unemployment in the Czech Republic, in contrast to other eastern/central European countries, has increased only modestly so far (Gottvald, Pedersen & Šimek, 1999). In Bohemia between 1995-1998, Prague continued to have the fewest unemployment problems while, with the exception of North Bohemia, other regions were below 7%. North Bohemia's high rate resulted from industrial and environmental problems, particularly those associated with brown-coal mining. Moravia had higher levels, particularly in the north with its ageing steel industry.

The question remains however why does the Czech Republic not attract even more foreign manufacturing companies, seeing that those there are already motivating the economy? A ready explanation may lie in the slack economy; perhaps a deeper reason is that foreign investors were not always encouraged. For example, there was apathy towards foreign investors during the government of Václav Klaus. The situation has not greatly changed under the Social Democratic government in spite of its acceptance that foreigners may require 'inducements' for locating their firm in the Czech Republic. Even so, once it has arrived it is highly likely that the foreign firm will be run by Czech managers, with minimal employment of foreigners (EIU, 1999a).

An important signal for the Czech government appears to be that FDI is more helpful than harmful. This is perhaps significant at a time when Czechs are confronted with economic stagnation under Miloš Zeman's weak minority government (EIU, 1999b). At the end of 1998 industrial output had declined by over 9% compared with the previous year and if the 1999 recession continues it will render an overall 3.5% government budget deficit. As the economy dips there is increasing pressure to reform the banking system, which is suffering from huge losses (Anon, 1999a). Clearly, bank privatisation will attract western interest; improved investment incentives and ongoing EU enlargement talks could help pull in FDI worth 1.6bn in 1999 (EIU, 1999b), providing it can overcome the current deep recession (Anon, 1999b). Yet in spite of all the odds, a strong inflow of FDI during the first half of 1999 from US$ 227m to US$ 608m may bode well for helping the ailing economy pull out of recession (Anon, 1999c).

b) Hungary

The regional pattern of FDI during the first half of the 1990s revealed an uneven investment spread, partly the result of a high concentration of the economy and population in Budapest and its surroundings. Numerically, however, almost all the country's administrative divisions (komitats) attracted some important FDI enterprises in the early 1990s (Dzemianowicz, 1993). Most, both in number and capital value, were located in Budapest and Pécs in the south-west, while komitats with the fewest joint venture companies (Nógrád, Heves, and Jász-Nagykun-Szolnok) were located immediately to the east of the Budapest agglomeration. As regards FDI distribution the major centres, after Budapest and Pécs, were the komitats of Fejér to the west of the capital, and Borsod-Abaúj-Zemplen bordering on Slovakia in the north-east. Lowest FDI capital was recorded in the komitats of Tolna (south-west) and Heves (north) (Table 4) (Fig 3a).

Table 4. Hungary: Regional Distribution of FDI Companies, 1993

Region	Firms with 10% or more FDI share		of which: Manufacturing	
	No.	%	No.	%
Central	607	60.1	227	49.3
North West (N. Transdanubia)	121	13.4	87	18.9
South West (S. Transdanubia)	47	5.2	38	8.3
North East (N. Alföld)	37	4.1	30	6.5
South East (S. Alföld)	45	5.0	37	8.0
North	48	5.3	41	8.9
T O T A L	905	100.0	460	100.0

Source: H. van Hastenberg (1996b), Table 3, p.130.

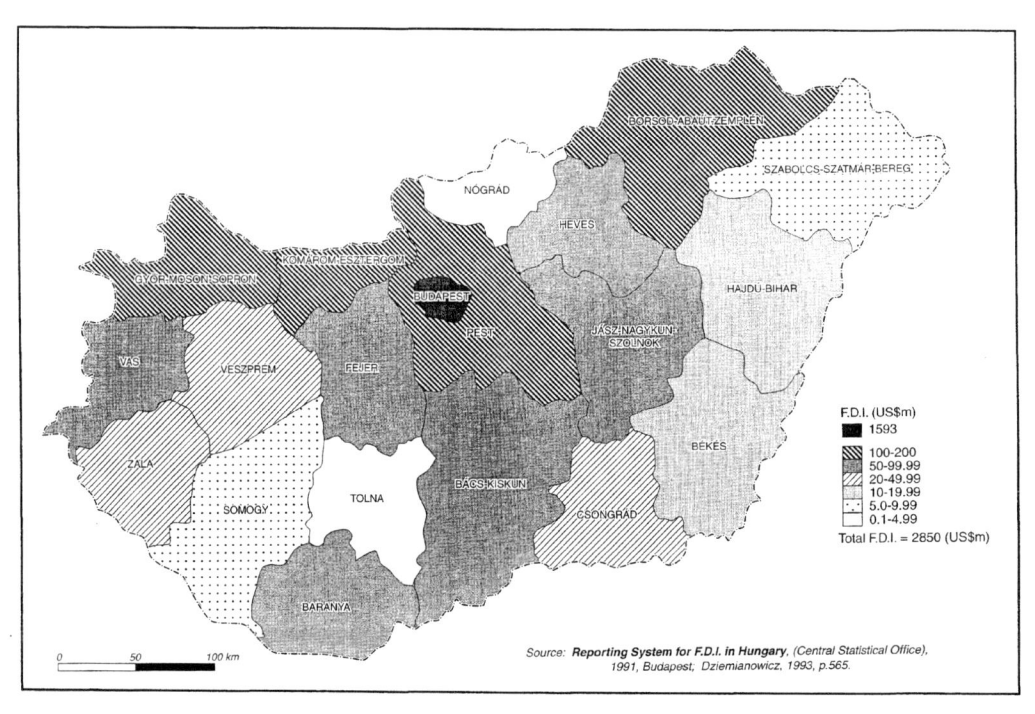

Figure 3a. Hungary: Foreign Direct Investment by Region 1991 (US$ million)

In 1993, the Central region (including Budapest and its agglomeration) was dominant, having three-fifths of the total for those firms with more than a 10% FDI share; North Transdanubia came a poor second, with the rest mustering about a fifth. Moreover, half of the manufacturing sector, which attracted most FDI, was located in the Central region, followed by a fifth in North Transdanubia and nearly a third spread over the rest of the country (van Hastenberg, 1996b).

Budapest and its agglomeration remained the major destination for foreign investment throughout the early 1990s having over two-fifths of all Hungarian FDI companies. This suggested just how much the country's economic life was concentrated on the capital, which held a fifth of the country's inhabitants. Numerically, it had the highest number of companies per capita (23 : 1,000) compared with only 8 : 1,000 for the rest of Hungary (Nemes-Nagy, 1994; 1995). However, the dominant position of Budapest and to a lesser extent the Northwest, proved a little deceptive. For example, General Electric/Tungsram's light bulb company was only registered as located in Budapest but, in reality, consisted of four separate branches. Only two were located in the Central region, one in the capital and another at Vác in Pest komitat. The additional plants were in the North East region at Hajdúböszörmény in Hajdú-Bihar komitat, and Kisvárda (Szabolcs-Szatmár-Bereg).

Vas komitat was another interesting anomaly recording relatively more FDI than any other komitat in Hungary outside Budapest. This erroneous impression was linked to Vas komitat's advantageous geographical situation near the Austrian border. After 1990, it attracted only a few, but considerably large, wealthy FDI companies. One of them was 'General Motors Austria' which, in 1990, formed two joint ventures with the Hungarian Rába company. Starting on a greenfield site in 1992, with an annual production capacity of 200,000 engines and a labour force of 650 local employees, the Opel factory was located at Szentgotthárd close to the Austrian frontier. Its other joint venture for car sales, was based in Budapest (Kapitány & Kállay, 1990; Anon, 1992).

Three similar vehicle production projects were located in western Hungary based on large amounts of FDI. Suzuki established a car assembly plant north of Budapest at Esztergom, situated along the Danube on the Hungarian/Slovak border. During negotiations, certain strict environmental guarantees were demanded from 'Magyar Suzuki' by the Hungarian negotiators; the Japanese investors, after a long period of negotiation, reached an acceptable agreement which was largely concerned with the installation of air purification equipment. Ford built a components factory at Székesfehérvár to the south-west of Budapest. Here production concentrated on the manufacture of ignition coils and fuel pumps for export, in exchange for car and commercial vehicle imports. Finally, Volkswagen/Audi constructed an engine assembly plant on a greenfield site at Györ to the west of Esztergom at a cost of US$ 420m. A major location factor here was lower wage levels which, at that time, were between 10%-12% less than in Germany (Kápitany, 1992; Sadler & Swain, 1994).

By mid-decade the regional distribution of FDI in Hungary was causing some concern amongst the country's population. The reason was linked to the geographical location pattern of most invested FDI capital, which had either gone to the capital region, or to western parts of the country, namely those komitats closest to EU/Western markets.

After 1995, regional FDI development in Hungary mainly centred around how to reduce the stark economic contrasts between the western and eastern halves of the country. Discussion gathered momentum in 1998 after the May election successes of the Fidesz Hungarian Civic Party. As part of its pre-election campaign the new government had declared its intention of correcting the country's regional imbalances and promote economic growth in the outer komitats. Once in power they started to address this problem, which revolved around the regeneration of eastern Hungary. Over the past decade it had symbolised the worst aspects of the country's post-communist transition. Signs are that it has begun to experience some regeneration, with multinational corporations eager to exploit the region's unused source of cheap, skilled labour, and the new government's declared aim to reduce the economic gap between the country's two halves.

One welcome initiative has come from the US-Eastern Hungary Partnership involving the US Trade and Development Agency. A project has been established in several northern/eastern cities, whereby American commercial representatives will try to promote US trade and investment. In fact, over the last decade US FDI companies have invested more than US$ 200m in eastern Hungary leading to over 3,000 new jobs. Even so, this did not eradicate the FDI pattern's unevenness. For example, between 1995-1996 the combined FDI of two eastern komitats (Hajdú-Bihar and Szabolcs-Szatmár-Bereg) only equalled one tenth of the US$ 10.5 bn poured into Budapest. Such irregularities in the FDI pattern caused local businessmen to complain about the unfair treatment some regions received. For example, the Industrial Park at Nyíregyháza, established two years ago, still lies empty despite resolute efforts by the local authorities to encourage investment. Poor quality roads are one of the biggest problems; over the next four years it is planned to replace them and will include a 70km eastward extension of the M3 motorway (Langenkamp, 1999).

The US Trade and Development Agency has also recently completed a feasibility study of Salgótarján's steel works in Nógrád komitat. This study examined the possibilities for manufacturing corrugated metal piping widely used in road and railway construction. If the findings are accepted it could lead to an initial FDI of US$3-4m, along with further prospects of American financial interest in this poorly developed north-eastern region. It is hoped that the presence of a highly experienced and creative workforce, together with Nógrád komitat's proximity to Budapest, will encourage FDI to be placed in other towns to the west of Salgótarján, including Balassagyarmat, Rétság and Szécsény. Such activity may be encouraged by the newly proposed government FDI tax incentives to help companies locate in eastern Hungary; already several foreign companies have established themselves there, including Ross Mould (glass), Michelin (tyres), Nestlé (food/beverages), AES (power), Butler Manufacturing (steel), Delco Remy (car parts) and ICN Pharmaceuticals (Anon, 1999d).

Another success story has taken place in the city of Miskolc during early 1999 when it enticed the Japanese 'Shinwa' electronics company to build a car stereo plant there, based on a US$ 20m FDI, which is eventually planned to employ 1,000 local people. For the Japanese employer the main advantage was low labour expenditure with wages costing, on average, about 25-30% less than in western Hungary. For the local region the benefit came from potential reduction in the unemployment rate (16%, or double the national average) which FDI would bring to this part of Borsod-Abaúj-Zemplén komitat. Also unemployment growth has been partly reduced at Ózd, a town in north-eastern Hungary devastated by the closure of state-owned industrial enterprises, thanks to General Electric's construction of a US$ 27m FDI in an electrical components factory (Langenkamp, 1999).

Nevertheless, by the late 1990s lack of employment opportunities continued to be a serious problem in north-east Hungary, particularly in the komitats of Borsod-Abaúj-Zemplén, Nógrád and Szabolcs-Szatmár-Bereg, as well as parts of the Alföld. More favourable employment opportunities continue to exist in the Budapest region and the western border komitats of Győr-Moson-Sopron, Vas and Zala (Fazekas, 1993; Varga, 1999) In some extreme cases here, FDI has contributed to the complete disappearance of unemployment in certain cities. For example in Győr, labour shortages are so critical that the Audi car manufacturing company has to transport employees from nearby towns to its factory by bus (Langenkamp, 1999).

In the western half of the country evidence of greater prosperity continues. The inflow of greenfield FDI has given new life to existing sectors like electronics and pharmaceuticals and created entirely new industrial sectors such as motor car assembly and motor components (Robinson, 1997a; Wright, 1998). Hungary is proving a fertile ground for leading car producers (Swain, 1998). General Motors factory at Szentgotthárd is experimenting with its shift system/ overtime, which could raise production to over half a million engines annually without further investment. It is also planning a new transmission plant scheduled to begin production in 2001. Audi has begun small volume car assembly in Győr, again taking advantage of flexible labour conditions amongst its 3,400 workforce, and wage levels five times lower than in Germany. Suzuki at its Esztergom plant succeeded in producing nearly 66,000 cars and capturing a quarter of the domestic market in 1998, 43,000 going for export. Over half the value of its assembled cars is provided from domestic supply bases (Done, 1998). Production will be further boosted by plans to invest US$ 74m in the production of a new microvan by 2000 (Anon, 1999e). Meanwhile, Hungary's well-known pre-1990 bus manufacturer 'Ikarus', has combined with Renault/Fiat Iveco to form a joint company in August 1999, with an annual production target of 1,500-2,000 buses annually, together with a new passenger car model (Anon, 1999f).

Recent FDI interest in Hungary has centred around research and development (R&D). The majority of R&D enterprises have been purchased in the fields of computer technology and telecommunications. They include General Electric/Tungsram (US$ 70m) for light source research, and Electrolux Sweden, (US$ 60m) for refrigerator development at Jászberény, east of Budapest. R&D departments valued at between US$ 5-10m have also been established by Audi, Graphisoft, Knorr-Bremse AG, Microsoft Hungary and Motorola. The IBM company is developing a regional research centre in the INFOPARK area south of the Buda district in Budapest, as is Nokia of Finland. The locational factors for such activity included the presence of highly qualified specialists, large intellectual resources and a developed information technology network; these have ensured cuts in telecommunications and computer engineering costs and closer links between industry and academia (Anon, 1999g).

Considerable FDI interest has also been shown in the Hungarian power industry. In 1995, Germany's Bayernwerk bought a controlling stake (US$ 108m) in Hungary's regional electricity distributor 'Dédász', which supplied the state-owned Dunaferr Steelworks with over a tenth of its energy needs. More recently foreign investors in energy production have included the US 'El Paso' company, and the UK's 'PowerGen' which bought a 43 MW plant on Csepel Island south of Budapest for US$ 300m; the intention is to modernise it and increase capacity to 390 MW. Austria's 'Energie Versorgung Niederösterreich' company plans to build an 80 MW plant at Nagykanizsa costing US$ 115m, west of Lake Balaton and close to the Former Yugoslavian border. Between 1995 and 1997 alone therefore, US$ 515m of FDI had been allotted to Hungary's power generation, particularly in the south-western part of the country (Langenkamp & O'Leary, 1997).

Finally, it is proposed to divide Hungary's FDI location pattern into five regional groups for the late 1990s, each having similar amounts of FDI and based on the country's nineteen 'komitats', or administrative regions (Fig. 3b).

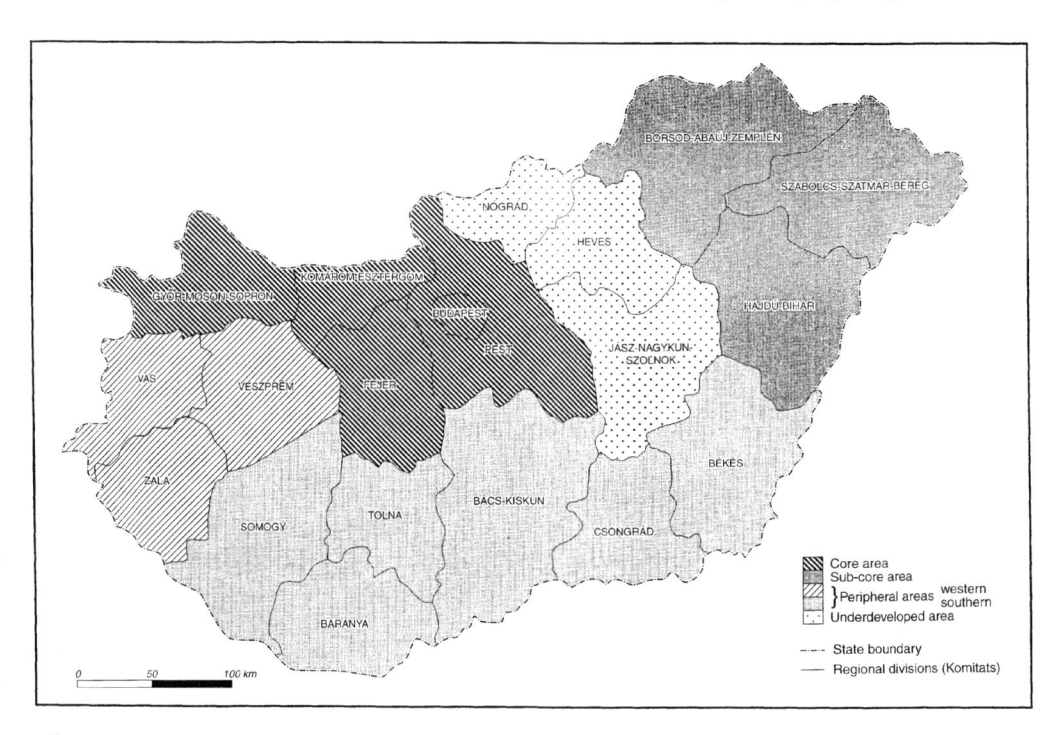

Figure 3b. Hungary: Regions of Comparable Foreign Direct Investment, 1998

The first, designated as the core area, consists of Budapest and its agglomeration, Fejér, Györ-Moson-Sopron and Komárom-Esztergom, all enjoying Hungary's highest GDP rates (Rechnitzer, 1996). This area contains the majority of Hungary's population, Pest itself having nearly one million inhabitants. Hungary's FDI is highly concentrated in the service sector, most of it clustered in Budapest, together with other urban centres creating a corridor stretching from the capital through Tatabánya, Komárom, Győr and Sopron towards Vienna. This corridor also acts as an investment magnet for other economic branches such as light industry/ engineering, especially in Győr and the Budapest region. The core area has a favourable transport and communication infrastructure, inherited from Austro-Hungarian days, with major road/railway links connecting Budapest with its western neighbours. The second, or sub-core area possesses similar attributes to the core. It is located in the komitats of Borsod-Abaúj-Zemplén, Szabolcs-Szatmár-Bereg and Hajdú-Bihar, which contain a large percentage of Hungary's chemical industry and the rapidly growing textile/clothing manufacturing branches, which enjoy the availability of considerable FDI capital sources. Further possibilities for infrastructural sector growth may come to this area once Hungary has joined the EU, particularly as it will form part of the EU's eastern border, giving access to the Ukraine, Slovakia and Romania (Nyerki, 1998).

The third, or peripheral area, can be divided into two sub-peripheral regions; the first consisting of Vas, Zala and Veszprém komitats forming part of Hungary's western border area with Austria (Deußner, 1996). At present FDI is not very large here, mainly due to a dependence on agriculture. It may also be the result of EU reluctance to invest in this area, in an attempt to preserve the agricultural sector for itself, in spite of the many problems it causes members states. Once Hungary is part of the EU more investment may be forthcoming as the EU will be obliged to give increased support to this region (Somfai, 1996). The second sub-periphery area encompasses the more economically prosperous Bács-Kiskun and Csongrád komitats in southern Hungary, along with the neighbouring komitats of Tolna, Békés, Somogy and Baranya. Collectively these komitats, especially Békés and Csongrád, constitute the agricultural heart of Hungary. As the textile industry increases its significance in the region, more FDI is likely in future, especially in urban centres such as Szeged, Békéscsaba, Gyula, Hódmezővásárhely, Kiskunhalas and Kecskemét. Finally, there is a fifth underdeveloped FDI area which, at present, attracts least FDI in the whole country, namely the komitats of Nógrád, Heves and Jász-Nagykun-Szolnok (Horváth, 1999). This poorly developed region has a low population, its density having suffered intensive out-migration to Budapest. It is possible that in future younger people may wish to return home after success in the capital, offering potential foreign investors the advantages of lower labour costs and house rents. This will most likely be in Szolnok, due to its advantageous transport links with Budapest.

c) Poland

At a regional level Poland's FDI pattern had a distinct east-west orientation during the first half of the 1990s. Since 1977 there had been a tradition of foreign firms in Poland which were largely confined to six voivodships (provinces) namely, the capital Warsaw, Bielsko-Biała, Cracow, Częstochowa, Siedlce and Wałbrych (Skalimowski, 1988). In the early 1990s, just as in other East European countries, no attempt was made through tax relief and similar inducements, to utilise FDI for encouraging growth in the country's most underdeveloped regions. As a result FDI became concentrated in only a limited number of advantageous locations (Fig. 4a). No government investment policy existed for those areas possessing poorer infrastructures, which often had less dynamic/efficient local governments, and exorbitant transport costs (Dobosiewicz, 1992; Gorzelak, 1993).

Foreign Direct Investment (US$m)
- 278.3
- 50.1 - 100
- 20.1 - 50.0
- 10.1 - 20.00
- 5.1 - 10.0
- 0.0 - 5.0

Total Foreign Direct Investment = 694 (US$m)

---- State boundary
____ Regional boundary before 1998

Source: Agency for Foreign Investments (PAIZ); Dziemianowicz, 1993, p565.

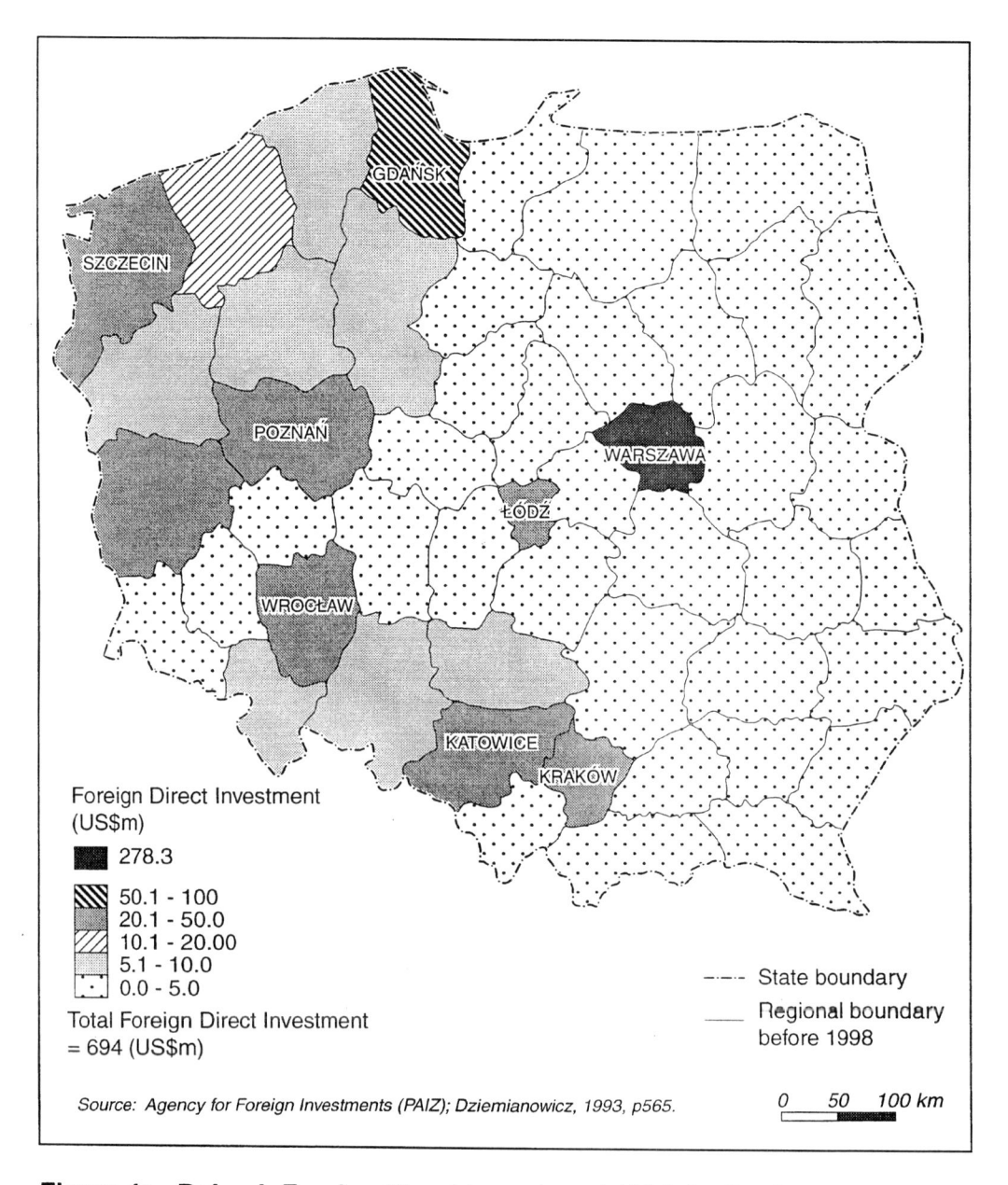

Figure 4a. Poland: Foreign Direct Investment 1991, by Region

According to Zbigniew Dobosiewicz, the geographical structure of FDI in Poland was largely fortuitous, but there does appear to have been some locational logic in choice. The spatial pattern of the early 1990s revealed that

FDI companies were more preponderant in the better developed voivodships such as the capital Warsaw, Poznań and Szczecin. Spatially by the middle of 1990, the largest FDI company capital stock was found in the Warsaw voivodship (mainly Warsaw itself), followed by those with large ports (Gdańsk, Szczecin), and the more industrialized regions of Cracow, Katowice, Poznań, Wrocław and Zielona Góra (Dziemianowicz, 1993; Mazurski, 1995). This suggests a threefold pattern of FDI was emerging, firstly centred on Poland's capital and principal ports, a second group with less FDI located in voivodship capitals and/or industrial centres and thirdly, the less attractive FDI regions, which absorbed two-fifths of the foreign capital but were spread thinly over the remaining 42 voivodships. They were mainly located in the poorer eastern parts of the country and on average had only 14 foreign firms and US$ 4,141,000 FDI each (Table 5).

Table 5.
Poland: Joint venture companies by Voivodship (Province) (30/6/1990)

Voivodship	No. of companies (%)	Initial capital value (US$ '000s) (%)
Warsaw	453 (29.45)	97,721 (22.06)
Gdańsk	88 (5.72)	64,504 (14.56)
Szczecin	113 (7.34)	54,504 (12.30)
Poznań	127 (8.25)	15,246 (3.45)
Katowice	98 (6.38)	14,035 (3.17)
Zielona Góra	33 (2.15)	12,421 (2.81)
Olsztyn	23 (1.50)	10,551 (2.39)
Others (42)	603 (39.20)	173,906 (39.26)
T O T A L (49)	1,538 (100)	442,888 (100)

Source: E. Sadowska-Cieślik, Analysis of Licences Granted by Foreign Investment Companies, (Foreign Investment Agency), Warsaw, 1990, Table 6.

With the progress of time, increasing numbers of foreign firms were installing themselves in the larger voivodship centres; most were located in Warsaw and more generally in the western and northern voivodships. These particularly included the Cracow, Gdańsk, Katowice, Łódź, Poznań, Szczecin and Wrocław regions. The Warsaw voivodship had the largest concentration of FDI by 1993 with a quarter (567 companies) of all those firms involved in foreign participation, followed by the voivodships of Gdańsk and Katowice. Similarly, most of the FDI (US$ 71m) had been invested in the Warsaw voivodship, followed by those of Poznań and Szczecin (Anon, 1995). The FDI pattern in 1993 compared with that of 1990, revealed a noticeable rise in the number of joint venture companies in some eastern voivodships such as Lublin and Kielce; however, there was a group of voivodships including Krosno, Łomża, Ostrołęka, Przemyśl, Tarnobrzeg and Zamość which still had minimal FDI totals and joint venture numbers.

Proof of this east-west split in Poland's FDI came in 1994 when the Gdańsk Institute for Market Economics undertook research into FDI attractiveness for all voivodship regions. The study took account of the industrial base, local market (including labour supply), infrastructure (including business environment) and availability of incentives. The ensuing map showed FDI preference for the Warsaw metropolitan area reflecting the power of the capital and major cities like Cracow, Gdańsk, Katowice, Łódź, Poznań, Szczecin and Wrocław. At the other end of the scale came the typically agricultural voivodships of eastern and central Poland with their underdeveloped industrial and infrastructural bases, the marginal impact of new reform programmes and suffering from inadequate markets. It is very noticeable that many of the regions with low FDI attractiveness were in the central, east and north-east parts of the country. These included Biała Podlaska, Ciechanów, Konin, Łomża, Ostrołęka, and Włocławek. The possible reason stems from the historical division of the country by three foreign empires from the late eighteenth to early twentieth centuries, when much of this area was part of Russian Poland. The southern and western regions tend to be more advanced with their history of Austrian or Prussian administration. Furthermore, those regions with low FDI indices have suffered from investment indifference in the past, which could lead to a widely asymmetric pattern of economic development at any future national scale (Dąbrowski, Dworzecki, Gawlikowska-Hueckel & Wyżnikiewicz, 1994).

In sum, the first half of the 1990s clearly demonstrated the FDI 'haves' and 'have nots' on a regional basis. On the positive side were regions with high industrial development thanks either to bounteous natural resources like Upper and Lower Silesia or a legacy of nineteenth century industrial tradition (e.g. textiles). Others had been blessed with a beneficial geographical situation such as a favourable coastal location for shipbuilding. Regions with some of these locational benefits like Warsaw, Cracow, Gdańsk, Katowice, Łódź, Poznań, Szczecin and Wrocław were amongst Poland's best developed voivodships and comparably much more advanced than other regions. They also possessed a superior market structure, improved transport facilities and a more advanced telecommunications infrastructure, all providing greater potential for future FDI prospects; in addition many were also more adaptable to structural and ownership changes, as well as support from higher educational centres. It is therefore no wonder that these regions contained much of Poland's FDI.

In stark contrast, the mainly agricultural regions of eastern Poland were much more poorly developed, characterised by a high degree of employment overmanning and an industrial structure bound up with agriculture. These poorer regions were crying out for new employment openings, together with radical changes in infrastructure, but many were characteristically identified with high unemployment rates and feeble market structures. In turn, this created an impression of low capacity and hence diminished investment potential. The situation was further aggravated by deficiencies in both transport and telecommunication networks. Ironically, in spite of poor industrial development, eastern Poland also suffers from high environmental pollution levels resulting from considerable use of artificial fertilizers and the impact of acid rain resulting in the expansion of soil erosion areas and declining quality of arable land. It is therefore understandable why these regions failed to entice much FDI in the early 1990s, despite the belief then of an enormous potential CIS market over the adjacent border.

Already by mid-decade there was concern in Poland that such regional dissimilarities would be augmented, and further enlarge the east-west disparity in the country. More than three-fifths (61.2%) of Poland's 49 pre-1999 voivodships were below the national average income, while those more economically advanced regions above them (38.8%) were still well below the European average on the whole (Gawlikowska-Hueckel, 1995).

In an attempt to reverse such regional disparities, a new initiative was inaugurated in 1995 with the creation of special economic zones (SEZs), to enhance the economies of those poorer regions which inherited ageing heavy industries from former communist times. The first SEZ was established in Mielec (S. Poland) a former centre of aircraft manufacture. Four more were planned near Częstochowa, Katowice, Łódź and Suwałki in 1996. It was hoped that such zones in the Katowice voivodship would attract large numbers of investors, because they had a huge productive capacity. Three zones were originally planned in the area, near Jastrzębie, Tychy and a joint zone in Dąbrowa Górnicza and Sosnowiec (Dutkowiecz, Lavell & Sowińska, 1996). By 1998, 17 SEZs had been established and promised, substantial advantages for investors through tax exemptions. However, many foreigners were discouraged by the system of different preferential taxes for each SEZ, which demanded a detailed knowledge of the legal regulations and careful tax management, as well as increasing opposition by the EU to their very existence (Anon, 1998; Kubińska, 1998; Jelonkiewicz, 1999b).

According to an investment risk index of Central and Eastern Europe in 1996, out of a grade scale of 5, Poland scored an impressive 2.6, better than the respective indexes of other countries. This improvement in the investment risk index and in other economic parameters, resulted in increasing the appeal of Poland to foreign investors. Areas with highest investment attractiveness were the voivodships of Warsaw, Cracow, Gdańsk, Katowice, Łódź, Poznań, Szczecin, and Wrocław (EIU, 1999c; GUS, 1998; Możejko, 1998; Hardy, 1998). This pattern supports the view that strong regional contrasts in FDI are emerging with national capitals becoming particularly dynamic, accompanied by rapid land development (Gorzelak, 1996; Dowell, 1996). On the other hand there is consternation that the evolving spatial pattern consists of a few dominant FDIs, encircled by many smaller ones, which are there merely to test a location's economic viability (Hardy & Rainnie, 1996). Most of the FDI has gone into the food processing industry, iron and steel, household chemicals, catering, advertising, wholesale machinery and office equipment, banking and building construction. In contrast, those sectors which have clearly been overlooked include agriculture, insurance and those industrial branches linked to fossil fuels and ore extraction (M. Ślenczek, 1997). Nevertheless, the debate on permitting foreigners to buy land and buildings continues (Anon, 1999h). In 1998 foreigners legally bought 4,355 ha. compared with 2,942 ha in 1997, a 150% increase. These figures form part of a combined total of 16,851 ha. sold over the 1990-1998 period, a considerable size when compared with Poland's total area of 312,700 km². It is arousing traditional fears amongst Poles of losing their hard-won land (Jelonkiewicz, 1999a).

The pattern of FDI in Poland by late 1998 confirms the view that western regions of the country are more prosperous than those in the east, and therefore have been more successful in obtaining foreign investment (Fig. 4b).

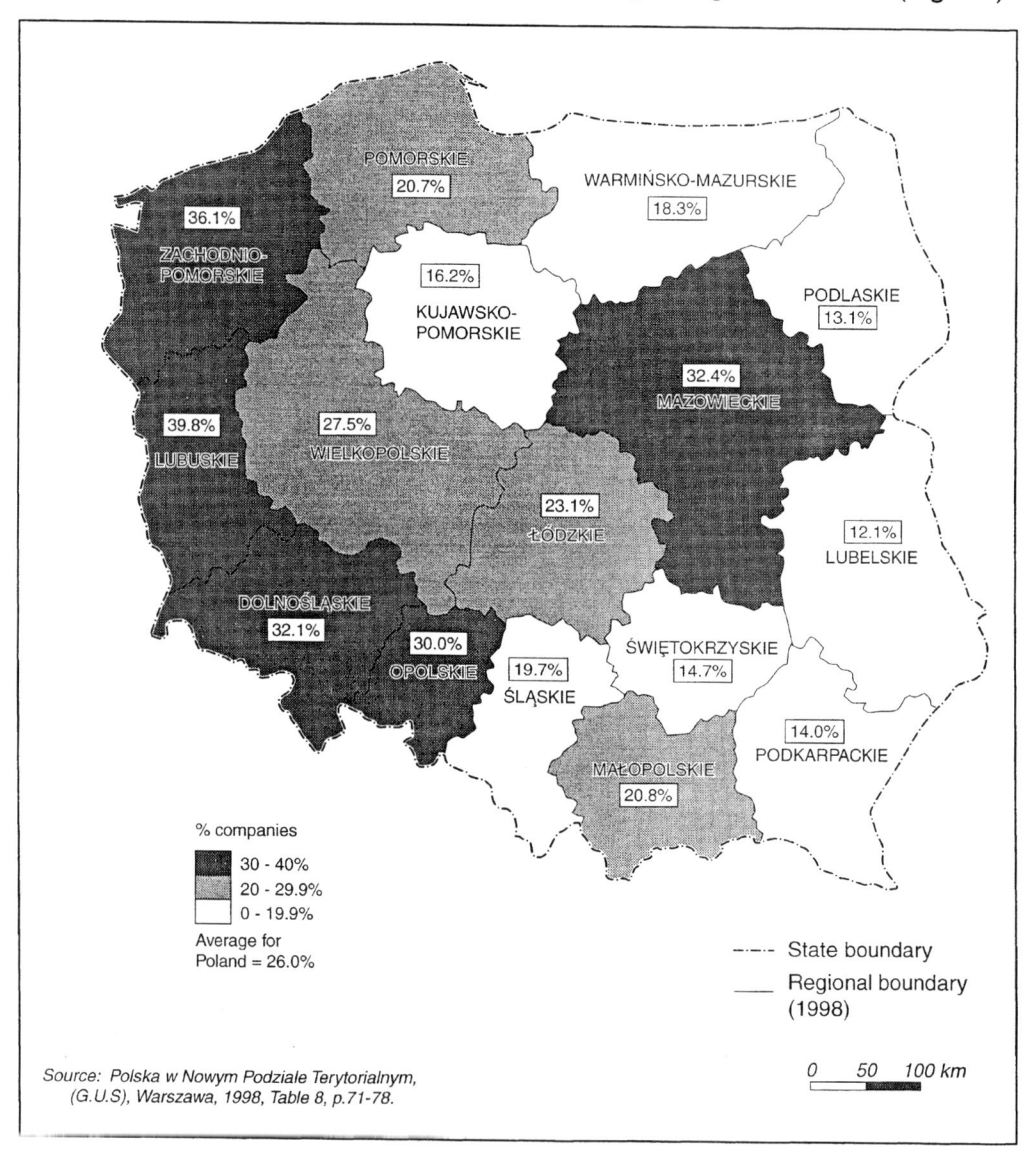

Figure 4b. Poland: Percentage of Companies with Foreign Direct Investment, by Region (31/12/98)

This zone stretches from Gdańsk on the Baltic coast to Warsaw in the centre and Cracow in the south. One possible reason for this division relates to the most easterly areas having had minimal political leverage or investment under communism. These poorer regions, usually referred to as Poland "B" during communism, were largely reliant on agriculture in contrast to the more industrialised regions of Poland "A". The post-1990 transition decade has done little to alter this scenario, with "B" still afflicted by a weaker infrastructure and longer distances from west European markets, which This has resulted in them having the country's lowest average incomes and highest unemployment rates (GUS, 1997). Sections of the eastern frontier have experienced fleeting prosperity thanks to uncontrolled transborder trade (Komornicki, 1998) but, on EU insistence, this ended abruptly with the Poland's imposition of tighter visa regulations in 1998, and the serious economic predicament in Russia. Even so, Poland's eastern regions may yet act as part of an influential "bridge" between the EU and Russia sometime in future (Piskozub, 1998).

High unemployment in the north-east of Poland has also influenced the failure to attract FDI. By mid-1998, the highest regional percentage of unemployed (nearly a fifth) was recorded in the Suwałki district whilst west of Gdańsk, the Słupsk and Koszalin voivodships had similar totals. The reasons for such unemployment here are often related either to the location of a few heavy industrial complexes with high employment in urban areas, or problems linked to areas with inherently weak infrastructures due to geographical isolation. More ambitious regional plans have tried to revitalise local economies in some areas (e.g. SEZs) hoping to attract more FDI, but this has achieved only limited success.

d) Slovakia

During the early 1990s the regional pattern of FDI in Slovakia was extremely uneven. Where investment had occurred it was extremely concentrated, but the spin-off proved advantageous for learning about technology transfer, progress in skills for local employees and positive results for local subcontractors and the labour market (Smith, 1994). Even so, FDI had primarily established at best 'cathedrals in the desert' and at worst had thwarted local efforts to gain sustainable forms of regional economic development (Smith, 1997). In the early 1990s most foreign enterprises were located in Bratislava, the country's new capital. Major foreign interest had come from Germany and at the beginning of 1992, its contribution formed two-thirds of the capital's FDI (Dubská, 1992). For example in Bratislava, Volkswagen bought the Bratislavské automobilové závody (BAZ) assembly and components factory (Ferenčíková, 1995; 1996a). Nevertheless, at the time of the Czech-Slovak 'Velvet divorce' in January 1993, Slovakia had attracted only a meagre US$ 300m of foreign investment, and was clearly the FDI cinderella of the Central-East European region (Ferenčíková, 1996b). Half this investment had gone into the manufacturing sector and another quarter in trade. However during 1993 interest in Slovakia grew, especially from neighbouring Austria, and opportunities for increasing FDI appeared favourable.

Bratislava continued to dominate with three-fifths (60.36%) of 1994's FDI total. This is not surprising seeing it was the country's major economic centre, which persuaded many well known firms, among them Unilever, Kmart, Volkswagen and Henkel, to establish branches there (Anon, 1996). Elsewhere, the pattern suggested a west-east split of the top ten FDI districts (Table 6; Fig. 5a).

Table 6. Slovakia: Top ten districts attracting FDI in 1994

District	No. of firms (%)	FDI (%)
Bratislava	49.63	60.36
Poprad	1.01	6.56
Humenné	0.51	5.94
Nitra	2.63	3.86
Banská Bystrica	3.63	3.23
Rožňava	0.42	2.44
Trnava	3.33	2.33
Košice	5.34	1.96
Vel'ký Krtíš	0.39	1.80
Senica	1.45	1.68
Other 28 districts	31.66	9.84
T O T A L	100.00	100.00

Source: E. Mikelka (1995), 'Integrácia Slovenska do európskej a svetovej ekonomiky', *Ekonomický Časopis*, Vol. 43, No. 7-8, Table 6, p.654

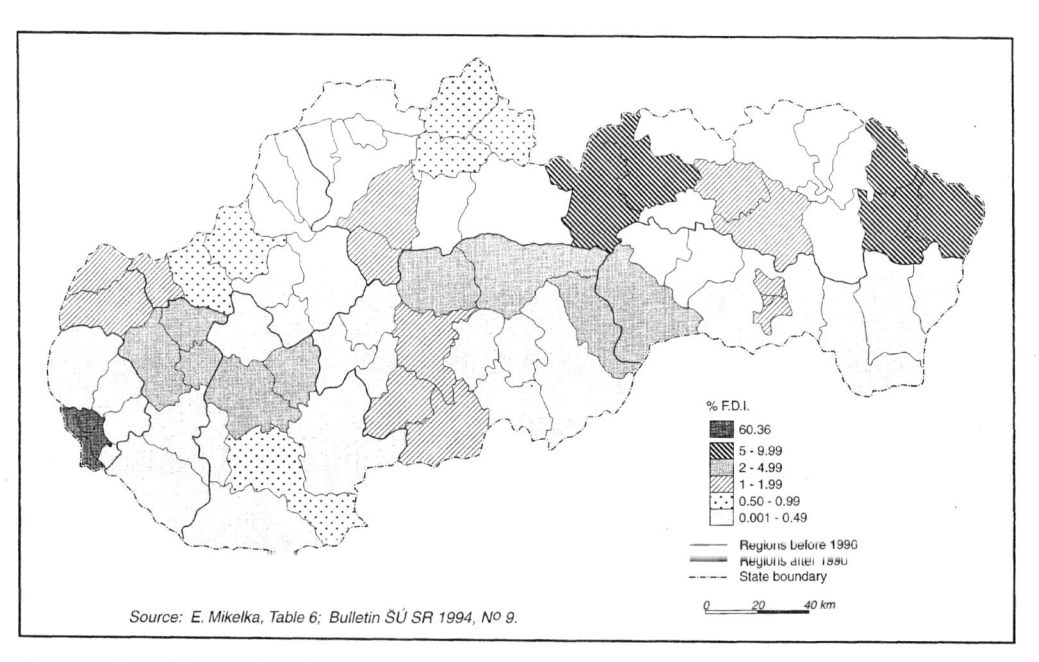

Figure 5a. Slovakia: Percentage of Foreign Direct Investment by District, 30/9/1994

Four of these districts were in the east (Humenné, Košice, Poprad, and Rožňava regions) and between them attracted nearly 17% of FDI in 1994, proving highly beneficial for local industries and services in East Slovakia (Žárska, 1996). FDI provided a welcome economic stimulus to the country's poorest third, especially in areas recently effected by the closure of state factories (e.g. arms manufacture) and subsequent rise in unemployment (Carter, 1998; Paulov, 1996; Smith, 1994). The Central Slovakian districts of Banská Bystrica and Veľký Krtíš were less successful, receiving only 5% of the amount available between them. West Slovakia clearly dominated FDI obtaining over two-thirds of the total (68.23%) through, besides Bratislava, the industrial districts of Nitra, Senica, and Trnava. Of the remaining 28 districts they attracted less than 10%, yet contained nearly a third of the firms, emphasising their small size overall. Generally, there seemed to be a strong investment bias towards metropolitan areas and the major urbanised districts of the north-west. Unfortunately, foreign investors showed little interest in the southern districts, much to the chagrin of the predominantly Hungarian minority residing there (Šaková, 1994; D. Turnock, 1995).

FDI in Slovakia during the second half of the 1990s experienced considerable changes. In 1996, Slovakia's privatization programme continued with direct sales the dominant mode, following the abrupt abandonment in 1994 of the voucher programme's second stage. By the end of that year it was estimated that over nine-tenths of all Slovak manufacturing firms were privatized (Djankov & Pohl, 1998), but the foreign investment climate was not conducive for FDI. The reasons related to political instability, a difficult privatisation policy, which prohibited foreign investors until the completion of privatisation, and an underdeveloped capital market. FDI interest waned further as a result of limited domestic markets, bureaucratic red tape, unclear ownership rights, an inadequately structured banking and information system, and poor accounting procedures.

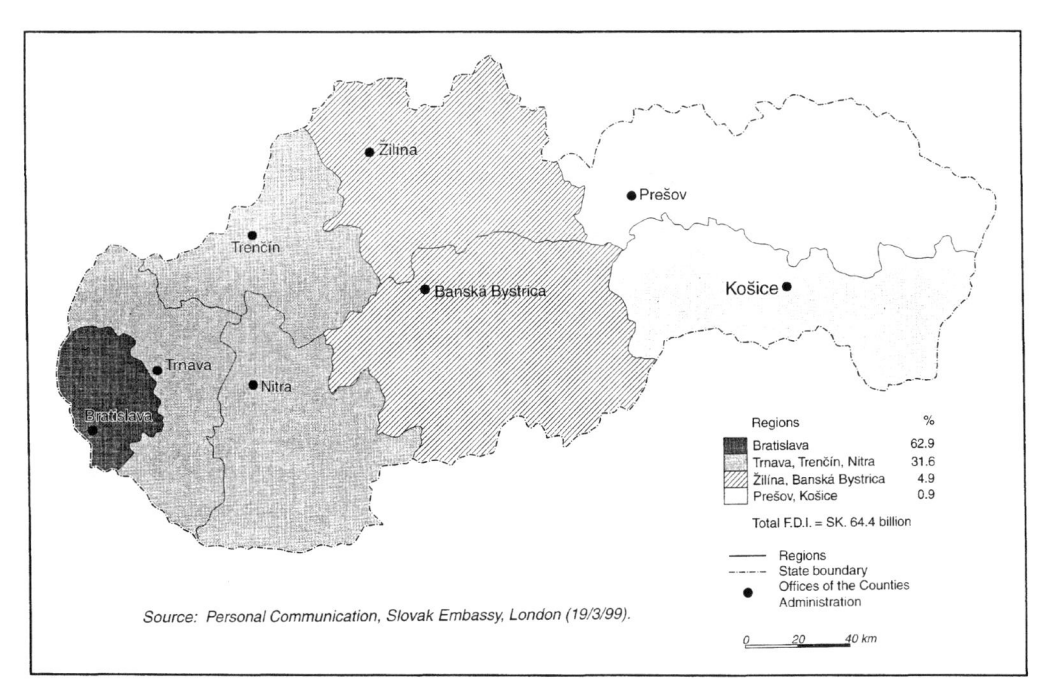

Figure 5b. Slovakia: Percentage of Foreign Direct Investment by Regions, September 1998

The FDI allocation pattern in 1998 (Fig. 5b) again highlighted the dominance of Bratislava and its immediate surroundings, with over three-fifths of the total. However, compared with 1994, there appears to have been a strengthening of the west-east pattern (Fig 5a). Districts like Trnava, Trenčín and Nitra only summoned up 7% of total FDI in 1994, but four years later overshadowed the rest of the country with nearly a third, giving West Slovakia (with Bratislava) a grand total of 94.5%. The central (Žilina, Banská Bystrica) and eastern (Prešov, Košice) regions had less than 6% between them. Central Slovakia only recorded a slight decline over 1994, although it has some of the country's economically least developed areas, with GDP per capita less than half the national average. For example, in the districts of Rimavska Sobota and Lučenec, FDI was below 0.2% in 1998, but unemployment rates were amongst the country's highest (25-30%); even in Veľký Krtíš, FDI did not exceed 2% (Novotný, 1998). East Slovakia experienced a catastrophic fall from 17% in 1994 to less than 1% in 1998, perhaps confirming the long term lack of faith by foreign investors in this poorer region, with districts like Rožňava attracting less than 2% FDI in 1998. On top of this, the country's largest steel manufacturer, the East Slovakian Steelworks (Východoslovenské Železiarne) at Košice, recorded a fiscal loss of US$ 120.5m in 1998 as well as loan problems, in spite of having a U.S. joint venture partner (Anon, 1999i). These longer term changes suggest that earlier suspicions of a west-east division in Slovakia's FDI regional pattern have been confirmed.

This pattern has, to some extent been supported by an analysis of income distribution for 1997 (Table 7).

Table 7. Slovakia: Income range in '000s Sk by district, 1997 (%)

Regions	>15	15-51	51-75	75-99	99+
Bratislava	12.8	8.8	16.8	21.6	45.8
Trnava	6.4	10.1	11.4	16.3	8.3
Trenčín	14.7	11.7	10.5	8.7	3.5
Nitra	10.6	14.4	13.1	11.8	5.1
Žilina	10.8	12.9	12.7	10.5	10.5
B. Bystrica	10.8	12.5	13.1	11.8	11.7
Prešov	16.1	15.2	9.7	6.2	6.6
Košice	17.8	14.7	12.7	13.1	8.5
Slovak Republic	100.0	100.0	100.0	100.0	100.0

Source: *Vybrané údaje o regiónach v Slovenskej Republike v roku 1997*, Bratislava (April) 1998; Pauhofová & Bauerová, Table 3, p. 900.

The table shows that a third (33.9%) of Slovakia's population with an annual income of 15,000 Sk or less, lived in the poorer eastern regions of Košice and Prešov. In sharp contrast, nearly half (45.8%) of the Slovaks enjoying a salary above 99,000 Sk lived in Bratislava, compared to only 15.1%

in the two eastern regions. In 1997 only 2% of Slovakia's population had disposable incomes in the highest bracket; in contrast, 4.7% earned less than 15,001 Sk, whilst most (71%) earned between 15.000 and 51,000 Sk; the other two categories received 18.3% (51-75,000 Sk) and 4% (75-99,000 Sk) respectively (Pauhofová & Bauerová, 1998). Spatially, the western region (Bratislava, Trnava, Trenčín, Nitra) dominated the salary income pattern with over half the total (52.48%), compared to over a fifth (23.46%) in the central region (Žilína. Bankská Bystrica) and nearly a quarter (24.12%) in the east (Prešov, Košice).

Conclusion

In the post-communist world of Central-East Europe, the belief that FDI would provide the engine for economic prosperity has not been proved entirely true; overall FDI levels have been less than originally projected, but remain considerably more than in South-East Europe. There has also been some disillusionment amongst the region's inhabitants who saw FDI as a panacea for all earlier disappointments. Some believed that overnight, FDI would bring to their nascent post-communist systems the equivalent of an American living standard, the benefits of a Swedish welfare state, and democratic institutions like in the UK.

Admittedly, there have been improvements but the level has depended on where you live, as supported by evidence from the regional FDI pattern analysis. Capital cities and more westerly areas have fared much better economically than their respective districts to the east. This follows a common pattern of a decrease eastwards in Central-Eastern Europe accompanied by increasing distance from the European Union (Hamilton, 1999). It should be remembered that FDI investors need faith, wealth and a taste for risk, but the potential is enormous. Also expectations play a crucial role, because the location decisions of firms are often very expensive to reverse; in deciding where to locate in Central-East Europe, future government policy (or its uncertainty) could be as important as the current political situation.

Initially, the motives of FDI world companies were influenced by opportunities to extend into the newly established East European markets, the possibilities offered by privatisation, and the chance to exploit low production costs. FDI personnel were lured to Central-East Europe by the presence of a relatively cheap, well-educated labour supply and proximity to crucial West European markets. Besides the overall economic prospects, other decision-making requisites for FDI included the presence/absence of a sound institutional structure and proven political stability, were government credibility could play a major role. Thus confirmation that a particular Central-East European country had been accepted to join the EU early was seen as a positive sign of transition progress and hence an endorsement to future stability. This has had profound positive effects on industrial location. It is these sort of factors over the past decade that have contributed to the steady growth of FDI stock in some of the countries studied here.

The future role of the EU may be vital in the continuance of this trend. The phased enlargement of the EU could most probably trigger a redirection of FDI inflows towards certain Central-East European countries. For example, Poland, the Czech Republic and Hungary, who will acquire early membership, may increase their FDI totals at the expense of later entrants such as Slovakia. The present inclination for foreign investors to concentrate on early EU entrants, particularly those topping the accession list (Poland, Hungary, Czech Republic), could be further strengthened by yet more FDI inflows from more recent EU members like Sweden and Austria, following the longer German and Dutch FDI tradition over much of the decade.

Of course, staged EU enlargement carries with it certain risks, which may lead to a divided development pattern. Those countries like Slovakia which have temporarily been excluded from the early EU entry could lag behind economically, if not regressing in absolute terms. However, factors such as proximity to large markets provides strong incentives for firms to locate in countries like Slovakia. The general implication for Central-East European countries is that proximity to West European development centres, gives such states as Slovakia a greater chance of luring industry and FDI. This proved especially important in the early 1990s for those Central-East European countries sharing common borders with an EU state(s), giving them a locational advantage for enlarging their economic activity. For example, opportunities arose for transfrontier cooperation through joint ventures, subcontracting, local/regional policy coordination and the expansion of transport/telecommunications infrastructure.

It appears that the ramifications of future development of FDI patterns in Central- East Europe revolve around certain considerations. First, countries that continue to be relatively attractive for FDI will have a better chance to surmount/survive economic recession. This will be achieved either through their pace of transition, or economic growth opportunities from privatisation. Secondly, new competitors among the transition latecomers, may attract additional FDI inflows to the region, without damaging prospects for the currently most attractive states. For example, the privatisation potential of the four Central-East Europe countries studied here, still remains untapped or not yet exhausted completely. In the near future, FDI investment could play a significant role in the development of these countries in spite of aberrations like the Kosovo crisis. Thirdly, the four countries analysed here will, or soon may be EU members. They will become more attractive for FDI as their economic systems and regulatory frameworks become more compatible with other EU member countries (UNCTAD, 1998). Then, and only then, will the more dynamic consequences of EU membership agreements begin to manifest themselves on the spatial pattern of FDI in Central-East Europe.

Acknowledgements

The author would like to thank the Cartographic Unit at University College London for the skill shown in preparation of the maps.

References

Alcroft, D.H. & Morewood, S. 1995. *Economic Change in Eastern Europe since 1918*. E. Elgar Publ., Cheltenham/Northampton, MA (quoted: p. 207)

Amin, A., Bradley, D., Howells, J., Tomaney, J. & Genth, C. 1994. 'Regional incentives and the quality of mobile investment in the less favoured regions of the EC', *Progress in Planning*, Vol.41, No.1, p.9-112.

Amin, A. & Thrift, N. 1995. 'Institutional Issues for the European regions; from markets and plans to socioeconomics, and powers of association', *Economics & Society*, Vol.24, p.41-66.

Andor, L. & Summers, M. 1998. *Market Failure: A Guide to the East European 'Economic Miracle'*. Pluto Press, London/Chicago (quoted: p.78-79)

Anon, 1992. 'Birth of the Hungarian Opel', *The Hungarian Observer*, Vol.5, No.7, p.11-12.

Anon, 1995. *Poland: Your Business Partner*, Warsaw, p.49-50.

Anon, 1996. 'Capital destiny'. *British Czech and Slovak Association: Newsletter*, No.30, London, p.5.

Anon, 1998. 'Tax Free Investment in Poland', *Polish Business*, Nov./Dec.1998, London, p.12-13.

Anon, 1999a. 'Czech central bank cuts its key repo rate again as economy sags', *New Europe*, 10-16/5/1999, London, p.10.

Anon, 1999b. 'IMF says concerned by Czech fiscal deficit outlook', *New Europe*, 10-16/5/1999, London, p.11.

Anon, 1999c. 'Strong FDI welcome in Czech Q1 BOP data', *New Europe*, 14-20/6/1999, London, p.10.

Anon, 1999d. 'Foreign investment on the rise in research and development sector', *New Europe*, 10-16/1/1999, London, p.14.

Anon, 1999e. 'US trade agency aims to increase investments in Hungary', *New Europe*, 14-20/2/1999, London, p.15.

Anon, 1999f. 'Suzuki unit to invest HUF 16 million in new microvan', *New Europe*, 14-20/6/1999, London, p.15

Anon, 1999g. 'Hungary Ikarus establishes venture with Renault Iveco', *New Europe*, 28/6-4/7/1999, London, p.15.

Anon, 1999h. 'The Poles bargain with Europe', *The Economist*, 31/7/1999, p.34.

Anon, 1999i. 'VSZ to maintain downward trend in second quarter', *New Europe*, 17-23/5/1999, London, p.16.

Bradshaw, M.J. 1997. 'The Geography of Foreign Investment in Russia, 1993-1995', *Tijdschrift voor Economische en Sociale Geografie*, Vol.88, No.1, p.77-84.

Buckwalter, D.W. 1995. 'Spatial Inequality, Foreign Investment, and Economic Transition in Bulgaria', *The Professional Geographer*, Vol.43, No.3, p.288-298.

Cantwell, J. (ed.) 1999. *Foreign Direct Investment and Technological Change*, 2 vols. E. Elgar Publ., Cheltenham/Northampton, MA, 1056 pp.

Carter, F.W. & Turnock, D. 1996. *Environmental Problems in Eastern Europe*, Updated Edition, Routledge, London/New York, 291 pp.

Carter, F.W. 1998. 'Geographical problems in east Slovakia', *Region and Regionalism*, No.3, 1998, Łódź/Opole, p.187-203.

Carter, F.W. 1999. 'The role of foreign direct investment in the regional development of Central & South-East Europa', *Regional Prosperity and Sustainability*, 3rd Moravian Geographical Conference, Slavkov u Brna, p.16-22.

Carter, L., Sader, F. & Holtedahl, P. 1996. *Foreign direct investment in Central and Eastern European infrastructure*, World Bank: Foreign Investment Advisory Service, Occasional Paper, No.7, 28 pp.

Dąbrowski, J.M., Dworzecki, Z., Gawlikowska-Hueckel, K. & Wyżnikiewicz, B. 1994. 'Powered by Promotion', *Warsaw Voice*, 25/9/1994, p.B6.

Deußner, R. 1996. 'European Networks and the East Austrian and West Hungarian Border Regions', *Discussion Papers*, No.1 (Institute of Social and European Studies), Budapest-Kőszeg-Szombathely, p.31-36.

Djankov, S. & Pohl, G. 1998. 'The restructuring of large firms in the Slovak Republic', *Economics of Transition*, Vol.6, No.1, p.67-85.

Dobosiewicz, Z. 1992. *Foreign investment in Eastern Europe*. Routledge, London/New York, p.20-24;102.
Done, K. 1998. 'Automotive Industry; Accelerating away', *Financial Times* (Survey: Hungary), 7/12/1998, London, p.IV.
Dowall, D.E. 1996. *The Warsaw economy in transition*. Avebury Press, Aldershot, 235 pp.
Dubská, D. 1992. 'K regionálnímu rozdělení joint ventures v čs. ekonomice' I/II, *Národní Hospodářství* (Prague) No.10, p.23-25; No.11, p.31-32.
Dutkiewicz, J., Lavell, T. & Sowińska, M. (eds) 1996. *Fine-Tuning the Market Economy: Poland Consolidates Its Progress*, Warsaw Voice, Warsaw, p.58-64.
Dziemianowicz, W. 1993. 'Foreign capital in Czecho-Slovakia, Poland and Hungary, 1989-1992', Ch. in *Regional Question in Europe*, G. Gorzelak & B. Jałowiecki (eds), Regional and Local Studies No.10 (EIRLD, Warsaw Univ.), Warsaw, p.537-570.
EIU [Economist Intelligence Unit] 1999a. 'To FDI for', *Business Eastern Europe*, 11/1/1999, p.1.
EIU, 1999b. 'Czech Republic', *Business Central Europe: The Annual 1998/1999*, London, p.23.
EIU, 1999c. *Eastern Europe's emerging cities*. Jan.1998, London, 40 pp.
Fazekas, K. 1993. 'A munkanélküliség regionális különbségeinek okairól. A foglalkoztatási térségek tipizálása', *Közgazdasági Szemle*, Vol.40, No.7-8, p.694-712.
Ferenčíková, S. 1995. 'Vstup zahraničného kapitálu do slovenskej ekonomiky na príklade vybraných joint ventures', *Ekonomický Časopis*, Vol.43, No.2, p.140-153.
Ferenčíková, S. 1996a. 'Niektoré skúsenosti z pôsobenie zahraničných investorov', *International Business Cooperation*, Vol.7, No.2-3, p.13-14.
Ferenčíková, S. 1996b. 'Efekty a pôsobenie priamych zahraničných investícií na príklade Slovenskej republiky', *Ekonomický Časopis*, Vol.44, No.6, p.450-465.
Gács, J., Holzmann, R. & Wyzan, M.L. 1999. *The Mixed Blessing of Financial Inflows: Transition Countries in Comparative Perspective*. E. Elgar Publ., Cheltenham/Northampton, MA, 272 pp.
Gawlikowska-Hueckel, K. 1995. 'Poland and Europe', Ch. 10 in *Monitoring Economic Transition: The Polish Case*, G. Blazyca & J.M. Dąbrowski (eds), Avebury Press, Aldershot, 1995, p.159-175
Gorzelak, G. 1993. 'The Regional Patterns of Polish Transformation', in *Regional Question in Europe*, G. Gorzelak & B. Jałowiecki (eds), Regional and Local Studies, No.10 (EIRLD, Warsaw Univ.), Warsaw, 1993, p.503-535.
Gorzelak, G. 1996. *The regional dimension of transformation in Central Europe*. Jessica Kingsley Publ., London, 204 pp.
Gottvald, J., Pedersen, P.J. & Šimek, M. 1999, 'The Czech labour market in transition; Evidence from a micro study', *Bulletin of Economic Research*, Vol.51, No.1, p.39-65.
Grabher, G. 1994. 'The disembedded regional economy: the transformation of east German industrial complexes into western exclaves', in A. Amin & N. Thrift (eds), *Globalization, institutions and regional development in Europe*. O.U.P., Oxford, p.177-196.
Grabher, G. 1997. 'Adaption at the Cost of Adaptability? Restructuring the Eastern German Regional Economy', in *Restructuring Networks in Post-Socialism: Legacies, Linkages and Localities*, G. Grabher & D. Stark (eds), O.U.P., Oxford, p.107-134.
GUS [Główny Urząd Statystyczny] 1997. *Bezrobocie rejestrowane w Polsce I kwartał 1997*. Warszawa, 57 pp.
GUS, 1998. *Działność gospodarcza spółek z udziałem kapitału zagranicznego w 1997 roku*. Warszawa, 88 pp.
Hamilton, F.E.I. 1995. 'Re-evaluating Space: Locational Change and Adjustment in Central and Eastern Europe', *Geographische Zeitschrift*, Vol.83, No.1, p.67-86.
Hamilton, F.E.I. 1999. 'Transformation and space in Central and Eastern Europe', *Geographical Journal*, Vol.165, No.2, p.135-144.
Hardy, J. & Rainnie, A. 1996. *Restructuring Kraków: Desperately seeking Capitalism*. Mansell Publ., London, 310 pp.
Hardy, J. 1998. 'Cathedrals in the Desert? Transnationals, Corporate Strategy and Locality in Wrocław', *Regional Studies*, Vol.23, No.7, p.639-652.
Horváth, G. 1999. 'Changing Hungarian Regional Policy and Accession to the European Union', *European Urban and Regional Studies*, Vol.6, No.2, p.166-177.

Jelonkiewicz, W. 1999a. 'Foreign Land Acquisition: What Worth the Earth?', *Warsaw Voice*, 6/6/1999, p.17.
Jelonkiewicz, W. 1999b. 'Special Economic zones: To Be or Not to be ...', *Warsaw Voice*, 6/6/1999, p.12.
Kápitany, Z. & Kállay, L. 1990. 'Hungary's Automative Sector: Looking for Markets and Suppliers', *International Motor Business*, October, p.14-23
Kápitany, Z. 1992. 'Hungary's Trade and Motor Industry: Dilemmas of Transition', *NOMISMA: Economic Journal of East Europe and the Soviet Union*, Vol.1, Bologna, p.49-57.
Komornicki, T. 1998. 'Boundaries of Poland as Spatial Barriers', in *European Integration and Transborder Co-operation*, K. Ivanička (ed.), Vol.1 (Faculty of Political Sciences and International Affairs, University of Matej Bel Banská Bystrica), Banská Bystrica, p.51-61
Kubińska, J. 1998. 'Special Economic Zones', *Polish Business* (London), Feb. 1998, p.30-32.
Langenkamp, D. 1999. 'The regeneration of Hungary's east', *New Europe*, 1-7/3/1999, London, p.15.
Langenkamp, D. & O'Leary, J. 1997. 'El Paso power grab in south Hungary', *Prague Business Journal*, 17-22/2/1997, p.20.
Lankes, H.P. & Stern, N. 1998. *Capital inflows to Eastern Europe and the Former Soviet Union*, Working Paper, No.27, EBRD, London, 21 pp.
Mazurski, K.R. 1995. 'Die Transformation der Wirtschafts- und Gesellschaftsordnung Polens', *Geographie und Schule* (Köln), Vol.17, p.20-30.
Michalak, W.Z. 1993. 'Foreign direct investment and joint ventures in East-Central Europe: a geographical perspective', *Environment and Planning A*, Vol.25, p.1573-1591.
Michalak, W.Z. 1995. 'Foreign aid and Eastern Europe in the "New world order"', *Tijdschrift voor Economische en Sociale Geografie*, Vol.86, No.3, p.260-277.
Możejko, E. 1998. 'Inwestuj w Łodzi!', *Życie Gospodarcze*, 15/1/1998, Warszawa, p.28-29.
Murphy, A.B. 1992. 'Western Investment in East-Central Europe: Emerging Patterns and Implications for State Stability', *Professional Geographer*, Vol.44, No.3, p.249-259.
Novotný, J., 1998. 'Cross-Border Co-operation in the Regions of Gemer-Malohont Novohrad and Hont', in *European Integration and Transborder Co-operation*, K. Ivanička (ed.), Vol.1 (Faculty of Political Sciences and International Affairs, University of Matej Bel Banská Bystrica), Banská Bystrica, p.150-151.
Nyerki, J., 1998. 'Hungary's Approach toward Cross-border Co-operation and European Integration', in *European Integration and Transborder Co-operation*, K. Ivanička (ed.), Vol.1 (Faculty of Political Sciences and International Affairs, University of Matej Bel Banská Bystrica), Banská Bystrica, p.93-95.
Pauhofová, I. & Bauerová, E. 1998. 'Income Situation and Consumer Habits Formation in Transforming Society', *Ekonomický Časopis*, Vol.46, No.6, p.894-912.
Paulov, J. 1996. 'The Transformation Process in Slovakia: Some thoughts on spatio-temporal regularities, regional pattern and possible regional shift', *Acta Facultatis Rerum Naturalium Universitatis Comenianæ: Geographica*, No.37, p.113-120.
Pavlinek, P. 1995. 'Regional Development and the Disintegration of Czechoslovakia', *Geoforum*, Vol.26, No.4, p.351-372.
Pavlinek, P. 1998. 'The Role of Foreign Direct Investment in the Czech Republic's Transition to Capitalism', *The Professional Geographer*, Vol.50, No.1, p.71-85.
Pisková, H. 1998. 'The Flow of Foreign Direct Investments Remains on the 1996 Level', *Czech Business and Trade* (Prague), No.2, p.1-4.
Piskozub, A. 1998. 'Polska jako przestrzeń cywilizacyna i geopolityczna w zjednoczonej Europie. Prognoza na wiek XXI na tle wniosków i doświadczen dziejowych', in *Polska i jej sąsiedzi wobec przemian cywilizacyjnch i geopolitycznych*, M. Jakubowski (ed.), (Geopolitical Studies Vol.4), IGSP, P.A.N., Warszawa, p.57-80.
Pollert, A. 1999. *The New Market Economies of Eastern Central Europe*. Sage Publ., London, 256 pp.
Pye, R.B.K. 1997. 'Foreign Direct Investment in Central Europe The Czech Republic, Hungary, Poland, Romania and Slovakia: Results from a Survey of Major Western Investors', *Working Paper Series* (FWP: A.97/1), City University Business School, London, p.23-28.
Rechnitzer, J. 1996. 'The main elements of national planning strategy in North-West

Transdanubia', *Discussion Papers*, No.1 (Institute for Social and European Studies), Budapest-Kőszeg-Szombathely, p.24-30.
Robinson, A. 1997a. 'Greenfield projects play a key role', *Financial Times* (Survey: Hungary), 9/12/1997, London, p.II.
Sadler, D. & Swain, A. 1994. 'State and market in eastern Europe: regional development and workplace implications of direct foreign investment in the automobile industry in Hungary', *Transactions of the Institute of British Geographers*, Vol.19, p.387-403.
Šaková, B. 1994. 'Motivácia či demotivácia zahraničných investorov u nás?', *Ekonomické rozhľady*, Vol.24, No.4, p.41-48.
Skalimowski, W. 1988. 'Rozprzestrzenianie się przedsiębiorstw zagranicznych w Polsce w latach 1977-1986', in *Percepcja, scenariusze i przedsiębiorczość*, B. Jałowiecki (ed.), Warszawa, p.25-35.
Ślenczek, M. 1997. 'Pochodzenie i wielkość inwestycji zagranicznych w Polsce w latach 1989-1996', *Czasopismo Geograficzne*, Vol.68, No.3-4, p.373-382.
Smith, A. 1994. 'Uneven Development and the Restructuring of the Armaments Industry in Slovakia', *Transactions of the Institute of British Geographers*, Vol.19, No.4, p.404-424.
Smith, A. 1996. 'From convergence to fragmentation: uneven development, industrial restructuring, and the 'transition to capitalism' in Slovakia', *Environment and Planning A*, Vol.28, p.135-156.
Smith, A. 1997. 'Inward investment and the political economy of regional development in Slovakia', paper presented at *R.G.S./I.B.G. Annual Conference*, Exeter, 23 pp.
Somfai, A. 1996. 'Developmental Alternatives for Western Transdanubia in the Process of European Transformation', *Discussion Papers*, No.1 (Institute for Social and European Studies), Budapest-Kőszeg-Szombathely, p.37-42.
Swain, A. 1998. 'Governing the Workplace: The Workplace and Regional Development Implications of Automotive Foreign Direct Investment in Hungary', *Regional Studies*, Vol.32, No.7, p.653-672.
Tarzi, S. 1999. 'Host countries and foreign direct investment from the emerging markets', *International Relations*, Vol.14, No.4, p.15-32.
Turnock, D. 1995. 'Regional development in the new Eastern Europe', *Geofile* No.260, p.3.
Uhlíř, D. 1995. *Nadnárodní korporace, zahraniční investice a regionální rozvoj: obecná východiska a konkrétní situace České republiky*. Unpublished Master's thesis, Charles University, Prague.
Uhlíř, D. 1997. 'Internationalisation of enterprise and regional change in the Czech Republic since 1989', paper presented at *R.G.S./I.B.G. Annual Conference*, Exeter, 20 pp.
United Nations Conference on Trade and Development (UNCTAD), 1998. 'Trends and Determinants; Central and Eastern Europe', *World Investment Report 1998: Investment, Trade and International Policy Arrangements*, New York, p.271-289.
van Hastenberg, H. 1996a. 'Foreign Direct Investment in Central and Eastern Europe; Experiences and Prospects', in *Workshop Transformation Processes in Eastern Europe*, H.B.G. Ganzeboom (ed.), ESR/NWO, The Hague, p.49-67
van Hastenberg, H. 1996b. 'Regional and Sectoral Characteristics of Foreign Direct Investment in Hungary', *Workshop Transformation Processes in Eastern Europe*, H. van der Wusten (ed.), ESR/NWO, The Hague, p.121-136.
Varga, Z. 1999. 'The Hungarian diversification strategy. Constraints and opportunities', *GeoJournal*, Vol.46, No.3, p.217
Williams, A.M., Baláž, V. & Zajac, S. 1998. 'The EU and Central Europe: The Remaking of Economic Relationships', *Tijdschrift voor Economische en Sociale Geografie*, Vol.89, No.2, p.131-149.
Wolf, K. 1998. *Podruhé a naposled aneb mírové dělení Československa*. G plus G, Praha, 141 pp.
Wright, R. 1998. 'Pharmaceuticals; Russia's bitter pill', *Financial Times* (Survey: Hungary), 7/12/1998, London, p.IV
Žárska, E. 1996. 'Význam lokálnej úrovne v ekonomickom rozvoj', *Ekonomický Časopis*, Vol.44, No.6, p.466-480.

Structure, regional distribution and selected effects of foreign direct investment in Polish manufacturing in the 1990s

Bolesław DOMAŃSKI (Kraków)

Abstract

The focus of this paper is on foreign direct investment (FDI) in the Polish manufacturing sector between 1990 and mid-1998. The following topics are dealt with: size and structure of FDI in Poland; major types of investments; regional distribution of FDI; local embeddedness of FDI; all that with reference to existing theories and empirical literature.

The author's findings include: the existence of a disproportionate spatial concentration of manufacturing FDI in the Warsaw metropolitan region and in the major urban agglomerations; and low investment in eastern Poland, but also in the Polish-German borderland. The economic consequences of FDI are assessed to be predominantly positive.

Struktur, räumliche Verteilung und ausgewählte Effekte der Ausländischen Direktinvestitionen im Industriesektor Polens in den 1990er Jahren

Kurzfassung

Der Aufsatz untersucht die ausländischen Direktinvestitionen (FDI) in der Industrie Polens zwischen 1990 und Mitte 1998. Folgende Themen werden vor dem Hintergrund einschlägiger theoretischer und empirischer Arbeiten behandelt: Größe und Struktur der FDI in Polen; wichtigste Typen von Investitionen; regionale Verteilung der FDI; Einbettung der FDI in die lokale Wirtschaft.

Der Autor gelangt u. a. zu folgenden Ergebnissen: Es gibt eine überproportionale räumliche Konzentration der industriellen FDI auf die Hauptstadtregion Warschau und auf die größten städtischen Ballungsräume, und wenig Investitionen in Ostpolen, aber auch im Grenzgebiet zu Deutschland. Die ökonomischen Konsequenzen der FDI werden als überwiegend positiv bewertet.

One process that has begun to affect the economies of Central and Eastern Europe since the collapse of communism is foreign direct investment (FDI). Several questions have been raised in this field. To what extent does FDI intensify existing regional disparities or contribute to changing the organisation of the economic space of these countries (e.g. Murphy 1992; Sadler and Swain 1994; Buckwalter 1995; Smith and Ferencikova 1998; Pavlinek 1998)? What are location factors of greenfield foreign investment in Central and Eastern Europe (e.g. Meyer and Qu 1995)? Does state regional policy have any impact on FDI (Sadler and Swain 1994)? How far are new foreign investments embedded in the local economy (Grabher 1994; Hardy 1998; Pavlinek and Smith 1998)? What are the major economic and social effects of FDI in host countries in the 1990s (e.g., Dobosiewicz 1992; Dunning 1993)?

The aim of this paper is to explore some of these problems in the Polish context in the light of the existing research and the author's own studies. The focus is on foreign direct investment in manufacturing in Poland between 1990 and mid-1998. The author begins with an overview of the size and structure of FDI in Poland and of major types of investments. Regional distribution of the foreign capital is discussed at some length in terms of the new administrative division of the country, some hypotheses are put forward, and comments concerning location factors of new factories are made. Finally, selected positive and negative consequences of FDI are examined and the issue of local embeddedness is addressed in particular.

Size and structure of foreign direct investment in Poland

The influx of foreign capital into Poland in the early 1990s was rather slow, slower than into some smaller countries of the region, especially Hungary. The process has gathered momentum in recent years and reached $5.5 billion in 1996, $6.6 billion in 1997 and roughly $10 billion in 1998 (Fig. 1). This rapid increase contrasts with the rather steady foreign investment of $1–2 billion a year in Hungary and the Czech Republic at the same time and makes Poland the largest recipient of FDI in Central and Eastern Europe in absolute terms – about $29 billion since 1990. Still, in terms of FDI per capita Poland lags behind Hungary, Slovenia and the Czech Republic. Several reasons may lie behind the recent surge in foreign investment in Poland. In the first place, it may reflect an appreciation of the size of the Polish domestic market, the continuous fast economic growth since 1991 accompanied by rising consumption of durable goods and a high investment rate, uninterrupted by the financial crises that hit Hungary and the Czech Republic. Thus Poland may be a confirmation of the argument that domestic economic growth is the precondition for FDI on a large scale. After the initial shock phase of 1989–1991 the Polish economy has been developing at a very fast rate, which is particularly true of manufacturing (8,3% average annual increase). The proximity of Germany, and a relatively skilled and cheap labour force are undoubtedly important too, though they do not provide Poland with any special advantage vis-a-vis the Czech Republic or Hungary. Foreign capital has been coming to Poland despite the strongest and most militant trade unions in Central and Eastern Europe, high taxation and an unstable legal system, bureaucratic procedures slowing down investment processes, inadequate infrastructure and poor financial services. Tax concessions

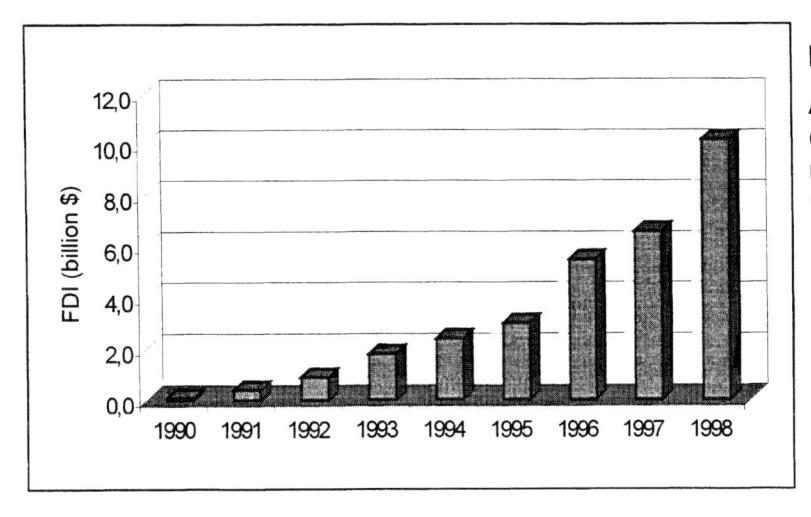

Figure 1:

Annual foreign direct investment in Poland, 1990 – 1998

are believed to have had little impact on attracting large, long-term investors into Poland. The Act of December 1988 granted foreign joint ventures in Poland universal three-year tax holidays, but they were abolished in June 1991 and replaced with individual tax exemptions occasionally awarded by the Ministry of Finance. A study carried out in 1995 indicated that only 8,2% of large foreign-owned companies enjoyed tax holidays in Poland, while 7,6% took advantage of the benefits of the 1988 Act (Błuszkowski and Garlicki 1995).

Manufacturing has attracted by far the most capital. According to the Polish Agency for Foreign Investment (PAIZ) approximately 63% of total FDI in Poland through 1997 took place in manufacturing. The financial sector runs second with about a 13% share.

The production of food and drinks and the automobile industry are two sectors that have received more investment than any other – 21 and 17,6 per cent of manufacturing FDI respectively. They are both primarily oriented towards the Polish market, though the export of cars and car components keeps growing. The domestic market is also crucial for the substantial investment in chemicals (especially detergents and cosmetics, industrial gases), rubber and plastics, tobacco as well as printing and publishing (Tab. 1). On the other hand, export plays an important role in the production of other non-metallic products, e.g. cement, construction materials, paper and board, as well as consumer electronics and electrical equipment.

Nearly one-fourth of the capital invested in Polish manufacturing stems from the United States. The role of German capital is significant (15%), though it represents only half the German share of Polish exports and imports. Italian, British, Swedish and Swiss companies were among the first large investors in Poland, whereas greater activity by French firms is a more recent phenomenon (each of these countries accounts for 5-10% of FDI). Austrian firms contribute roughly 1% of the foreign manufacturing capital, which contrasts with their greater involvement in Hungary and the Czech Republic[1]. All in all, the Euro-

---

[1] The presence of the Austrian capital has been more visible in finance (Creditanstalt, Raiffeisen), construction and hotels (Bau Holding, IAEG, Porr).

pean Union is the source of 57% of the inward investment, Europe as a whole of about two-thirds. Asian investors comprise 7,5% of the capital, most of which comes from Korea, while Japanese companies, with few exceptions, have adopted a wait and see strategy[2].

Table 1: Foreign direct investment in Polish manufacturing by sector, 1990 – mid 1998

NACE code	Sector	Percentage of manufacturing FDI	Major companies
15	Food and drinks	20,9	PepsiCo, Coca Cola, Nestle, Mars, Unilever, Ferrero, Carlsberg, Heineken, Cargill, Cadbury
34	Cars and components	17,6	Fiat, Daewoo, General Motors, Ford, Volkswagen, Isuzu, Volvo, MAN
26	Glass, cement & construction materials	11,0	Pilkington, Saint Gobain, Dyckerhoff, Lafarge, Heidelberger, Readymix, Owens Illinois, BTS
24	Chemicals	8,7	Glaxo Wellcome, British Oxygen, Pliva, Procter & Gamble, Praxair, Linde, Unilever, Akzo Nobel
21	Paper and allied products	6,7	International Paper, Mondi, Intercellulosa, Trebruk, SCA Mölnlycke, Kappa Packaging
16	Tobacco products	5,5	Philip Morris, Reemtsma, BAT, Reynolds, Seita, House of Prince
25	Rubber and plastic products	4,1	Michelin, Goodyear, Bridgestone, Nordisk Wavin, Rubbermaid
32	TV, radio and telecommunications	3,9	Thomson, Daewoo, Lucent Technologies, Alcatel, Siemens, Philips,
31	Electrical equipment	3,4	ABB, Philips, Siemens, Exide, Legrand, Ahlstrom, Matsushita, Bosch
22	Printing and publishing	2,8	Passauer Neue Presse, Orkla, Donnelley, H.Bauer, Axel Springer, Gruner und Jahr
	Other sectors	15,4	Kronospan, Lucchini, Electricite de France, F & P Holding, Schmalbach, Ikea, Danfoss
	All manufacturing	100,0	

Source: author's calculations based on questionnaire surveys, PAIZ data and press releases.

Types of investment

We can distinguish four major sources of foreign capital invested in Poland: transnational corporations (TNCs), medium-sized and small enterprises, venture capital organisations, and international financial institutions. The vast majority of the 33,460 companies with foreign capital registered in Poland (1997) are small and medium-sized firms that amount to approximately 15% of FDI, whereas TNCs (including transnational banks) represent about three-fourths of the total value of foreign investment and slightly more in the case of

---

[2] A new Isuzu diesel engine plant in Tychy is the newest, largest Japanese FDI (worth $115 m in the first stage). Other important investors include Bridgestone, NSK and Matsushita.

manufacturing alone. The share of venture capital can be estimated at 4% and is similar to that of international institutions such as the European Bank for Reconstruction and Development and International Finance Corporation, which had committed $930 million in Poland by mid-1998.

Foreign small businesses were the first to enter Poland, long before the collapse of state socialism. They could be established in Poland since 1976, but their limited number and size made their impact negligible (Matykowski and Stryjakiewicz 1993). There were a mere 867 foreign companies registered in December 1989. Their number then soared, especially since the Act on Firms with Foreign Capital of June 1991, which abolished legal and financial barriers that existed earlier.

It took much longer for TNCs to decide to invest in Poland. The first major multinational corporation that took the plunge was Swiss-Swedish ABB, which purchased the majority share of the Elbląg-based turbine manufacturer, Zamech, in May 1990, and established joint ventures with Dolmel in Wrocław (generators and electric drives) a few months later. In the next two years, ABB invested in the chief Polish producers of transformers and railway control systems. Another Swedish company, Intercellulosa, set up a joint venture with the paper and pulp factory in Ostrołęka. In 1991, Philips bought the largest producer of electric bulbs in Piła, Thomson purchased a closed factory of TV cathode-ray tubes, while Unilever and Henkel took over detergent plants and PepsiCo the leading confectionery firm. They were joined by the Italian Fiat and Lucchini groups and the American AT&T (now Lucent Technologies) and International Paper in 1992. It is only since 1993 that a larger number of transnational companies have begun manufacturing activities in Poland. The TNCs that arrived first have expanded their operations and continue to be leading investors in the country, e.g. ABB controls 13 factories and Philips 7 plants manufacturing a wide range of products (Tab. 2).

It is worth noting that all the early TNC investments in Poland involved equity purchase from the Polish state or contribution to a joint venture company that took over the assets of an existing factory. The former solution has been preferred by the Polish government. This reflects a specific attitude towards privatisation, where the sale of state firms is treated not only as means of enhancing their economic efficiency (which was an overwhelming concern during the rapid Hungarian privatisation), but also as a significant source of revenue for the national budget. There are no such revenues in the case of joint venture agreements, where the entire foreign capital goes to an individual enterprise. Joint venture agreements were especially widespread in the case of TNC investment in ailing companies, e.g. Thomson and Lucchini, as well as two prominent investors in the automobile industry – Fiat and Daewoo. In addition, all the privatisation contracts include the commitments to fu rther capital input by the foreign investor. Such commitments tend to be relatively higher in the case of joint ventures (e.g above $1 billion by Fiat and Daewoo). Reasons for the concern with the maximisation of state revenues from equity sale, sometimes at the expense of the investor's commitment to the company, included the volatile political situation (weak coalition governments) and the populist use of the "cheap sell-off" argument in public debates on privatisation (see the interesting discussion of state bargaining with TNCs in Iceland by Skulason and Hayter, 1998).

Table 2: Major transnational companies that undertook early investment in Polish factories

Company	Date of first major investment	Product	Original value of investment (million $)	Total value of investment as of June 1998 (million $)	Number of factories as of June 1998
A B B	May 1990	turbines	12	310	13
Intercellulosa	Oct. 1990	paper and pulp	10	108	3
Philips	May 1991	electric bulbs	17	130	7
Unilever	June 1991	detergents	20	140	5
Pepsico	July 1991	confectionary	24	412*	6
Thomson	Sept. 1991	TV tubes	35	185	3
Henkel	Dec. 1991	detergents	10	37	4
Intenational Paper	Aug. 1992	paper and pulp	120	370	2
Fiat	Sept. 1992	cars	180	1248	6
Lucchini	Nov. 1992	steel	35	81	1
A T & T	Oct. 1992	telecommunications equpiment	28	80	1

* including investment in restaurant chains
Source: author's compilation based on PAIZ data and press releases.

Another feature of Polish privatisation has been the deliberate exclusion of certain sectors for political reasons. For example, the first investors in tobacco companies were allowed in late 1995, and some industries still await a full opening to private capital, e.g. oil refineries, power generation and steel plants.

The first greenfield investments by TNCs took place in 1992 and were undertaken by large American manufacturers of consumer products for the Polish market – Coca Cola, Mars, Levi Strauss and Colgate Palmolive. This type of investment permits the legacies of the local firm, especially existing labour relations and work practices, to be circumvented (Massey 1984; Barnes et al. 1990; Hardy 1998). On the other hand, the purchase of a large and viable Polish company may not only be a cheaper and faster solution, but can also yield ready access to the domestic market.

The author's estimates indicate that greenfield projects comprised about 25% of total FDI in Polish manufacturing between 1990 and mid-1998; far more investment took place in existing plants. The greenfield developments had relatively greater significance in the production of consumer goods, especially in the food and drink industry. There is an interesting difference between the behaviour of American and European investors here. The former were more prone to erect new factories, which constituted roughly 40% of the total American investment, in comparison to 22% of the European FDI.

A distinction is commonly drawn between two broad categories of FDIs, based on the fundamental reasons for overseas production: market-oriented and cost-oriented investments (e.g. Dicken 1998). The former constitutes a form of horizontal expansion of the firm across national boundaries undertaken in order to serve the Polish domestic market. The bulk of manufacturing FDI in Poland belongs to this category. Still, there are also cost-driven investments, where the location of production in Poland is part of a broader TNC strategy of exploiting geographical cost differentiation, low labour costs in particular: most of the products are exported, especially to the European Union. This type of investment has been made, for example, by Thomson and Daewoo (TV sets and components), Isuzu and Volkswagen (diesel engines and electric car components), and is typical of numerous German furniture and garment companies in Poland. The dichotomy of market and low cost investments is obviously a simplification. For example, factories acquired or erected in order to serve the Polish market could gradually be expanded and incorporated within a broader multinational corporate network assuming export functions, e.g., Philips's production of TV sets, electric bulbs and batteries (the latter together with Matsushita).

We may note here that the current growth of personal income in many Central and East European countries is a process encouraging domestically-oriented FDIs, whereas it erodes the rationale for cost-oriented investments.

Regional distribution of foreign capital in Polish manufacturing

There is very limited research exploring the uneven distribution of FDI within the countries of Central and Eastern Europe (Murphy 1992; Michalak 1993; Pavlinek 1998). The discussion of this issue here presents only the preliminary results of a broader project in progress.

Figure 2 shows the spatial differentiation of manufacturing FDI by the 16 new provinces (voivodeships) introduced in Poland in January 1999. Almost half of the investment took place in three voivodeships: Mazowieckie (with Warsaw), Wielkopolskie (with Poznań) and Śląskie (with Katowice). The disproportionate concentration of foreign investment in the capital region has been noted in many countries and accounted for, among other things, by the best availability of information (Hamilton 1974). Wielkopolskie is another area with one of the highest general economic growth rates in Poland in the 1990s, benefiting from its relatively well-developed infrastructure, differentiated economic base and high standard of living, as well as its location between Berlin and Warsaw. Both Mazowieckie and Wielkopolskie comprise industrialised areas, but they

Figure 2

Foreign direct investment in Polish manufacturing between 1990 and mid-1998 (in dollars per capita)

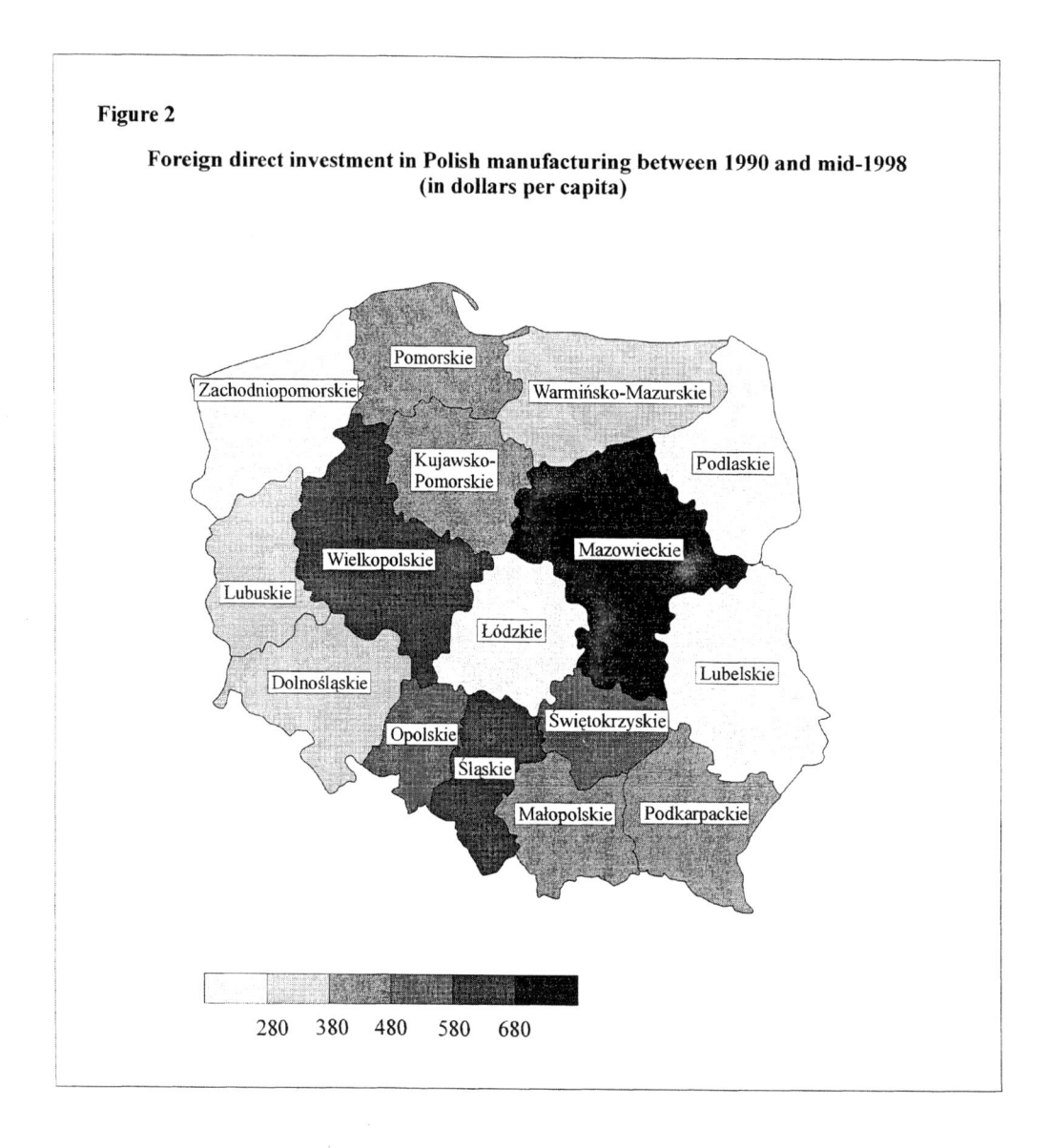

280 380 480 580 680

have never been dominant industrial districts of the country. Their current industrial growth, of which foreign capital is an important part, is a process that may establish them as leading areas of modern manufacturing in Poland.

Śląskie includes the Upper Silesian industrial district, the largest concentration of manufacturing and mining in Poland, which used to be dominated by the coal and steel industries, and the adjacent industrial areas of Bielsko Biała and Częstochowa. In contrast to Mazowieckie and Wielkopolskie, the influx of foreign capital to this old industrial region has had a strong sectoral bias – more than half of it concerns automobile production. There are car factories in Bielsko Biała and Tychy modernized and expanded by Fiat, a greenfield integrated GM auto assembly plant, as well as a growing number of car component manufacturers.

The industrialised southwestern voivodeship of Dolnośląskie as well as the traditional textile district of Łódź are characterised by moderate investment. On the whole, limited foreign capital has been invested in areas along the Polish-German border[3], especially in the northwest, and still less in the least industrialised region, eastern Poland.

An analysis based upon large, internally differentiated voivodeships is hardly sufficient to draw conclusions about the impact of FDI on uneven regional development. A substantial part of the investment is concentrated in major urban agglomerations, e.g. those of Warsaw, Poznań, Wrocław (Dolnośląskie) and Cracow (Małopolskie), there are also other local contrasts. The research carried out so far at different geographical levels makes it possible to advance the following hypotheses for verification in the project:

1. FDI generally contributes to the reproduction of the existing regional differentiation of the country, especially between western and eastern parts of Poland and between urban agglomerations and more peripheral areas. This corresponds with Dziemianowicz's (1997) conclusion that foreign capital buttresses strong regions in particular.

2. Foreign investors tend to avoid old industrial districts, the position of which is gradually deteriorating. This was evident in the case of the Sudeten Mountains in the south-west, the Łódź district, and Upper Silesia in the early 1990s. However, a recent rise in FDI in the latter two areas casts some doubt on this hypothesis.

3. The location of greenfield TNC investments may sow the seeds of new industrial spaces on a local scale, especially on the outskirts of major metropolitan areas and sometimes in more peripheral regions.

The regional contrasts are particularly striking in the case of greenfield investment (Fig. 3). It is here that the heavy concentration of foreign capital in the broad metropolitan region of Warsaw is most evident – Mazowieckie voivodeship has captured roughly 30% of the greenfield manufacturing FDI in Poland. The availability of quality producer services and skilled labour are crucial advantages of Warsaw and, to a lesser degree, other main regional centres as well. In addition, the Warsaw region benefits from its central location in the country. The importance of good accessibility for the location of new factories often attracts them to the vicinity of major cities that enjoy the comparatively best road connections. There are, for example, characteristic clusters of foreign greenfield investments along future motorways west of Poznań (Tarnowo Podgórne) and south of Wrocław (Kobierzyce).

Figure 3 illustrates an extreme east-west disparity in greenfield FDI in Poland – the investment in the eastern voivodeships is from five to fifteen times smaller in per capita terms than in many western regions. However, it is important to note that it is definitely not areas along the Polish-German border that attract large investment. Opinions about the *maquiladora* type of FDI in Central

---

[3] The border zone benefits in the first place from the development of indigenous small businesses in trade and service activities serving German customers (see Stryjakiewicz 1998).

Figure 3

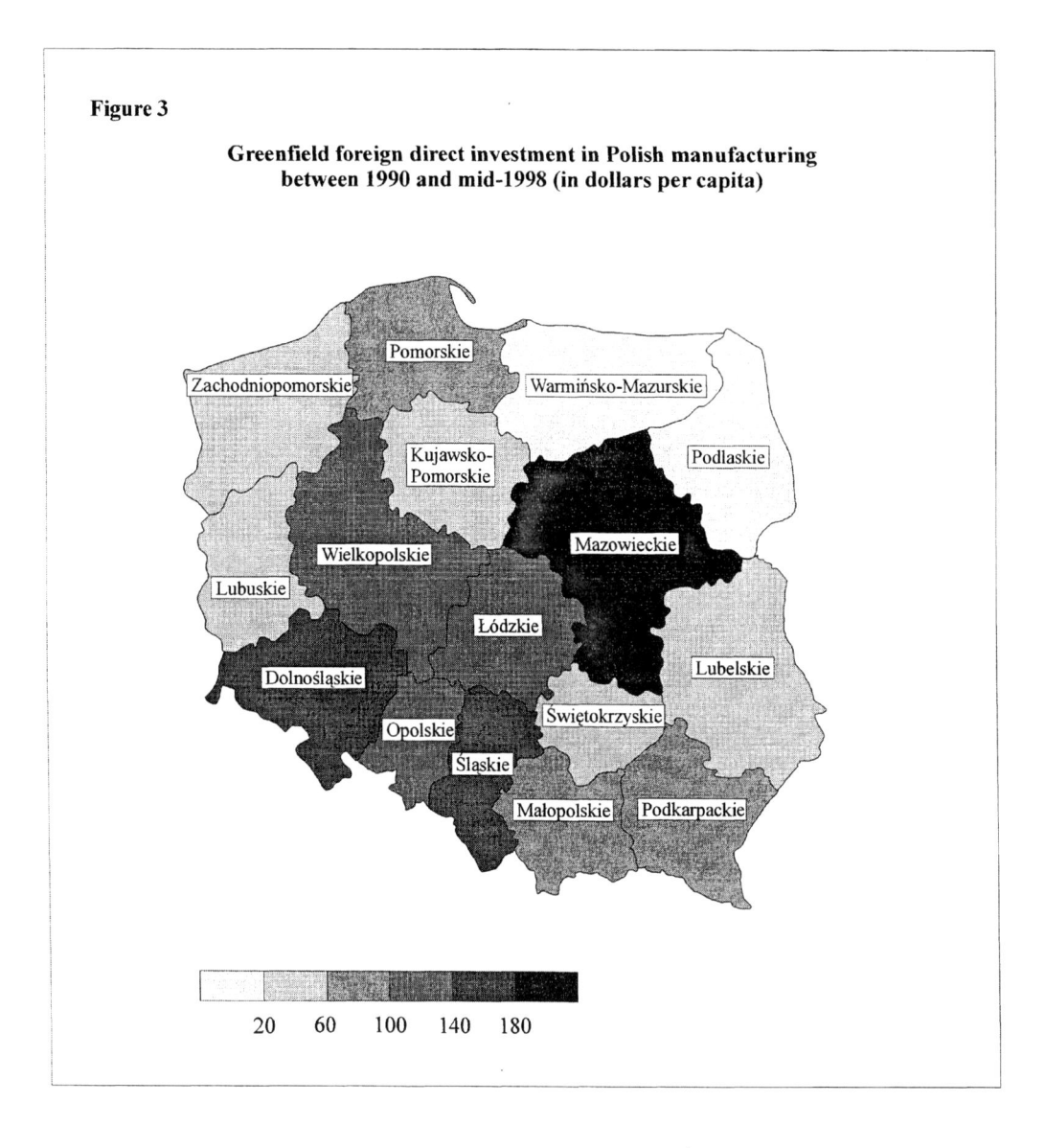

Greenfield foreign direct investment in Polish manufacturing between 1990 and mid-1998 (in dollars per capita)

[Map of Poland showing FDI per capita by voivodeship, with shading scale: 20, 60, 100, 140, 180]

and Eastern Europe scarcely find support in Poland[4]. We can point to at least two geographical factors behind the limited investment in the western borderland. First, the border regions on both the Polish and German sides are relatively less developed and populated than regions situated farther from the boundary. Second, Poland is not a large enough country to provide marked time or cost advantages in the case of border locations. Last but not least, the sectoral structure of FDI confirms that investment that is both export-oriented and labour-cost-sensitive constitutes a small part of FDI in Poland so far[5].

---

[4] The joint venture established by Volkswagen and Siemens in Gorzów, which manufactures electric wiring for cars, is a unique large development that could fit this type of FDI.

[5] Benacek and Zemplinerova (1997) also conclude that cheap labour has not been a prime target for FDI in the Czech Republic.

One may note that the highest proportion of greenfield investment in the total FDI (above 40%) is found in Dolnośląskie and Łódzkie, that is, in regions that include old industrial districts. On the other hand, Wielkopolskie has four times as much investment in existing factories as in new plants.

All things considered, it is likely that manufacturing FDI in Poland may bring about both deeper spatial concentration and greater dispersal of production in various areas and at different geographical levels.

Institutional relationships and greenfield locations of TNCs in Poland

The first serious attempt of the Polish state to influence location choice of large foreign companies was the introduction of special economic zones (SEZ). The first zone was established in the south-eastern town of Mielec in 1995, where layoffs in the military aircraft factory produced mass unemployment. A further 16 SEZs were set up in various localities in the country in 1996 and 1997. Except for the Mazowiecki and Cracow technological parks, the aim of the zones is to stimulate creation of new jobs in areas of actual or potential high unemployment. Ten-year tax exemptions plus 50% tax relief for another ten years are incentives for companies investing at least 350,000 or 2,000,000 ECU (depending on the zone) or employing 40 or 100 people.

By 1998, the SEZ comprising areas within six towns of the Upper Silesian industrial region has attracted more capital than all the other SEZs. The value of investment projects that are in progress in this zone exceeds one billion dollars and they are to bring more than 10,000 jobs, two-thirds by foreign companies, representing predominantly the automotive industry. It is to be emphasised that the vast majority of this investment is taking place in the prosperous towns of Gliwice and Tychy included in the SEZ, and not in towns seriously affected by job reductions in traditional industries (Domański 1998a).

Manufacturers of car components are also chief investors in the SEZs in the south-western copper mining region (Volkswagen in Polkowice) and in the underdeveloped north-east (Daewoo in Ełk). Both regions have high unemployment. The oldest SEZ in Mielec gained about 2,000 new jobs as a result of foreign investment. Other zones have not captured significant FDI in the first years of their functioning.

All things considered, it is too early for a comprehensive evaluation of the regional policy based on SEZs. Still there are already serious doubts about the prospects for attaining the fundamental goal of new jobs in areas of unemployment. There are probably too many places included in SEZs to attract investors to some of them. To make matters worse, there are indications that the bulk of FDI within SEZs may be captured by towns that were granted governmental SEZ incentives, but would have developed smoothly without them as well. Finally, there is also a salient question as to whether Polish SEZs lure greater foreign capital into the country in general, or merely shift its location within Poland.

The Polish experience of greenfield FDI in the 1990s confirms the considerable role played by local institutions in the process of location choice by TNCs. The success of Kobierzyce, Tarnowo Podgórne, Gliwice, and Polkowice, to name just a few, rests not simply on their attractive conditions but to a large extent on the activity of their local governments. This means most of all the ability to provide the investor with fast and reliable information as well as support in dealing with various state and local institutions, for example utility companies, and in some cases a vigorous promotional campaign too (e.g. Kobierzyce).

There are two further conclusions to be drawn from studying towns and rural communities that have attracted several major foreign companies. First of all, it seems that some sort of local success typically preceded the investment of the foreign firm. This could be economic growth based on endogenous factors and/or a remarkable improvement in local infrastructure (e.g. Domański 1998b). Secondly, there was a clear snowball or demonstration effect, where the location of one TNC reduced uncertainty on the part of other potential investors and created a local institutional setting and network of relations conducive to further inward investment[6].

Local embeddedness of FDI in Poland

The issue of local embeddedness of foreign investment in Central and Eastern Europe is a complex one (see e.g. Dicken et al. 1994; Swain and Hardy 1998), while empirical evidence is rather scarce. We can focus here on supplier relationships regarded as the salient indicator of local embeddedness (Dicken et al. 1994). On the one hand, Sadler and Swain (1994) find that the new automotive investments in Hungary generated limited regional supply chains. Grabher (1994) describes the early manufacturing investment in east Germany and Hardy (1998) FDIs in the Wrocław region as "cathedrals in the desert", that is, enclaves with few linkages backwards or forwards. On the other hand, Pavlinek and Smith (1998) provide examples of both foreign firms isolated from their local environments and investments relatively integrated into regional economies in the Czech Republic, the latter supported by Uhlir (1998) as well.

One can easily find contrasting cases in Polish manufacturing too, depending on sector, type of production (e.g. disembedded assembly activities) and company strategy. It is particularly interesting to note that automobile production by TNCs in Poland has to a significant degree relied on local component supply chains from the beginning. The apparent contrast with Hungary may result from a different mode of entry (acquisition of the local firm vis-a-vis greenfield location) as well as the longer tradition of passenger car manufacturing in Poland. Fiat Auto Poland retained and developed a healthy network of 267 domestic suppliers, which contributed 73% of parts bought by the company in 1996[7]. Firms from the Katowice voivodeship alone (before the administrative

---

[6] There are also joint initiatives of neighbouring communities in this field, for example a special centre was established in co-operation with a regional development agency in Bielsko Biała in order to provide companies with information on investment opportunities and legal procedures.

[7] On the other hand, Daewoo began its activity in newly acquired Polish establishments in 1995 with the rudimentary assembly of cars, which had originally been assembled in Korea, shipped to a Slovenian port and dismantled there in order to circumvent the Polish tariffs on complete vehicles! The Korean corporation signed an agreement to increase the share of Polish components in its passenger cars to 40% by the end of 2000, it also continues production of old Polish makes, which are predominantly based on domestic parts.

reform) provided one-third of Fiat's domestic supply. The location decision of General Motors to build a new factory in Gliwice in 1996 triggered a sort of rush for automobile investment in Poland, and in Upper Silesia in particular. By late 1998 there were at least seventy companies manufacturing car components with foreign capital above $1 million, and twenty-seven greenfield plants constructed by foreign firms in Poland (including investments in progress), only three of which were erected before 1996. Similar spread effects took place earlier in the Czech Republic following Volkswagen's acquisition of Skoda (Pavlinek 1998).

There is a question as to what lies behind the marked spatial concentration of new producers of car components in the vicinity of Fiat and GM plants, in a region that by and large lacked a tradition in this sort of production, and furthermore has some of the highest wages and strongest unions in Poland. Can this be accounted for by manufacturers' preference for short distances in just-in-time deliveries in a country plagued by poor roads? To what extent is this affected by the benefits of the SEZ?

Pavlinek (1998) suggests that export-oriented FDIs attracted by cheap labour are less likely to have significant linkages with local firms and contribute to durable regional economies in the Czech Republic. There is some contrary evidence in Poland, e.g. the production of electrical equipment by Alstom, Philips, or Legrand. This question deserves broader empirical verification[8].

Predominantly local linkages are typical of sectors relying on local raw materials, for example manufacturers of furniture, paper, glass, construction materials and various food products, but they rarely entail long supply chains. Tobacco giants that took over Polish cigarette factories (Philip Morris, Seita, Reemtsma) have launched training programmes for tobacco farmers and provide special funding to support their modernisation efforts, all of which sustain the use of Polish tobacco. These activities exceed foreign manufacturers' commitments in privatisation contracts and may be motivated not only by immediate commercial concerns, but also by the pursuit of a positive public image for the company.

Dicken et al. (1994) raise a question about the extent to which social provisions by some TNCs for the community are underlain by their narrow self-interest, or rather reflect some sort of community spirit. There are ventures such as the construction of sports facilities and sponsorship of cultural activities and schools, for example those carried out by Coca Cola in Niepołomice near Cracow or Pepsico in Pniewy south of Warsaw, which are hardly irrelevant from the point of view of local embeddedness. The sketchy evidence suggests that company provisions of this sort can often be found in small communities, where subsidiaries or branch plants of powerful TNCs are the major employer and tax-payer[9].

---

[8] This also contrasts with Welfens's (1994) opinion that inward-oriented FDI in Latin America had limited success whereas export-oriented FDI in many Asian countries contributed to their general economic performance.

[9] On the whole, there is an almost universal agreement among the representatives of local authorities that foreign companies bring more benefits than costs to local communities (89% positive opinions and 2% negative ones), as a study of 102 Polish communities has shown (Błuszkowski and Garlicki 1996).

Finally, one may note that local content requirements are part of special economic zone regulations. However, the condition of a 30-percent-share of materials manufactured within the particular zone itself in the product value is practically impossible to fulfil. Consequently, investors are exempt from this stipulation as a rule, unless the ministry supervising the zones wants to reject them, which happened twice under the pressure of Polish manufacturers opposing a new competitor (a German steel products maker in Sosnowiec and an Italian producer of home appliances in Łódź).

The discussion on local suppliers often ignores non-material linkages. The study carried out by the author among 71 foreign-owned companies in the Cracow region in 1996 shows that local (in a narrow territorial sense) multiplier effects of their development may often be generated more through service linkages than suppliers of parts and components (Domański 1996). From the point of view of a community or a small region, there are usually limited prospects of orders being placed with local manufacturing establishments, so it is really vital how far the foreign subsidiary or branch plant uses local repair, construction, and transportation as well as software, financial and consulting services, etc., or rather contracts them out to Warsaw or abroad.

Other selected economic and social effects of FDI

The vast majority of FDIs bring direct positive consequences for the acquired company itself. They include technological upgrading, new managerial skills, marketing know-how and sometimes access to new markets (Young *et al.* 1996; Bąk and Kulawczuk 1996; Jarosz 1996; Benacek and Zemplinerova 1997; Dziemianowicz 1997; Hardy 1998). Companies with large foreign capital commonly experience sales growth, introduce new products and improve their quality (Domański 1998c). The author's analysis of TNCs that arrived in Poland a few years ago reveals that their activity very rarely ends with a single initial investment. It is rather a process of gradually increasing outlays on the modernisation and expansion of production capacity, construction of new plants or the take-over of further Polish companies. The PAIZ survey of 1997 shows that 80% of profits are reinvested in Poland at the moment. So far, there have been no case of a major plant closure in Poland by TNC in the process of global reorganisation of production, although small branch plants in multi-plant companies have been liquidated (mostly in food processing).

The impact on labour markets is often considered a vital yardstick in the assessment of FDI. Most studies of large companies in Poland report extensive training of the staff following foreign investment in the firm, accompanied by a wage rise vis-a-vis local enterprises (Surdej 1996; Jarosz 1996). There is limited evidence in Poland for the large-scale development of FDI based on "the deskilling and concomitant wage-reducing effects of the further fragmentation of the production process", which was described by Grabher (1997, p. 126) in the former East Germany. Pavlinek (1998) finds low-skilled, young female labour performing assembly-type operations for German companies particularly in small firms along the Czech-German border. We lack similar investigation of small FDIs in Poland. Cheap labour force as a requisite of export-oriented production is characteristic of Polish garment manufacturing. There is undoubtedly scope for a wider analysis of changes in labour markets in the post-socialist era in terms of segmentation theories. A specific, yet unexplained, problem are differences in hiring locals in senior management positions, e.g. Italian companies seem to be specially inclined to "import" the bulk of managerial staff to their Polish subsidiaries.

New jobs created by foreign capital result from greenfield developments or the vast expansion of production capacity. Technological modernisation of factories without a major increase in production inevitably leads to reductions in employment. Two- or three-year employment guarantees, which are a standard element of privatisation contracts in Poland, can hardly prevent this. They function as a buffer delaying layoffs or providing redundant workers with financial compensation – a generous gratuity offered to people who resign from their jobs is a common practice.

Specific advantages of being an employee of a privatised firm in contemporary Poland include free shares (15% at the moment). The foreign investor normally buys the shares allocated to the employees by the state, which gives them extra revenues sometimes equivalent to several years' pay. There is only anecdotal evidence of a profound impact of the godsend of five or ten million dollars on consumer spending in the community, especially in small or medium-sized towns.

TNCs taking over Polish companies also acquire a specific market share, although they do not gain a monopoly position, which has been reported in certain sectors of Czech manufacturing, e.g. passenger cars, tyre, tobacco and chocolate production (Pavlinek 1998). Some foreign investments have ended monopolies that were a legacy of socialist central planning. Still, oligopolistic domination of the Polish market by a couple of TNCs is characteristic of many industries.

Foreign companies accounted for 38% of Polish exports in 1996. Nonetheless, they generate even more imports and are regarded one of chief sources of the current negative Polish trade balance. This reflects both flows of components and materials to foreign owned factories and imports of machines and equipment contributing to the technological modernisation of Polish manufacturing (Jarosz 1996).

Conclusions

The geographical picture of foreign direct investment in Poland, as in all of Central and Eastern Europe, is a partial one and, indeed, selective in the evidence available. Hence it would be wrong to slip into far-reaching conclusions based on our preconceptions. On the one hand, there are great expectations with respect to the impact of foreign capital on the transforming of post-socialist economies. On the other, there are notions of truncated industrialisation, *maquiladora* type investment, and the reproduction of regional development patterns from the past. Comprehensive empirical studies exploring detailed spatial distribution of foreign capital and employment as well as local linkages of FDIs are needed in order to reach broader generalisations here.

It is necessary to reject misconceptions about both footloose transnational corporations (see Allen 1995) and passive actors in deregulated post-socialist economies. It is an intriguing task to unravel a complex web of bargaining relationships between TNCs and various institutions in host countries at the national, regional and local level. Actual strategies and practices are underlain by, and exert their influence on, power relations based upon control over various economic, political and cultural assets[10]. The historically-rooted place-specific institutional structures and their "culture" make themselves felt in all aspects of foreign firm activities. The resultant structures and processes are never superimposed by the overseas newcomer, but rather planted into the pre-existing ones. For example, supply networks of automobile giants such as Fiat and Daewoo reproduce many of the linkages of their state-owned predecessors, transforming them and forging new ones incorporating new local partners while attracting others from abroad.

There seems to be reliable support for the hypotheses about the disproportionate spatial concentration of FDI in the Warsaw metropolitan area and in major Polish urban agglomerations, low investment in eastern Poland, and the lack of considerable foreign manufacturing capital in Polish-German borderland. FDI appears to facilitate some shift of manufacturing from major cities to small town and rural communities. The latter process raises a question about the degree to which greenfield locations outside existing industrial centres result from labour control strategy, that is the wish on the part of the foreign-owned enterprise to hire new workforce and create new labour agreements at a new site (see Hayter 1997; Swain 1998). Generally, surprisingly little is known about attempts to introduce new work practices by overseas employers in Poland.

One can point to a number of other interesting problems related to FDI in Poland, which deserve wider discussion impossible in a short paper. These include, for example, foreign capital liability for environmental clean up, impact on R&D activity, overall financial costs and benefits including tariff concessions, profit reinvestment, taxes and transfer pricing. Last but not least, there is a practical issue of monitoring and assessing social and economic effects of the regional policy implemented by means of special economic zones over next couple of years.

References

Allen J 1995 Crossing borders: footloose multinationals? (in:) J Allen and C Hamnett (eds.) *A shrinking world?* Oxford: Oxford University Press 55-102

Barnes T, Hayter R and Crass E 1990 MacMillan Bloedel: corporate restructuring and employment change (in:) M De Smidt and E Wever (eds.) *The corporate firm in a changing world economy: case studies in the geography of enterprise.* London: Routledge 145-165

Benacek V and Zemplinerova A 1997 Foreign direct investment in the Czech manufacturing sector. *Prague Economic Papers* 6 141-155

Bąk M and Kulawczuk P (eds.) 1996 *Wpływ inwestycji zagranicznych na gospodarkę Polski.* Warsaw: Instytut Badań nad Demokracją i Przedsiębiorstwem Prywatnym

Błuszkowski J and Garlicki J 1995 *Inwestorzy zagraniczni w Polsce. Raport z badań opinii inwestorów zagranicznych o społecznych i ekonomicznych warunkach działalności w Polsce.* Warsaw: Indicator

---

[10] See Hayter (1997) for a broad discussion of TNC's bargaining with governments, communities and labour.

Błuszkowski J and Garlicki J 1996 *Companies with foreign participation in their local environment.* Warsaw: Friedrich Ebert Foundation

Buckwalter D W 1995 Spatial inequality, foreign investment, and economic transition in Bulgaria. *Professional Geographer* 43 3 288-298

Dicken P 1998 *Global shift: the internationalization of economic activity.* 3rd ed.

Dicken P, Forsgren M and Malmberg A 1994 The local embeddedness of transnational corporations (in:) A Amin and N Thrift (eds.) *Globalization, institutions, and regional development in Europe.* Oxford: Oxford University Press 23-45

Dobosiewicz Z 1992 *Foreign investment in Eastern Europe.* London: Routledge

Domański B 1996 Wpływ inwestycji zagranicznych na gospodarkę województwa (in:) *Raport o stanie inwestycji zagranicznych w województwie krakowskim.* Cracow: VRG Strategy 55-68

Domański B 1998a *Upper Silesia in the postsocialist economy: inevitable decline or prospects for success?* Paper presented at the Seminar on Processes and Problems of Spatial Economic Restructuring in Poland, School of Slavonic and East European Studies, University of London

Domański B 1998b Gliwice/Gleiwitz, Oberschlesien: Erfolgssuche in einer Problemregion. *Geographische Rundschau* 50 35-41

Domański B 1998c *Foreign investments in the Cracow Province.* Cracow: Cornelius

Dunning J 1993 The prospects for foreign direct investment in eastern Europe (in:) P Artisen, M Rojec and M Svetlicic (eds.) *Foreign investment in Central and Eastern Europe.* London: Macmillan 16-33

Dziemianowicz W 1997 *Kapitał zagraniczny a rozwój regionalny i lokalny w Polsce.* Warsaw: European Institute for Regional and Local Development

Grabher G 1994 The disembedded regional economy: the transformation of east German industrial complexes into western enclaves (in:) A Amin and N Thrift (eds.) *Globalization, institutions, and regional development in Europe.* Oxford: Oxford University Press 177-195

Grabher G 1997 Adaptation at the cost of adaptability? Restructuring the eastern German regional economy (in:) G Grabher and D Stark (eds.) *Restructuring networks in post-socialism: legacies, linkages and localities.* Oxford: Oxford University Press

Hamilton F E I (ed.) 1974 *Spatial perspectives on industrial organisation and decision making.* London: Wiley

Hardy J 1998 Cathedrals in the desert? Transnationals, corporate strategy and locality in Wrocław. *Regional Studies* 32 639-652

Hayter R 1997 *The dynamics of industrial location: the factory, the firm and the production system.* Chichester: Wiley

Jarosz M (ed.) 1996 *Kapitał zagraniczny w prywatyzacji.* Warsaw: Institute for Political Studies, Polish Academy of Science

Matykowski R and Stryjakiewicz T 1993 Foreign enterprises in an „economy in transition": the example of Poland (in:) E W Schamp, G J R Linge and Ch Rogerson (eds.) *Finance, institutions and industrial change: spatial perspectives.* Berlin: de Gruyter 162-182

Massey D 1984 *Spatial divisions of labour: social structures and the geography of production.* London: Macmillan

Meyer S and Qu T 1995 Place-specific determinants of FDI: the geographical perspective (in:) M B Green and R B McNaughton (eds.) *The location of foreign direct investment.* Aldershot: Avebury 1-13

Michalak W Z 1993 Foreign direct investment and joint ventures in East-Central Europe: a geographical perspective. *Environment and Planning A* 25 1573-1591

Murphy A B 1992 Western investment in East-Central Europe: emerging patterns and implications for state stability. *Professional Geographer* 44 249-259

Pavlinek P 1998 Foreign direct investment in the Czech Republic. *Professional Geographer* 50 71-85

Pavlinek P and Smith A 1998 Internationalization and embeddedness in East-Central European transition: the contrasting geographies of inward investment in the Czech and Slovak Republics. *Regional Studies* 32 619-638

Sadler D and Swain A 1994 State and market in eastern Europe: regional development and workplace implications of direct foreign investment in the automobile industry in Hungary. *Transactions, Institute of British Geographers* 19 387-403

Skulason J B and Hayter R 1998 Industrial location as a bargain: Iceland and the aluminium multinationals. 1962-1994 *Geografiska Annaler* 80 B 29-48

Smith A and Ferencikova S 1998 Inward investment, regional transformations and uneven development in East-Central Europe: enterprise case studies from Slovakia. *European Urban and Regional Studies* 5 155-173

Stryjakiewicz T 1998 The changing role of border zones in the transforming economies of East-Central Europe: the case of Poland. *GeoJournal* 44 203-213

Surdej A 1996 Wpływ inwestycji zagranicznych na rynek pracy w województwie (in:) *Raport o stanie inwestycji zagranicznych w województwie krakowskim* Cracow: VRG Strategy 32-54

Swain A 1998 Governing the workplace: the workplace and regional development implications of automotive foreign direct investment in Hungary. *Regional Studies* 32 653-671

Swain A and Hardy J 1998 Globalization, institutions, foreign investment and the reintegration of East and Central Europe and the former Soviet Union with the world economy. *Regional Studies* 32 587-590

Uhlir D 1998 Internationalization, and institutional and regional change: restructuring post-communist networks in the region of Lanskroun, Czech Republic. *Regional Studies* 32 673-685

Young S, Hood N and Peters E 1996 Multinational enterprises and regional economic development. *Regional Studies* 28 657-677

Welfens P J J 1994 Foreign direct investment and privatisation (in:) A Schipke and A M Taylor (eds.) *The economics of transformation: theory and practice in the new market economies.* Berlin-Heidelberg: Springer 129-169.

Kaliningrad and the Changing Geopolitics of the Baltic (*)

William STANLEY (Columbia, SC) and Elke KNAPPE (Leipzig)

Abstract

The paper examines the situation of the Russian exclave of Kaliningrad, originating from the end of World War 2. Since then, many things have changed. The once politically powerful emigrant East Prussians no longer count for much in German domestic politics. More startling is the disappearance of the Soviet Union. Its wartime acquired most western-protruding window, the northern portion of former East Prussia know today as Kaliningrad, once was the most militarized region in the USSR. Today, Kaliningrad lacks even a contiguous border with the remainder of Russia. It is having to adjust to a new Europe and to a Baltic Region undergoing radical transformation. Kaliningrad's once significant ocean fishing fleet and manufacturing sector whose production was primarily for the military no longer count for much in the new dispensation. The region is finding it difficult to adjust to new markets and new ideas. That former Politburo member and later Head of State, Mikhail Kalinin still has his name enshrined on a piece of Russian geography could be reflective of the decision-making processes in both Kaliningrad and Moscow. – The paper traces some of the socio-economic and political issues impacting the region.

Kaliningrad in der geänderten geopolitischen Situation des Baltikums

Kurzfassung

Der Beitrag untersucht die Situation der russischen Exklave Kaliningrad, die ein Produkt des zweiten Weltkriegs ist. Seit damals hat sich vieles verändert. Die einst politisch einflußreichen Emigranten aus Ostpreußen haben heute in der deutschen Innenpolitik kaum mehr ein Gewicht. Ein weit überraschenderes Faktum ist das Verschwinden der Sowjetunion. Ihr im Krieg erworbener am weitesten nach Westen vorspringender Vorposten, der nördliche Teil des ehemaligen Ostpreußen, jetzt meist als Kaliningrad bezeichnet, war das stärkst militarisierte Gebiet der UdSSR. Dieses Gebiet besitzt heute keine Landverbindung mit dem übrigen Rußland. Es muß sich an ein neues Europa und an eine Region Baltikum anpassen, die in radikaler Umgestaltung begriffen ist. Kaliningrads einst bedeutende Hochseefischereiflotte und sein Produktionssektor, der in erster Linie für das Militär produziert hatte, zählen in der neuen Konstellation kaum mehr. Das Gebiet hat es schwer, sich an neue Märkte und neue Ideen anzupassen. Daß ein ehemaliges Politbüromitglied, das spätere Staatsoberhaupt Michail Kalinin, bis heute im Namen eines Stücks russischen Territoriums verewigt ist, kann man als symptomatisch für die Entscheidungsprozesse sowohl in Kaliningrad als auch in Moskau ansehen. – Die Arbeit behandelt einige der sozioökonomischen und politischen Themen, die das Gebiet betreffen.

(*) Cf. author's note at the end of the paper.

The post-Cold War vernacular has seen the revival of a word once shunned in some circles because of its perceived association with Third Reich expansionism. Geopolitics, the geography of politics, is increasingly employed to explain political change in areas rife with real or latent instability (Swerew 1996). The margins of the former Soviet Empire offer numerous examples of instability, situations where political change is both conditioned by and responsible for geographical realignments. Russia has the world's longest border (60,933 km) and shares borders with more countries (16) than any other nation (Grandberg 1999: 75). Following the break-up of the Soviet Union in 1991, new border regions came into being. Eight former Soviet republics became independent states at the same time that Russia lost direct borders with six East European and Near Eastern states.

Geopolitical Instability?

An excellent model of latent instability is the Russian oblast of Kaliningrad, the northern portion of former German East Prussia. In this case the instability is in part the result of the physical separation of Kaliningrad from mother Russia now that Lithuania has gained its independence. It also is due to the fracturing of economic interconnections (Economist 1996: 36; Rupert 1997: 1) developed when the larger area was part of the Soviet Union and in no small measure to the negative implications of economic and social uneasiness throughout Russia. More disturbing despite the scope and intensity of discussions related to NATO expansion eastward (Albright 1997: 4,7) and the risks of antagonizing Russia is the fact that she will share a common boundary with an NATO state once Poland is part of the alliance. It is as if strategic planning in certain circles blithely ignores the organic relationship between Kaliningrad and Russia. Furthermore, the three Baltic states and Poland seem destined for eventual admission into the European Community. When that occurs, there will be increased pressure for Kaliningrad to enter into some manner of association with her neighbors (Korneyevets 1996: 26) if only to safeguard an already fragile economy. How Moscow will choose to respond to what still is a hypothetical situation should have considerable impact upon the future tranquility of the Baltic region (Prevelakis 1995: 2). The issue could well evolve into a contest between economic pragmatists and hard line nationalists.

Poland is Kaliningrad's immediate neighbor to the South and, officially, appears to be unconcerned for her remaining boundary with Russia. Churchill stated in 1943 that Poland should receive all of German East Prussia as war compensation and Stalin, never one to refuse gifts, raised the issue of *Königsberg* and *Memel* at Yalta. He stated that the USSR should be given both port cities and adjacent territories. Roosevelt's key foreign affairs advisor went so far as to state that „a new western frontier for the Soviet Union will solve rather than create political and economic conflicts" (Welles 1946: 119). The transfer of these lands was made official at the Potsdam Conference. Poland was assigned the southern portion of East Prussia in addition to Germany's Silesia and Pommerania. Stalin presumably placated his western allies, but not necessarily the Poles, by pushing Poland's prewar boundary to the West and North at the cost of potential long term enmity with Germany over the loss of its eastern territories. This is how it seemed at the time (Davies 1981: Chapter 21). Later events, in particular Germany's seminal role within the expanding European Community and its acceptance of the new Polish boundary have defused much of animosity caused by the loss of its eastern territories. Nevertheless, the loss of East Prussia remains a troubling issue for many Germans. Davies, the chronicler of Polish History is obliged to comment on Poland's end-of-war territorial acquisitions by noting that:

„Of all Poland's neighbours, however, the Germans have the most reason to query the official version of polish History as propagated in Warsaw. Whatever they may feel about the irrevocable loss of their eastern provinces – and they seem to feel a mixture of guilt, resentment, and indifference – they cannot consign a substantial slice of their heritage to oblivion" (Davies 1981: 525).

Union until 1956 when, for the first time, The 200 km Kaliningrad-Polish frontier was permanently sealed by the Soviet Communist Party delegations from Poland were allowed to visit in the North. For Poles who replaced the German population in what had been southern East Prussia, the Soviet portion of former East Prussia was unknown territory. Cross-border movement did not exist (Sakson 1994: 180). As if to reinforce their claim, the Soviets constructed an imposing demarcation line of manned watch towers, plowed strips of land and considerable fencing. For nearly 45 years, Kaliningrad was sealed from the one country with which it shared an international boundary. In 1990-91, however, two international border crossings (Figure 1) were opened at Bagrationowsk (ex-Prussian *Eylau*) and Mamonowo (ex-*Heiligenbeil*). There is a third crossing at Goldap but only for local residents.

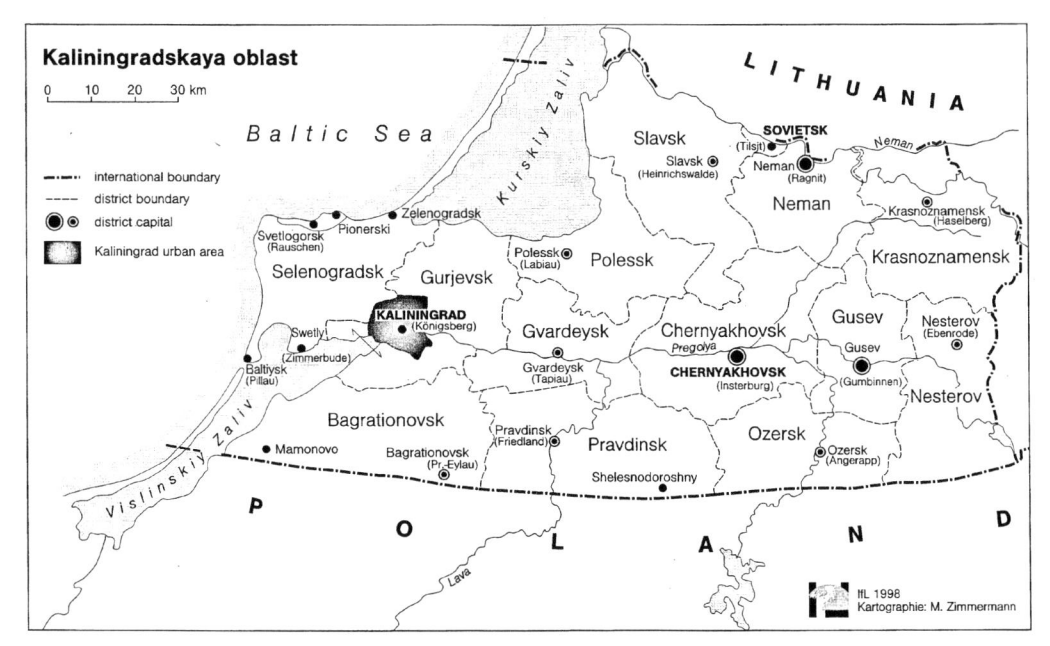

Figure 1: Map of Kaliningrad oblast

Taken near the end of World War 2 at no small cost to the Red Army and with terrible consequences for its resident German population (Dönhoff 1971; Werth 1964), this small territory until recently constituted the westernmost extension of the Soviet Union and presently serves the same role for Russia. Whereas added access to the Baltic clearly was a factor in Stalin's decision to acquire the region and the strategic, ice free ports of Baltysk (ex-*Pillau*) and Klaipeda (now Lithuania, ex-*Memel*), shrinking of Germany through removal of its easternmost territory also was an important consideration. This was no ordinary territory (Thadden 1987). *Königsberg*, capital of East Prussia, was the ultimate symbol of whatever constituted Prussian identity including militarism, for it was in this city's cathedral that the Prussian Kings were crowned. The fact that East Prussia had been German for 691 years did not make any difference (Guttzeit). The victorious USSR would define and enforce the changed political parameters for most of postwar eastern Europe. Furthermore, because he was not a party to the Atlantic Charter, Stalin was under no obligation to observe the 'no territorial acquisitions' statement (the first clause) of this lofty document formulated in 1941 by Churchill and Roosevelt. Being a signatory hardly constrained one's actions (Conquest 1991: 250-51). Churchill later in the war openly advocated territorial change at the expense of Germany.

Prior to 1990, a variety of factors made Kaliningrad into one of the most restricted areas in the Soviet Union. These ranged from Moscow's concern for real or imagined threats on the part of the United States, to secrecy about weapons deployed in the submarine flotilla based at Baltysk and at the numerous military installations. There also was concern for the several electronics manufacturing plants in Kaliningrad City which were organically connected to and sole suppliers of weapons used by the Soviet military. East bloc citizens were routinely denied access and internal movement controls within the USSR restricted its own citizenry. The more permissive environment since 1991 has not altogether removed restraints on travel. The present issue is one of money; travel by bus or rail is not free. Clearly, however, the secrecy formerly associated with Kaliningrad no longer exists. For example, with a modest cash payment the visitor from the West can photograph freely the rusting remnants of this once proud Baltic Fleet.

Prior to 1991, there were on average 300,000 soldiers based in this small region including air and naval units. This likely has fallen below 200,000 in spite of repositioning in Kaliningrad some of the units formerly stationed in East Germany. At one time, every third resident of Kaliningrad was a member of the Soviet military! Nevertheless, troop concentrations in this relatively small territory remain disproportionately high and represent a situation whose domestic and international implications warrant understanding. The visitor seldom escapes some visual reminder of this military presence. Also troubling is the environmental degradation identified at sites of now partially abandoned military installations.

Origins and phenomena of the Kaliningrad problem

The historical development of the region under German rule is well documented in Mortensen (ed., 1968). The economic geographical situation before World War 2 has been portrayed by Scheu (1936). The events in the final phase of the war can be summarized as follows. Ravaged by a seemingly unstoppable and revengeful Red Army starting in late 1944, East Prussians learned first hand some of the horrors of a conflict that knew few bounds. Unprepared for possible evacuation, many were overrun by the advancing Red Army. Once in motion, the evacuation of East Prussia assumed gigantic proportions and often tragic consequences, for the participants and for the German State. For a detailed account of the 'great tragedy 1944–46' see Applebaum (1995: 29), Bode (1995), Conquest (1991), Dobson (1979), Dönhoff (1971), Keiser (1978), and Solzhenitsyn (1974).

Devoid of the last remnants of its ever-dwindling German population whose forced evacuation after the end of hostilities in 1945–47 was more orderly if no less harsh than the chaotic wartime departures, Moscow proceeded to bring in scores of peasants and artisans to occupy its newly acquired territory (Vesilind 1997: 112). Drawn largely from areas in the Soviet Union that had suffered severe destruction in the war, these new settlers for the most part were conscripted for the transfer to former East Prussia. Set adrift by the authorities, sometimes with little more than a cow and their personal effects, in a chaotic end-of-war Soviet Union and conquered East Prussia faced with massive reconstruction, the new arrivals were largely dependent upon their own resources until the first crops matured. They surely realized that they were occupying a cultural-economic landscape quite different from the ones they knew in the Soviet Union. It also is conceivable that a few of the new arrivals might have questioned the length of their stay in this wartime acquisition with its non-Slavic, non-Soviet connotations.

Whereas this figurative looking over of one's shoulders may have affected some of the first generation of immigrants, those born in Kaliningrad (and there have been several generations) unquestionably consider themselves to be Russian. They know no other landscape as well as they do this one. Unlike other Russian residual and minority populations in the former republics of the Soviet Union, the Russians in Kaliningrad constitute nearly all of the population.

Many among the first Russian settlers, likely assisted by soldiers, vandalized much of the then existing German cultural landscape. Graves were violated on a scale that, in hindsight, can only be viewed as having been systematic and massive. This was done presumably in search of gold (teeth and rings) to be traded for food and other necessities on the black market. The visitor to Kaliningrad City or to any of the other towns and villages is fortunate to find even one German headstone, much less a German cemetery. There is, however, one notable exception. Honored by Russians as 'one of their own', to the dismay of some Germans, the grave of the great Prussian philosopher Immanuel Kant still has a place of honor next to one of the restored walls of what was once *Königsberg*'s Cathedral. One of the more striking aspects of contemporary change in Kaliningrad is an emerging interest on the part of Kaliningrad youth in better understanding the remaining German facets of this landscape. It is their homeland and they seek now to appreciate what many of their elders sought to destroy.

'Kantograd' frequently arises as a replacement name for Kaliningrad. A competitor is 'amber' (Bernstein) after the well known and still exploited deposits at Jantarnyi (ex-*Palmniken*). Stalin's name is gone from Stalingrad, Lenin's is gone from Leningrad and yet, one of the founding members (Kalinin) of the Bolshevik

Revolution is still commemorated in a city's name. It is almost as if the changing of a name might subject the region to still other, yet unknown and most likely unwanted forms of stress (Harris 1997: 60). It is better to do nothing.

Had it not been for reconstruction money provided by German churches, the previously roofless walls of *Königsberg*'s Cathedral and a few other churches might already have collapsed. Only 70 of the region's 224 churches were destroyed in wartime action. Twenty-six were demolished in the 1950s and 29 suffered the same fate in the 1960s, including 11 in Kaliningrad City. The process of cultural obliteration continued with the destruction of another 14 churches in the 1970s, followed by ten more during the 1980s (Bachtin 1994: 116-33). In a few cases, former churches were taken over for Russian Orthodox services but this was only possible after the restoration of freedom of worship. For the most part, the remaining shells stand empty and deteriorating, their sturdy red brick construction deterring all but concerted efforts to demolish. Only ruins remain to mark the castles built by the Teutonic Knights and the hundreds of well built and spacious warehouses constructed during the German period. The great majority were purposely destroyed after the war by Soviets more intent upon eradicating evidence of a German cultural landscape than in preserving structures for use by the arriving Soviet immigrants.

Unintended Complications

Systematic eradication of the former cultural landscape has caused unexpected problems. For example, the first wave of German tourists after 1991 was optimistically viewed by some Kaliningrad leaders as the harbinger of an economic renaissance based on tourism from Germany. In time, Germany and the European Community provided grants for infra structural improvements including the upgrading of transport facilities (Harris 1997: 60). Several Russian-German joint ventures were formed to build hotels, offer tours and generally cater to this new phenomenon comprised in the main of elderly nostalgic, former East Prussians and younger adults who, as children, fled with their families in 1944–45 or who were evicted after the war (Matthies 1991: 10). Quite naturally, the first German visitors were especially interested in visiting family graves. What they found, literally, were empty holes in the ground and fragments of former headstones. As if that was not sufficient shock, these same visitors often were unable to locate the villages which characterized the former landscape and served as their emotional connection to it.

Some 800 German villages were totally dismantled or destroyed by the Soviets. War time action would have been responsible for some of the destruction. In some instances, however, building stone salvaged from the purposeful dismantling of homes and shops was transported by rail to the Soviet Union to help in the rebuilding of towns or cities that had suffered wartime destruction (suggesting that, in the immediate postwar period, Soviet plans regarding this portion of former German East Prussia may not have been fully formulated). Many German settlements were destroyed because they no longer were necessary to a rural landscape soon to undergo massive collectivization.

Agriculture in Difficulty

East Prussia historically was one of Germany's premier agricultural regions, characterized in the main by grain cultivation and dairy cattle (Knappe 1993b). Knappe's informative map detailing land use near Znamensk (ex-*Wehlau*) before the war and in 1992 illustrates the enormity of crop land conversion to pasturage. Even with the agricultural reforms of 1991, less than four percent of cultivated land had been privatized two years later. This province also had the distinction of housing the greatest number of horses of any of the country's administrative units and for a locally bred draft horse known as *Trakehn*. Indeed, for some of the fleeing German farmers in 1944-45, there was considerable anguish in having to leave behind their beloved horses. The region's glacially formed moraine landscape is also noteworthy for its multitude of lakes and for soils requiring drainage. Unfortunately, few of the drainage systems built in the German time have been maintained by the new occupants. Furthermore, and contrary to perceptions that former East Prussia was a Junker landscape of great estates, dependent in the main upon a semi-feudal farm labor system, the reality is something else. Freehold farms and families, served by a well-connected network of small villages and towns, were increasingly the norm. In a recent „before and after" study of the Polessk area (ex-*Labiau* district) northeast of Kaliningrad City, some 5,000 family operated farms in the German time had been replaced by nine massive state farms (Knappe 1993a: 10). Not surprisingly, these nine factory farms collectively house fewer workers and their families than were provided for earlier by 5,000 farms. This may help to explain the redundancy of many of the former German agricultural villages once Soviet planners set forth to sovietize their new acquisition.

Agricultural output from the large collectives was seldom measured against the costs for inputs and hardly ever in relation to the declining productivity of the land. Crop rotations designed during the German time for nurturing productivity of soils were abandoned for mono-agriculture, primarily grain or milk production. This resulted in lower average yields per acre and declining milk output per cow (Kornejewez and Knappe 1996). Incredibly, and suggestive of the enormity of the collapse of the Soviet system, Kaliningrad's agricultural production in 1997 still had not returned to the production levels recorded in 1991 (Kaliningrad Region 1996: 53). The issue for the most part is one of accountability. Farm managers are no longer able to call upon Moscow or the local administration to make up financial shortfalls. After 1991, in theory at least, overdrafts would have to be repaid and with interest. Equipment maintenance was deferred and, in some cases, equipment was sold to raise money for current operations. In short, the agricultural component of the economy was grinding down to what might best be described as near subsistence level, largely dependent upon sanctioned or illegal bartering.

Collective farm managers were neither trained nor prepared to function in a free market nor to suffer its measures of accountability. Typically, these large scale enterprises might have a significant number of employees assigned to tasks tangential to the growing and processing of food. Realistic financial accounting has led to underemployment which, in some instances, threatens to turn into unemployment. Farm workers are not immune from the economic transformation and many seem destined to lose previously generous socioeconomic benefits. Housing, however, appears to be secure. Homes on the collective farms are generally of a much higher quality than urban housing.

Fishing

The once-thriving inshore fishing industry has been decimated by the combined effects of over fishing and outright pollution of the Kurskiy *Zaliv (Kurisches Haff)* and nearby portions of the Baltic. A trip astride the sea canal connecting Kaliningrad City to Baltysk offers an endless panorama of vessels in need of repair but with no repairs taking place, scenes of a once active shipbuilding and ship repair industry where much of the activity appears to have stopped in 1991. The local unemployment consequences of this industrial collapse surely are significant.

The USSR's largest ocean going and now largely inactive fishing fleet is based in Kaliningrad. Formerly, its catches together with some from fishing fleets based elsewhere in the country were processed in Kaliningrad canneries. This rusting fleet is a stark reminder of the need to modernize in a world consisting of numerous low cost operators. During the last 14 years of South African control over Southwest Africa (Namibia), there were upwards of 350 deep-water Soviet trawlers fishing in Namibian waters. The Southwest African Peoples Organization (SWAPO) received political and material support from the Soviet Union during its long conflict with South Africa. Accepting the presence of this massive fleet was one way in which the Soviets could be repaid. Today, a handful of these same vessels (rusting, visually in need of repair, and flying the Russian flag) remains to fish under contract for Namibian companies. The remainder of this once impressive fishing fleet is back in Kaliningrad City at anchor, a visual reminder that there are few politically free fishing grounds left in the world.

The Soviet City

Even *Königsberg* in its day did not dominate the region's urban hierarchy to the extent that Kaliningrad City does today (Knappe 1994: table p.20). Admittedly, in the case of the latter, its service area is less than half the size of what existed in prewar. The Soviets embarked upon a major industrialization program for Kaliningrad City, mirroring the centralized planning implemented earlier in other USSR cities. In this manner, a former regional service center-provincial capital, intertwined with a landscape of numerous decision-making centers, was converted into an administrative center in which practically all significant economic decisions were imposed from above. Thus Kaliningrad was connected to the labor, raw material, manufacturing, and marketing systems encompassing all of the Soviet Republics, and especially to the nearby ones of Lithuania, Latvia and Byelorussia.

Components of the USSR's external trade directed through the city and port were processed locally (Fjodorow and Korneyevets 1996: 45-7). Industrialization for Kaliningrad, however, did not entail heavy industry. This was to be a light industrial base, with a special emphasis upon the more sophisticated technological demands of the military. In addition, factories were built to process locally produced dairy products and grain. Before the collapse of the USSR, a factory in

Kaliningrad might have shipped the greater portion of its output to markets beyond the region without concern for the true costs. To the extent that production quotas were met, other issues could be ameliorated.

The urban setting offers little in the way of alternatives. Factory managers face many of the financial constraints as their agricultural counterparts. Furthermore, they likely have fewer socioeconomic perks to offer their employees during this period of economic transformation. Entrepreneurs abound, from the enterprising street peddler to what might be described as an emerging class of tycoons, but the mass of the urban population has even to begin the mental transformation necessary to enter an economy predicated upon market forces. In this regard, Kaliningrad mirrors the situation elsewhere in Russia.

As is the case elsewhere in Russia, post-Soviet, market-oriented economics have had distressing consequences. A visual reminder is the emerging affluent suburb comprising large, opulent homes interspersed with dwellings that once housed the German middle class. More distant from Kaliningrad City, but even more telling, are the residences surrounded by walled compounds with sophisticated security systems and guard dogs. These are the homes of the very wealthy 'New Russians'. There is a continuing debate amongst those not so fortunate as to the origins of this wealth. The stark contrast between these new, frequently gaudy, and comparatively opulent homes, and the drab, visually decaying, and nondescript apartment blocks that house the great majority of the population is overwhelming. There surely will be unpleasant socio-political connotations in the future if the trend continues unabated.

Tourist Potential? For Russians?

Kaliningrad became a favorite retirement location for Soviet military officers, which merits attention whenever the question of what to do with this region arises. An expression of the region's popularity is seen in the health spa of Svetlogorsk *(Rauschen)* on the North coast. Relatively undamaged in the war, this Kurort was expanded to accommodate annual summer visits from military personnel and workers at several industrial syndicates who maintained lodges or hotels. Svetlogorsk also was popular with non-Kaliningraders who lived closer to the Baltic than to alternative Black Sea resorts. Partial collapse of the Russian economy and reduced vacation benefits, together with the need to pay for their own transportation, have caused the number of visitors to decline.

Even in the best of times which these clearly are not, it is doubtful if tourism from abroad or from elsewhere in Russia would provide more than a modest and localized addition to Kaliningrad's economy. Moscow assigned Kaliningrad a free trade zone and, more recently, declared its westernmost oblast to be a Special Economic Zone (Fjodorow & Korneyevets 1996: 45). Still, a much expanded version of the marketing arrangement for amber (Jantar) is needed, not only to reconnect and improve upon former regional economic linkages established during Soviet control but to nurture new ones in this portion of the Baltic. The latter have more than passing potential with continued European integration. For example, the main road corridor envisioned to connect Finland to East-Central Europe likely will be through Estonia (by ferry), Latvia, Lithuania, Kaliningrad and Poland.

Borderland Trade

At the outset, refurbishing and, perhaps more important, legitimizing the still locally important trade between Kaliningrad and Lithuania should have first priority. This can be followed by rebuilding and developing mutually advantageous trade between Kaliningrad, Lithuania, Poland and Belarus. It is anticipated that Poland will seek an expansion of its once important linkages to Lithuania now that these two countries share a common border as well as shared religious and historical political connections. Belarus presently is a dubious proposition so long as its government continues to direct its development within Russia's economic shadow, while using the old Soviet model for inspiration and implementation. As for Kaliningrad-Lithuanian trade, more cooperation on the part of both entities is required to control a growing and unofficial, clearly profitable, illegal trade in guns, automobiles, cigarettes, alcohol and an almost endless list of items for everyday use. Not only are the frontiers between Kaliningrad and Lithuania porous, the suspected volume and value of illegal trade detract from customs duties and encourage corruption. A recent perspective on this border and how it compares with Russia's other new border areas was presented at a 1997 symposium at Finland's Joennen University entitled 'Economy and Security of the Border Region'. Substantial risk for the Kaliningrad-Lithuania border was identified in three of nine problem categories: Isolation or dependence upon passage through a neighboring country; Inevitable uniting of a border region, and Excessive border crime (Grandberg 1999: 85). The attractiveness for this illegal, cross border trade can only be enhanced as membership in the European Community beckons for four of Kaliningrad's neighbors.

Further Baltic cooperation associated with the likely expansion of the European Community will enhance Kaliningrad's potential, but only if Russia agrees to a formula which, in all probability, weakens its sovereignty over the area. To enhance the economic attractiveness of Kaliningrad (Fjodorow 1995) to the point where this region, better yet its port and urban area, were to compete seriously with St. Petersburg for the country's western external trade, poses a potential dilemma for Moscow. The easy solution would be to let the nationalists have their way and accept the consequences of a Kaliningrad in economic decline, without meaningful growth potential. This course of action could result in still other problems if doing nothing forces the residents of Kaliningrad to live in the shadow of strong and increasingly enticing neighboring economies.

Alternatively, an economically healthy Kaliningrad functioning within a special political arrangement with its Baltic neighbors or European Community might serve as Russia's window to future European integration. Kaliningrad's port offers foreign trade a seasonal and distance advantage relative to St. Petersburg and might prove to be a compelling route once the necessary economic pieces were in place. There is some room for optimism. Bayerische Motoren Werke recently announced that Kaliningrad would become the site of its first automobile assembly facility in Russia and headquarters of a national distribution network of 17 dealers (BMW

1999: 2-3). Assembling will be in cooperation with the local company Avtotor and comprise semi knocked down and completely knocked down vehicles. BMW is looking forward to the production (assembly!) of 10,000 units yearly.

Some would advocate that Kaliningrad could become the Hong Kong of the Baltic, a special status exclave whose multinational economic hinterland would enrich Russia much as adjacent Chinese territory benefits from Hong Kong's window to world markets. During the last half century, however, Kaliningrad has been more akin to a Gibraltar. This was territory taken in war, prepared for war and presumably, still armed for war. Given this history and offered the choice, neighboring countries would support some form of special economic status for Kaliningrad if only to defuse its potential as a „loose cannon" in the Baltic Region.

If economic recovery in Russia continues to lag behind that of its western neighbors, coincidental with new opportunities for intra-European trade expansion into the eastern Baltic, the Kaliningrad exclave could become a cancer on regional stability. Expansion of existing regional connections (Stanley 1997) and development of new trading relationships between Kaliningrad and the countries surrounding the Baltic is needed, not only to interconnect the economic and cultural diversity of the region (Wein 1994: 105-09), but to integrate or reconnect the region with a Kaliningrad whose instability can only increase with the reluctance of Moscow to initiate or respond to regional integration. The absurdity of the current situation can be seen in the delays occurred in developing a relatively small petroleum field in the eastern Baltic.

The offshore boundary between Lithuania and Russia (Kaliningrad) starts at a point where the River Neman enters the Baltic. There is contention on the part of Lithuania that the offshore boundary, as originally drawn, is predicated upon a northwesterly-southeasterly line, allocating the bulk of the suspected oil to Russian. In spite of a statement in 1994 by the Russian Ambassador to Lithuania that the offshore oil belongs to Russia, Lithuania contends that the boundary should be drawn by a straight, east-west line. This in theory would give it a portion of the suspected oil. Speculation is only enhanced by the fact that the exploration maps, prepared when the Soviet Union still existed, are housed at an institute in Riga, Latvia, formerly the documentation center for Soviet Baltic petroleum exploration. Latvia is unwilling to release maps and other documents to Lithuania unless it is guaranteed some of the future oil production (presumably, irrespective of whatever information is deduced from the documents) and Russia is not prepared to accept Lithuania's definition of their mutual offshore boundary. The result, not unexpectedly, is that this particular petroleum field still awaits development. Lack of development may be of little consequence to Kaliningrad or Russia, but is significant to a Lithuania or Latvia totally dependent upon imported oil. Nationalism still exists in the Baltic lands and should be countered by inducements for regional cooperation. One would have thought that the removal of Soviet control in 1991 would have stimulated if not mandated cooperation between the small Baltic countries.

Conclusion

Victory in World War 2 and the acquisition of northern East Prussia gave the Soviets an enhanced Baltic window while simultaneously depriving defeated

Germany of territory and a long military tradition. The recent demise of the Soviet Union, coupled with the loss of its eastern European colonies, leaves only Kaliningrad, southern Sakhalin and the Kurile Islands as spoils from the great Patriotic War. Much as France drew a proverbial line in the sand in Algeria after her 1954 defeat in Vietnam, nationalists in Russia appear determined to retain sovereignty over their remaining wartime acquisitions. All the same, no country is prepared to challenge Russia on its right to sovereignty over Kaliningrad. The German dream to return lives largely in the minds of a soon-to-be dead generation; the once powerful post war political strength of this group has dissipated through time. German youth appear to be unconcerned. *Lebensraum* at the end of century has more significance in the tourist industry than with potential colonists.

Poland and Lithuania have historic claims but it is difficult to assign any credence to potential irredentism. Some in Poland may harbor a desire to reunite former East Prussia and people both portions with Poles (but never to permit Volga German resettlement). Poland struggled to enter NATO knowing of what it means to exist adjacent to an expanding Germany or expanding Soviet Union/Russia. Just as Germany has accepted the loss of its eastern territories, knowing that far more can be achieved through economic cooperation than by militarism, so surely will Poland reach a similar conclusion with respect to an area where the historical record is contentious. Lithuania will tread carefully to avoid antagonizing powerful and neighboring Russia whatever might be her historical claim to a portion of Kaliningrad. Not only does Lithuania have an awkward, potentially dangerous, irredentism issue in its own substantial Russian speaking minority population, it also has a small Lithuanian population in Kaliningrad. After the death of Stalin in 1953, approximately 20,000 ethnic Lithuanians settled in Kaliningrad. They and their descendants are active in the growing and illegal cross border trade.

What to Stalin in 1945 seemed a golden opportunity could, for his successors in Moscow, become an intolerable burden, not to be sustained for reasons of domestic politics any longer than absolutely necessary. A frail President Yeltsin visited Kaliningrad during the last election campaign to deliver a speech emphasizing its Russian character. This was to dispel any notion that he might be weak regarding the sanctity of Russia's borders. The speech not only was meant to attract a portion of the active and retired military vote, it also was intended to attack his nationalist opponents on their own emotional turf.

The Soviet Union created Kaliningrad and it is for Russia in the first instance to find a role for it within the new Europe. There are no healthy alternatives. The transformation process currently underway in East-Central Europe could easily be detoured by a Kaliningrad still lacking a role in the new dispensation. Much was anticipated in 1995 when Moscow promulgated the revised law, formalized on January 5, 1996 granting Kaliningrad the privileges of a 'special economic zone' with customs dispensations and currency regulations favoring foreign investors (Harris 1999: 60). That this and other gestures failed to provide Kaliningrad with the momentum necessary to emerge from a former military cantonment to a Baltic economic miracle can be largely attributed to Russian politics and mismanagement of the economy. For real change to occur, Moscow must accept a special role for Kaliningrad and a role that very likely could mean reduced sovereignty. Whether enshrined as a fourth Baltic Republic or as a 'Free Port' containing some of the characteristics of a pre-war Danzig or contemporary Hong Kong, the existing situation is not conducive to either regional economic cooperation or political tranquility. One of the first steps leading to the transformation would entail a substantial reduction in Kaliningrad's military establishment. Unfortunately, the current environment within Russia does not bode well for such transfers. One reason for many commissioned personnel wanting to remain in Kaliningrad may relate to housing. Here at least they and their families do not have to constantly worry about the basics. Hopefully, European integration will not flounder on this issue.

(*) *Author's Note*

Most of us are aware that Kaliningrad/*Königsberg* / East Prussia are pieces of the same geography assigned different names as a result of war. It would not be an understatement to suggest that Karl Sinnhuber takes special interest in this particular geographical realm.

He first saw East Prussia in 1931 or 1932 with a group of school children on a recreational visit. His next visit was in 1939 with the Labor Corps where he was 'employed' in clearing drainage canals in a peat bog near the delta of the River *Memel* (Neman). This hardly prepared him for his third and most memorable visit which took place in late 1944 with winter setting-in. Luftwaffe Lieutenant Sinnhuber was set down somewhere between *Insterburg* and *Nemmersdorf* in command of a mixed infantry company comprised in large measure of teenagers whose assignment was to hold off the Red Army! Bombed, later shot in the leg and separated from his disintegrating command during its first fire fight in January, 1945, Karl Sinnhuber had the common sense and inner strength to head in a westerly direction. En route, the severity of his wound and an understanding senior officer allowed him to avoid another and altogether likely fatal infantry engagement in order that he might continue westward in search of medical assistance. For part of the journey to *Königsberg*, he rode semi-conscious in a radio vehicle and recalls hearing someone announcing that the first Russian tanks had at that very moment entered the *Pregel* River town of *Tapiau*. Challenged by a soldier manning the eastern perimeter of *Königsberg*'s outer defenses, Karl Sinnhuber avoided being shot in part by understanding the dialect of the sentry. Medical treatment in *Königsberg* was followed by an overland journey to the port of *Pillau* where our colleague's good fortune continued. Scheduled to be evacuated with other wounded soldiers and refugees on a large passenger liner, he was 'bumped down' to a smaller vessel. The larger ship was torpedoed and sunk. Arriving in Gdynia by sea, Karl Sinnhuber presented himself to Luftwaffe Headquarters as the pilot he was and eventually reached Berlin.

East Prussia, therefore, has a special connection to our esteemed colleague who is honored with this *Festschrift*. The story is not over and few of his friends will be surprised if pilot, infantry commander, geographer, ski enthusiast and world traveler Karl Sinnhuber decides to add this unusual piece of westernmost Russia to his future travel plans.

The authors have their own special connections to East Prussia. Dr. Knappe was one of the very first German academics permitted to visit Kaliningrad in 1991 following the collapse of the Soviet Union. Fluent in Russian, she quickly established her credentials with the local academic community and has contributed several scholarly publications, frequently based on detailed field measurements. Dr. Knappe's expertise, in turn, attracted the co-author to Leipzig where he spent a four month residency. They embarked upon a memorable visit to Kaliningrad in October-November, 1996.

References

Albright, Madeleine, W. Cohen, S. Berger and M. McCurry. 1997. *Press Briefing on NATO Summit* Madrid), 13pp.

Applebaum, Anne. 1995. *Between East and West – Across the Borderlands of Europe*, Prelude and Chapter 1, 'Kaliningrad/Königsberg' (Papermac: London).

Barran, Fritz. 1992. *Königsberg Kaliningrad aktueller Stadtplan 1:10,000* (Rautenberg: Leer).

Bachtin, Anatolu. 1994. 'Zur Situation der Baudenkmäler im Königsberger Gebiet am Beispiel der Sakralbauten', in: *Ein schicklicher Platz – Königberg / Kaliningrad in der Sicht von Bewohnern und Nachbarn*, F. Kluge, Hrsg. (Fibre: Osnabrück), 103-130.

Bayerische Motoren Werke Aktiengesellschaft. 1999. *News Release – BMW to have its own sales team and assembly plant in Russia*, March 17.

Bode, Thilo. 1995. 'Tötet, Ihr tapferen Rotarmisten, tötet! – Vor fünfzig Jahren: Millionen fliehen über die Ostsee', *Frankfurter Allgemeine*, February 28, 7.

Conquest, Robert. 1991. *Stalin: Breaker of Nations* (Phoenix: London).

Davies, Norman. 1981. *God's Playground – A History of Poland, Vol. II: 1795 to the Present* (Clarendon: Oxford).

Dobson, Christopher, J. Miller and R. Payne. 1979. *The Cruelest Night* (Little Brown: Boston).

Dönhoff, Marion. 1971. *Namen, die keiner mehr nennt – Erinnerungen an Ostpreußen* (Eugen Diederichs: Düsseldorf).

The Economist. 1996. 'Bargins in the Baltic', May 4.

Granberg, Alexander. 1999. 'Frontier Regions in the National Strategy for Development: The Russian View', in: *Curtains of Iron and Gold – Reconstructing Borders and Scales of Interaction*, (eds.) H. Eskelinen, I. Liikanen and J. Oska (Ashgate: Aldershot), 75-87.

Fjodorov, Gennadij. 1995. 'Die wirtschaftliche Entwicklung des Gebiets Kaliningrad und Konzeptionen der regionalen Entwicklung', *Berliner Osteuropa Info* 6, 31-33.

Fjodorow, Gennadiy and Valentin Korneyevets. 1996. 'Multilevel Interests for the Development of the Kaliningrad Region as an Enclave Territory of Russia', *IOER-Schriften* 17, 45-47.

Guttzeit, Emil J. (n. d.) *Ostpreussen in 1440 Bildern – Geschichtliche Darstellung* (Gerhard Rautenberg: Leer, o. J.).

Harris, Chauncy. 1997. 'Europa Regional: Focus on Former East Prussia' (Review), *Post-Soviet Geography and Economics* 38, 59-62.

Kaliningrad region in Figures – Concise statistical handbook. 1996. State Committee of the Russian Federation on Statistics; Kaliningrad region (Committee of State Statistics), 74pp.

Keiser, Egbert. 1978. *Danziger Bucht 1945 – Dokumentation einer Katastrophe* (Bechtle).

Knappe, Elke. 1993a. 'Der Wandel der Landnutzung im Kaliningrader Gebiet – Die Beispielregion um Labiau', *Europa Regional* 1, 7-15.

Knappe, Elke. 1993b. 'Der Wandel der Landnutzung in der Region Kaliningrad (Teil II, mit Kartenbeilage)', *Europa Regional* 2, 22-30.

Knappe. Elke. 1994. 'Der Transformationsprozeß in der Region Tschernjachowsk (Gebiet Kaliningrad)', *Europa Regional* 4, 20-30.

Korneyevets, Valentin. 1996. 'VASAB and the Enlargement of the Coordination Between International Projects at the Preliminary Stage', *IOER-Schriften* 17, 26.

Kornejewez, Walentin u. Elke Knappe. 1996. 'Die Viehwirtschaft im Gebiet Kaliningrad: Zum Transformationsprozeß im ländlichen Raum', *Europa Regional* 4, 24-30.

Matochkin, Yuri. 1995. 'The Most Western Region of Russia', *Foreign Trade* (Ministry of Foreign Economic Relations, Moscow) 9, 18-21.

Matthies, Helmut. 1991. 'Was wird aus der Exklave Königsberg?', *Frankfurter Allgemeine Zeitung*, September 18.

Mortensen, Hans (Hrsg). 1968. *Historisch-geographischer Atlas des Preußenlandes* (F. Steiner: Wiesbaden).

Orlenok, Wjatscheslaw (u.a.). 1994. *Natur, Wirtschaft und Ökologie der Stadt Kaliningrad* (Institut für Länderkunde: Leipzig), 56pp.

Prevelakis, George. 1995. 'Comments on the paper of Dmitri Trenin' [New Dimensions of Security Policy], *International Geo-Political Research Colloquium*, George C. Marshall European Center for Security Studies, November 13.

Rupert, James. 1997. 'Still Within Reach of Russian Bear, Borderlands Seek Identities', *International Herald Tribune*, January 6.

Sakson, Andrzej. 1994. 'Königsberg, Kaliningrad, Królewiec oder Karaliau_ius? Polnische Betrachtungen über eine russische Exklave', in: *Ein schicklicher Platz – Königsberg / Kaliningrad in der Sicht von Bewohnern und Nachbarn*, F. Kluge, Hrsg. (Fibre: Osnabrück), 179-192.

Scheu, E. 1936. *Ostpreußen – Eine wirtschaftsgeographische Landeskunde* (Königsberg).

Solzhenitsyn, Alexander. 1974. *Prussian Nights*, transl. Robert Conquest (Farrar, Straus & Giroux: New York).

Stanley, William. 1977. Assessment of 'Berlin's Position im europäischen Verkehr des 21. Jahrhunderts', *Europa Regional* 5, 45-50.

Swerew, Jurij. 1996. *Rußlands Gebiet Kaliningrad im neuen geopolitischen Koordinatenfeld* (Köln: Bundesinstitut für ostwissenschaftliche und internationale Studien), 35pp.

Thadden, Rudolf v. 1987. *Prussia: History of a Lost State* (Cambridge Univ. Press: New York).

Vesilind, Priit. 1997. 'Kaliningrad: Coping with a German past and a Russian Future', *National Geographic* 191, 110-123.

Wein, Norbert. 1994. 'Die Exklave Kaliningrad/Königsberg: eine geographische und geopolitische Bestandsaufnahme', *Zeitschrift für Wirtschaftsgeographie* 38, 101-109.

Welles, Sumner. 1946. *Where are We Heading?* (Harper: New York).

Werth, Alexander. 1964. *Russia at War 1941–1945* (Avon: New York).

Regionalisierung und Dezentralisierung in Rumänien – Möglichkeiten und Hindernisse [1]

Peter JORDAN (Wien)

Regionalization and Decentralization in Romania – Opportunities and Obstacles [2]

Abstract

Disintegration and regionalization are as important factors in contemporary Europe as integration. On the one hand Europe makes many efforts to become for the first time in history a kind of a political union. On the other hand former federations have been dissolved, countries which were rather centralized in the past have undergone or are just undergoing considerable decentralization and the theme of a Europe of regions is on the agenda prompting even countries without regional traditions to look for territorial decentralization.

This paper does not necessarily advocate regionalization and decentralization, but noting a European trend in this direction it asks, whether Romania, as a candidate for European integration, would be able to respond to this trend. It confronts Romania's natural and historical diversity with her tradition of administrative centralism, describes her current regional diversity which has even been accentuated by the transformation process and it asks for grounds that prevent Romania from becoming regionalized and decentralized. Grounds taken into consideration and being discussed are: Romania's unitarian traditions from the beginning, the "Transylvanian dilemma" and the Hungarian ethnic group.

Kurzfassung

Desintegration und Regionalisierung sind im heutigen Europa ebenso bedeutende politische Trends wie es die Integration ist. Einerseits unternimmt Europa viele Anstrengungen, um zum ersten Mal in seiner Geschichte eine Art politischer Union zu werden. Andererseits sind Föderationen zerfallen, unterzogen oder unterziehen sich Staaten, die sehr zentralistisch waren, zum Teil weitgehender Dezentralisierung und steht ein „Europa der Regionen" auf der politischen Tagesordnung, so daß selbst Länder ohne jede regionale Tradition sich um Regionalisierung bemühen.

---

[1] Dieser Beitrag erschien erstmals in englischer Sprache in dem nachfolgend angeführten Band der Südosteuropa-Studien. Die vorliegende deutsche Fassung wurde geringfügig aktualisiert und ergänzt.

[2] A previous version of this paper has been published in English in: HELLER, W. (ed.): Romania : Migration, Socio-economic Transformation and Perspectives of Regional Development. München 1998. = Südosteuropa-Studien, vol. 62, p. 271-288.

Dieser Beitrag soll nicht ein Plädoyer für Regionalisierung und Dezentralisierung sein. Er wirft aber die Frage auf, ob Rumänien als ein Kandidat für die europäische Integration den europäischen Trends in diese Richtung entsprechen kann. Der Beitrag stellt Rumäniens natürliche und historische Vielfalt seiner Tradition eines administrativen Zentralismus gegenüber, beschreibt seine heutige regionale Vielfalt, die sich im Laufe des Transformationsprozesses noch akzentuiert hat, und fragt nach den Gründen, die Rumänien heute von Regionalisierung und Dezentralisierung abhalten. Als solche Gründe werden diskutiert: Rumäniens Tradition des Unitarismus von Anfang an, das „siebenbürgische Dilemma" und die ungarische ethnische Gruppe.

1. Vorbemerkungen

Im heutigen Europa sind sowohl Integration als auch Desintegration, Dezentralisierung oder Regionalisierung in gleicher Weise als politische Tendenzen erkennbar. Einerseits bewegt sich Europa zum ersten Mal in der Geschichte auf eine Art politischer Union zu. Andererseits haben sich seit 1989 Föderationen (die Sowjetunion, Jugoslawien, die Tschechoslowakei) in ihre Teile aufgelöst, geht der Prozeß politischer Zersplitterung am Balkan weiter (Bosnien-Herzegowina, Kosovo, vielleicht auch Montenegro), regionalisieren sich Länder mit zentralistischer Tradition wie Spanien, Frankreich, Italien oder Großbritannien und existiert das Leitbild eines "Europas der Regionen" (FOUCHER et al. 1993, S. 34).

Regionalisierung erscheint attraktiv, verspricht sie doch die Aktivierung regionaler Kräfte und Ressourcen und gelebte Demokratie im überschaubaren Rahmen. Sie kann sich aber auch negativ auswirken, wenn z.B. wohlhabende Regionen sich weigern, ihren Wohlstand mit rückständigeren Gebieten zu teilen oder wenn Zentralismus bloß auf eine niedrigere Ebene verlagert wird, wo er vielleicht weniger der Kontrolle unterliegt und sich die politischen Kräfte unter Umständen weniger im Gleichgewicht befinden. Regionalisierung könnte so auch zu steileren ökonomischen und sozialen Gradienten führen und ein Europa der neuen Feudalherrschaften hervorbringen (FOUCHER et al. 1993, S. 34).

Es ist wohl auch zu bedenken, daß etwa die Hälfte Europas über keine Tradition von Regionen verfügt, wenn man unter Regionen subsidiäre, sich selbst verwaltende territoriale Einheiten mittlerer Größe versteht. Es wird daher auch nicht leicht sein, über den ganzen Kontinent ein homogenes System von Regionen zu spannen (FOUCHER et al. 1993, S. 34).

Dieser Beitrag soll nicht als ein Plädoyer für Regionalisierung und Dezentralisierung verstanden werden.[3] Angesichts eines europaweiten Trends in diese Richtung lohnt es sich aber wohl die Frage aufzuwerfen, ob Rumänien als ein Kandidat für die europäische Integration in der Lage wäre, diesem Trend zu entsprechen.

---

[3] Der Autor ist allerdings der Meinung, daß ein ausgewogenes Zusammenspiel von zentraler und regionaler Verwaltung besser geeignet ist, die Potentiale eines Landes zu wecken und zu entwickeln, als eine zentralistische Verwaltung.

2. Rumäniens natürliche und historische Vielfalt im Gegensatz zu seiner Tradition eines administrativen Zentralismus

2.1. Natürliche und historische Vielfalt

Während es ganz und gar nicht überrascht, daß das von Natur aus und historisch homogene Ungarn ein zentralistischer Staat ist, erscheint (zumindest aus österreichischer Sicht) der Zentralismus in Rumänien als "unnatürlich". Von Natur aus wird Rumänien durch den Karpatenbogen in zwei Teile geteilt, und zu beiden Seiten zeigt sich eine Vielfalt von Naturlandschaften. Die naturräumliche Vielfalt Rumäniens wird aus jeder topographischen Karte deutlich und bedarf keiner weiteren Erläuterung.

Diese naturräumlichen Verhältnisse, noch mehr aber die Lage des Landes im Großraum am Rande großer historischer Reiche und Einflußsphären haben politische Grenzraumsituationen und politischen Wechsel auf dem Gebiet des heutigen Rumäniens im Verlauf der Geschichte begünstigt. Die Gebiete des heutigen Rumäniens waren – jedenfalls bis zum Ende des Ersten Weltkriegs – eine klassische Pufferzone zwischen den Machtzentren in der Mitte, im Osten und im Südosten Europas.

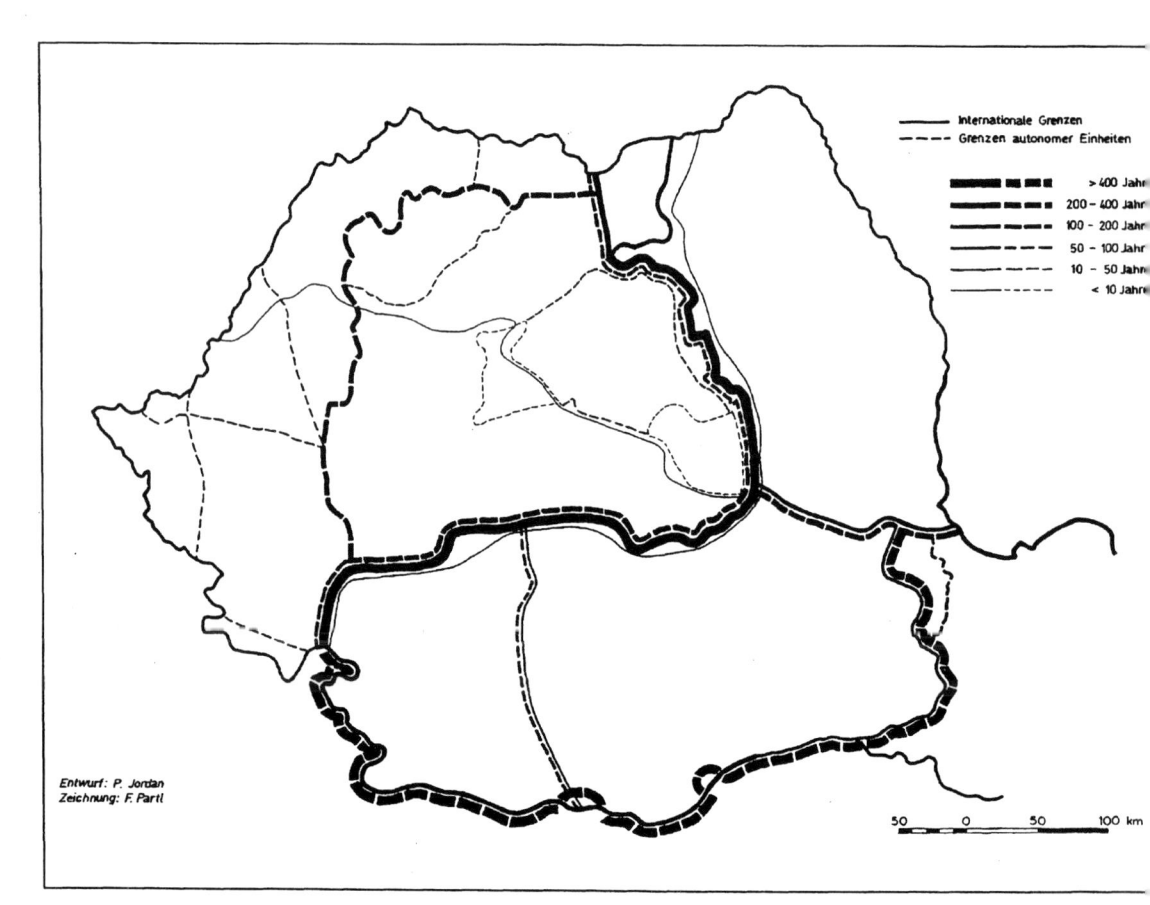

Abb. 1: Dauer internationaler Grenzen und von Grenzen autonomer Einheiten

Wenn man die Dauerhaftigkeit internationaler Grenzen und der Grenzen von autonomen politischen Einheiten auf dem Gebiet des heutigen Rumäniens untersucht (Abb. 1), erweist sich tatsächlich der das heutige Rumänien teilende Karpatenbogen als die historische Hauptscheidelinie. Mehr als vier Jahrhunderte lang bildete sein größter Abschnitt die östliche Grenze des Königreichs Ungarn und des Habsburgerreichs und somit die Scheidelinie zwischen starken westlichen Kultureinflüssen (westliches Christentum, Aufklärung) und der Dominanz von Byzanz und der Pforte. Nur im Bereich der südlichen Bukowina [Bucovina] teilt sich diese starke Trennlinie in zwei dünnere, die für kürzere Dauer stehen. Die östliche davon galt von 1775 bis 1918. Außer seiner Funktion als internationale Grenze bildete der Karpatenbogen zwischen 100 und 400 Jahre lang auch noch die Grenze zwischen autonomen Einheiten unter ungarischer (im Mittelalter) oder osmanischer (1541–1699) Souveränität, nämlich zwischen den Fürstentümern Siebenbürgen [Transilvania][4], Walachei [Țara Românească] und Moldau [Moldova]. Eine Variante dieser Gebirgsgrenze, etwas weiter im Süden und Osten und unterhalb der Gebirgspässe verlaufend, hatte nur von Mai bis Dezember 1918 Bestand. Zusammengenommen bildet der Karpatenbogen eine historische Scheidelinie, die an Dauerhaftigkeit von keinem Abschnitt der heutigen Grenzen Rumäniens übertroffen wird.

Jener Abschnitt unter den heutigen Außengrenzen Rumäniens, der schon am längsten ununterbrochen die Funktion einer internationalen Grenze ausübt, ist die Grenze an der Donau vom Eisernen Tor [Porțile de Fier] bis vor Tutrakan (bis zur Grenze der südlichen Dobrudscha), die seit der völligen Unabhängigkeit Rumäniens vom Osmanischen Reich im Jahr 1878 eine internationale Grenze ist. Sie bildete aber mit Ausnahme der beiden osmanischen Brückenköpfe von Turnu Măgurele und Giurgiu am linken Donauufer schon seit 1393 die Grenze der Walachei, als diese noch ein autonomes Fürstentum unter der Oberhoheit des Osmanischen Reichs war.

Bedeutendere historische Scheidelinien existieren auch zwischen der Moldau und der Walachei bzw. der Dobrudscha [Dobrogea]. Sie waren über mehr als 100 Jahre, nämlich vom 14. Jahrhundert bis 1511, als sich die Moldau osmanischer Oberhoheit fügte, internationale Grenzen und für weitere 350 bzw. 367 Jahre Grenzen zwischen den unter osmanischer Oberhoheit autonomen Donaufürstentümern Moldau und Walachei bis zu deren Vereinigung im Jahr 1859 bzw. bis zum Anschluß der Dobrudscha an Rumänien im Jahr 1878.

Ähnlich dauerhaft war die Grenze zwischen der Dobrudscha und der Walachei. Sie fungierte bis zur Unterordnung der Walachei unter osmanische Souveränität mehr als 100 Jahre lang als internationale Grenze und weitere 485 Jahre lang (1393–1878) mit Ausnahme eines Abschnitts nördlich von Hârșova, der 1829 abgeändert wurde, als Grenze zwischen autonomen Gebieten unter osmanischer Dominanz.

Im Gegensatz dazu war die östliche Grenze Olteniens [Oltenia] recht kurzlebig. Sie bildete im 14. Jahrhundert die Demarkationslinie zwischen unga-

---

[4] In diesem Beitrag wird als "Siebenbürgen" das Siebenbürgen im weiteren Sinn bezeichnet, also alle Gebiete des heutigen Rumäniens, die innerhalb des Karpatenbogens liegen. Wenn das historische Großfürstentum Siebenbürgen gemeint ist, wird explizit vom "Großfürstentum Siebenbürgen" oder vom "historischen Siebenbürgen" gesprochen. Die heutigen offiziellen Entsprechungen historischer Namen oder deutscher Exonyme stehen in eckigen Klammern.

rischen Oligarchien (Oltenien hieß damals Severin) und ab 1718 eine internationale Grenze, als Österreich Oltenien für 21 Jahre besetzte.

Innerhalb des Karpatenbogens ist als beständigste historische Grenze die westliche und nördliche Grenze des Großfürstentums Siebenbürgen zu nennen. Mit Ausnahme vorübergehender Veränderungen im 17. Jahrhundert und einer Verschiebung im Bereich des Gebiets von Sălaj im 19. Jahrhundert blieb sie mehr als 300 Jahre lang bis 1867 stabil.

Das Banat bildete unter dem Titel „Serbische Woiwodschaft und Temeser Banat" nur 11 Jahre lang eine autonome Einheit (1849–1860).

Andere Grenzen wie jene der Autonomen Ungarischen Region [Regiunea Mureş-Autonomă Maghiara / Maros Magyar Autonóm Tartomány] (1952–1968, 1960 in zwei Abschnitten verändert) und des ungarischen Nordsiebenbürgens (1940–1944) bestanden nicht viel länger oder sogar kürzer.

Man kann die Bedeutung alter Grenzen im Rahmen einer Diskussion um aktuelle Möglichkeiten zur Regionalisierung natürlich in Frage stellen. Zumindest die Grenzen des 19. und 20. Jahrhunderts sind aber wohl ohne Zweifel relevant, da sie das Land in einer sehr formativen Phase strukturiert haben.

2.2. Verwaltungszentralismus

Seit der Vereinigung der beiden Donaufürstentümer im Jahr 1859 treten die historischen Länder Moldau und Walachei nicht mehr als konstitutive Teile des neuen Staates oder auch nur als Einheiten eines administrativ-territorialen Systems in Erscheinung. Die Vereinigung im Jahr 1859[5] war radikal und hinterließ keine Spuren unterschiedlicher Verwaltungssysteme oder regionaler Selbstverwaltung. Tatsächlich hatten die beiden Fürstentümer trotz jahrhundertelang hauptsächlich aus dynastischen Gründen praktizierter Eigenstaatlichkeit immer schon sehr viel gemein (MAYER 1977, S. 44). In der ersten Hälfte des 19. Jahrhunderts näherten sie sich weiter an. Schritte dieser Annäherung waren die Entwicklung eines gemeinsamen rumänischen Nationalbewußtseins, einer gemeinsamen Schriftsprache und Schrift. Sie setzte sich mit der Verlautbarung zweier fast identischer Verfassungen [regulament organic] in den Jahren 1831 (Walachei) und 1832 (Moldau) und mit der Krönung von Alexander Cuza zum Herrscher beider Fürstentümer im Jahr 1858 fort (MAYER 1977, S. 47). Oltenien, das zeitweilig (14. Jahrhundert, 1718–1739) vom Fürstentum Walachei getrennt gewesen war, hatte sich bis dahin wieder voll in die Walachei integriert.

Der bei der Vereinigung der Donaufürstentümer praktizierte Zentralismus entsprach ganz den zeitgenössischen Tendenzen in Europa (Einigung Italiens!), war dem für die Rumänen stets sehr bedeutungsvollen französischen Modell nachempfunden und kann auch als eine Sammlung aller nationalen Kräfte zur Überwindung der osmanischen Vorherrschaft verstanden werden.

Die erste Verfassung der vereinigten Donaufürstentümer aus 1866 legte als administrativ-territoriale Gliederung des Landes ein Komitats- oder Bezirkssystem [judeţe] fest. Es wurde auf die Dobrudscha ausgedehnt, als diese im Jahr 1878 Rumänien zugesprochen wurde, erhielt sich aber ansonsten bis 1918

---

[5] Die Vereinigung wurde vom Osmanischen Reich und von den europäischen Mächten erst 1861 anerkannt.

fast unverändert. Es unterteilte Rumänien in 32 Komitate und berücksichtigte die historischen Bestandteile des jungen rumänischen Staates, also die Moldau, die Große Walachei (Muntenien), die Kleine Walachei (Oltenien) und die Dobrudscha insofern, als es die Komitate in deren Grenzen einfügte. Nach Größe, Zahl und Kompetenzausstattung waren diese Komitate aber nicht mehr als eine Art von dekonzentrierter Staatsverwaltung und durchaus keine Instrumente einer Dezentralisierung oder Regionalisierung.

Als Rumänien im Jahr 1918 um große Gebiete erweitert wurde, übernahm es in Siebenbürgen das ungarische Komitatssystem [megye] mit nur geringfügigen Modifikationen. Das war leicht möglich, weil das ungarische System dem rumänischen in Größe und Kompetenzausstattung sehr ähnlich war. Auf die bis dahin österreichische Bukowina wurde das rumänische System ausgedehnt. So gliederte sich das Gebiet des heutigen Rumäniens im Jahr 1930 in 58 Komitate oder Bezirke [județe]. Es unterblieb jeder Versuch, Gruppen von Bezirken zu Regionen zusammenzufassen. Zentralistische Einstellungen überwogen. Sie wurden v.a. von der National-liberalen Partei [Partidul Național-Liberal] unter Brătianu gefördert, die von 1922 bis 1928 und von 1934 bis 1937 an der Macht war. Diese Partei verstand sich als Anwalt der Interessen des „Alten Königreichs" (Moldau, Walachei, Dobrudscha) gegenüber den „neuen Provinzen". Nur eine kurze Zeit lang, von 1928 bis 1930, versuchte eine Koalition aus der National-liberalen Partei [Partidul Național-Liberal] Siebenbürgens und der Nationalen Bauernpartei [Partidul Național Țărănesc] im „Alten Königreich", geführt von Iuliu Maniu, eine Dezentralisierung. Maniu war aber zu kurz an der Macht, um dieses Vorhaben durchsetzen zu können. Im Oktober 1930 trat er aus Protest gegen die Rückkehr König Carol II. aus dem Exil zurück (RONNÅS 1984, S. 37).

Nach der ersten kommunistischen Verfassung aus 1948 veränderte die Verwaltungsreform des Jahres 1950 das administrativ-territoriale System Rumäniens grundlegend. Nach sowjetischem Vorbild schuf sie zum ersten Mal in Rumänien ein dreistufiges System, das sich aus 16 Regionen [regiunea] plus Bukarest [București] als der ersten Stufe, 150 (später 152) Rajons [raionul] als der zweiten Stufe und mehr als 4000 Gemeinden [comună] und Städten [oraș] als der dritten Stufe zusammensetzte. Die Regionen wären groß genug und historischen Landschaften[6] genügend angepaßt gewesen, um regionale Identifikation und Dezentralisierung in politischer und wirtschaftlicher Hinsicht zu bewirken. Das war aber nicht ihr Zweck. Ihre Kompetenzen waren wiederum auf die Transmission zentral getroffener Entscheidungen auf die regionale Ebene beschränkt. Außerdem verhinderte das monolithische und alle Sphären des sozialen und wirtschaftlichen Lebens durchdringende kommunistische Parteisystem mit einer strikt von oben nach unten gerichteten Entscheidungsstruktur ohnehin jede Dezentralisierung.

Als einzige Konzession an regionale Selbstverwaltung wurde eine autonome Region der ungarischen Volksgruppe im östlichen Teil Siebenbürgens eingerichtet. Dies geschah 1952 unter sowjetischem Druck und als Tribut an das in der kommunistischen Ära viel deklamierte Prinzip der internationalen Solidarität. Die Selbstverwaltung dieser Region hielt sich aber in engen Grenzen

---

[6] Einige von ihnen waren nach historischen Gebieten benannt: Banat, Crișana, Maramureș, Oltenia, Dobrogea.

und stellte die ungarische Minderheit nicht zufrieden. Nachdem die Region 1960 verkleinert worden war, wurde sie 1968 im Zuge des national-rumänischen Kurses der Ära Ceauşescu wieder aufgelöst.

Auf der Grundlage der Verfassung des Jahres 1965, die nationale Eigenständigkeit und historische Bezüge betonte, brachte die Verwaltungsreform des Jahres 1968 die Rückkehr zum traditionellen rumänischen Zweistufen-System, indem sie 39 Bezirke [judeţe] und 2706 Gemeinden [comună] einrichtete. Abgesehen von der Rückkehr zu traditionellen, ursprünglich rumänischen Verwaltungsstrukturen war es das Hauptziel dieser Reform, die räumlichen Disparitäten innerhalb Rumäniens zu vermindern. Das sollte durch Verteilung höherrangiger zentralörtlicher Funktionen über eine größere Zahl von Städten und durch Berücksichtigung zentralörtlicher Beziehungen bei der räumlichen Konfiguration der Bezirke erreicht werden. Auch die Kongruenz mit regionalen Identitäten und dem früheren Komitatssystem galten als Ziele, wenn auch nur in zweiter Linie.

Die Reform ergab eine Verwaltungsgliederung, die sich von der bis zum Jahr 1950 gültigen erheblich unterschied. Es verminderte sich gegenüber der alten Bezirksgliederung nicht nur die Zahl der Bezirke von 52 auf 39[7], man vollzog auch viele zusätzliche Grenzänderungen. Was Funktionen und Kompetenzen der Bezirke anbelangt, war das System des Jahres 1968 nicht stärker dezentralisiert als das alte Bezirkssystem. Alle Gremien blieben den zentralen Instanzen in Bukarest verantwortlich und hatten nur deren Entscheidungen umzusetzen (MAYER 1977, S. 83). Im Jahr 1981 ließ eine Reorganisation im Umland von Bukarest die Zahl der Bezirke auf 40 steigen (plus Bukarest), ansonsten blieb das System aber bis heute unverändert.

Auch die jüngste Diskussion um Makro- oder Entwicklungsregionen (Development regions), in denen jeweils 4 bis 7 Bezirke zusammengefaßt würden[8], wird an dieser Situation nichts ändern, da diese Regionen nicht als eine zusätzliche Verwaltungsstufe mit eigenen Gremien und Selbstverwaltungsrechten konzipiert sind, sondern lediglich flexible Zusammenschlüsse von Bezirken zum Zwecke gemeinsamer Planung darstellen würden (Romanian Government & European Commission 1997).

Eine Zusammenschau der Verwaltungsreformen seit 1919, welche die jeweils erste Stufe von Verwaltungseinheiten (Bezirke oder Regionen) berücksichtigt, bietet somit ein recht verwirrendes Bild (Abb. 2). Nur wenige Grenzen erhielten sich über diese ganze Zeitspanne hinweg, hauptsächlich „natürliche" Grenzen auf Gebirgskämmen und an Flüssen. Nur fleckenhaft verbreitet sind jene Gebiete, die stets vom selben Regionalzentrum aus verwaltet wurden.

Es ist das Verwaltungsmuster eines Staates, in welchem Verwaltungseinheiten nur Transmissionsriemen der Zentralgewalt und ihrer wechselnden Raumordnungskonzeptionen sind und weder Eigenständigkeit, noch Dauerhaftigkeit entwickeln können.

---

[7] Der ursprüngliche Plan sah 36 Bezirke vor. Brăila, Mehedinţi und Sălaj wurden in Entsprechung lokaler Wünsche hinzugefügt (RONNÅS 1984, S. 62).

[8] Die Vorschläge sehen 8 Entwicklungsregionen (Bukarest wäre eine eigene Region) vor, die sich deutlich an die historischen Gebiete oder Kulturlandschaften anlehnen, aber nicht deren Namen übernehmen. So würde die Region, die im wesentlichen dem Banat entspricht, „Entwicklungsregion West" benannt sein.

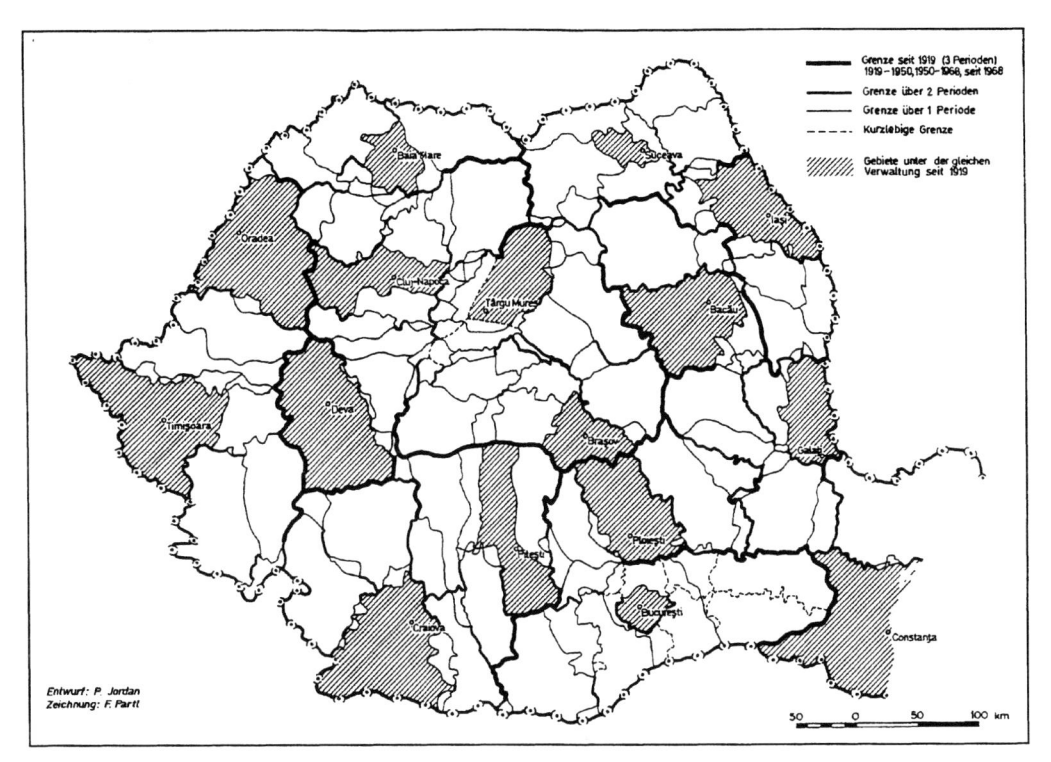

Abb. 2: Verwaltungsgliederungen 1919–1999 (Stabilität der Grenzen)

3. Regionale Identitäten heute

Drei grundlegende und etliche kleinere Veränderungen des Verwaltungssystems sowie eine Tradition des Verwaltungszentralismus konnten dennoch nicht das auf historische Gebiete bezogene Regionalbewußtsein tilgen (RONNÅS 1984, S. 22). Die französische Geographin Violette REY bemerkt nach dem politischen Umbruch zur Jahreswende 1989/90 sogar eine signifikant stärkere Identifizierung der Bevölkerung mit historischen Regionen unabhängig von ethnischen Zugehörigkeiten und interpretiert dies als Reaktion auf die Gleichmacherei in der kommunistischen Ära (REY 1994, S. 362).

Historische und Kulturregionen, die sich bis heute eine ausgeprägte Identität bewahrt haben, sind in Abb. 3 wiedergegeben. Wo ihre Grenzen von den aktuellen Grenzen aggregierter Bezirke abweichen, sind sie strichliert gezogen. Einige der Kulturregionen könnte man auch noch weiter unterteilen.

Das *Banat* ist immer noch eine im wesentlichen multiethnische Region mit einer wahrhaft multikulturellen Identität. Diese wurde durch die hauptsächlich im 18. Jahrhundert erfolgte fast gleichzeitige und gleichberechtigte Kolonisation eines davor kaum besiedelten und genutzten Landes[9] durch eine Vielfalt ethni-

---

[9] Das Banat war von seiner früheren ungarischen Bevölkerung schon zur Zeit der Eroberung durch die Osmanen größtenteils verlassen und durch die österreichisch-türkischen Kriege

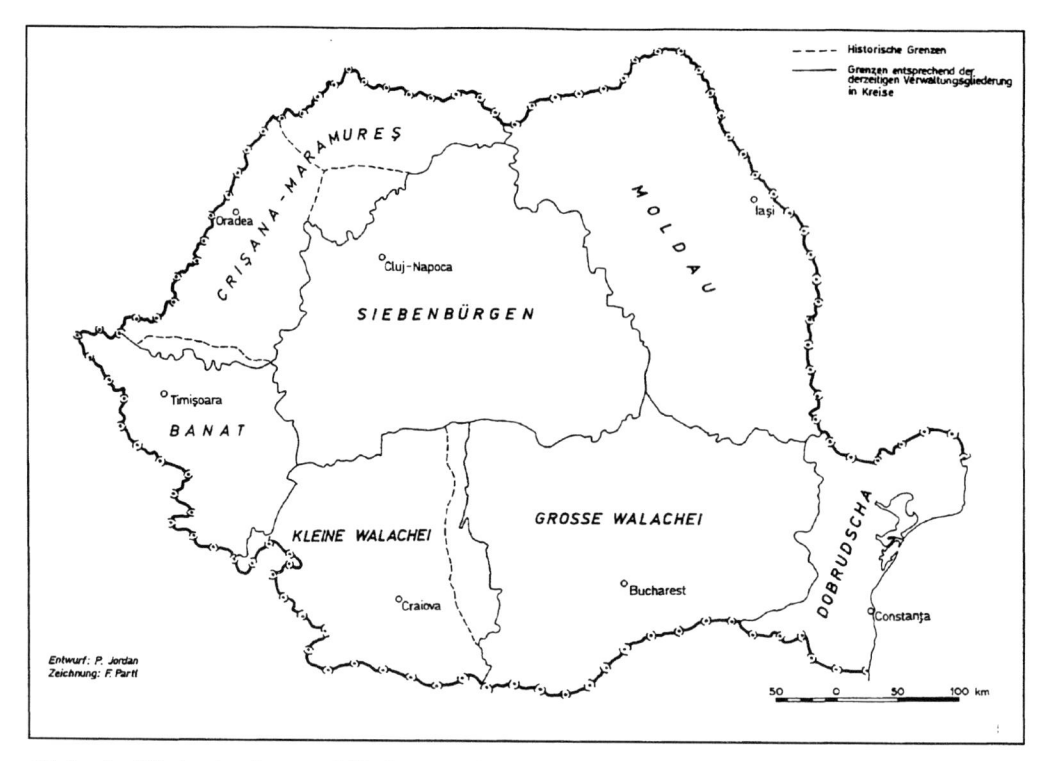

Abb. 3: Historische und Kulturregionen

begründet. Diese Identität wird noch unterstrichen durch die Ausdehnung der historischen Region und ihre Grenzlandrolle über bzw. zwischen drei Staaten, deren Staatsvölker drei verschiedenen Völker- und Sprachgruppen angehören.

Im Jahr 1989 und danach spielte das Banat und besonders sein Zentrum, Temesvar [Timişoara], in der rumänischen Revolution und als Brückenkopf westlichen Einflusses und westlicher Investitionstätigkeit in Rumänien eine bedeutende Rolle. Seine Westorientierung und seine verhältnismäßig gut entwickelte Wirtschaft sind ebenfalls Bestandteile seiner regionalen Identität.

Die Region *Kreischgebiet-Marmarosch* [Crişana-Maramureş] gründet historisch auf dem Partium, ist aber weniger homogen als das Banat. Man könnte sie zumindest in das Kreischgebiet [Crişana] und in die Marmarosch [Maramureş] unterteilen, in zwei Subregionen mit unterschiedlicher ethnischer Struktur. Während im Kreischgebiet die Ungarn die größte Minderheit sind, beruht die Identität der Marmarosch auch auf einer beachtlichen ruthenischen Minderheit. Auch der Bezirk Sălaj ist ein relativ eigenständiger Teil dieser Region. Er wechselte in der Geschichte häufig die politische Zuordnung. Das Sathmarer Gebiet [Satu Mare] hat auch deutsche Traditionen.

Westorientierung ist ein gemeinsames Merkmal der ganzen Region. Sie nimmt jedoch mit der Entfernung von der ungarischen Grenze ab und ist in der Marmarosch am geringsten entwickelt.

---

schwer in Mitleidenschaft gezogen worden. Die vom Wiener Hof in die Region gerufenen Kolonisten des 18. Jahrhunderts fanden zumeist versumpftes und verstepptes Land vor.

Die Identität des historischen *Siebenbürgens* [Transilvania] festigte sich durch die lange Selbstverwaltung der drei historischen „Nationen", der Szekler[10], der Sachsen[11] und der Ungarn. Weitere Komponenten sind die von den Sachsen begründete frühe städtische Kultur und die erhalten gebliebene Multiethnizität. Nicht zum wenigsten trägt auch das Regionalbewußtsein der rumänischen Bevölkerung zur regionalen Identität Siebenbürgens bei. Noch in der Zwischenkriegszeit bekannte sie sich zu einem großen Teil (1930: 30% der siebenbürgischen Bevölkerung) zur westorientierten griechisch-katholischen, mit Rom unierten Kirche.[12] Ab dem späten 18. Jahrhundert spielte Siebenbürgen wegen seines westlich beeinflußten, aufgeklärten Rumänentums die Rolle eines Piemont der rumänischen Nationalbewegung und nationalen Einigung. Auch heute noch ist den Rumänen Siebenbürgens den Rumänen außerhalb des Karpatenbogens gegenüber ein gewisses Sendungsbewußtsein eigen, das sich auch in einem Überlegenheitsgefühl äußern kann.

Die Identität der *Moldau* ist die des historischen, politischen und kulturellen Kernlandes der Rumänen. Viel größer als heute (einschließlich des späteren Bessarabiens), konnte sie sich im 15. Jahrhundert unter Stephan dem Großen [Ştefan cel mare] (1457–1504) aus ungarischer Dominanz lösen und als politisch mächtiges Land auch kulturelle Kraft entfalten. Sie präsentiert sich heute als eine Schatzkammer rumänischer Kulturdenkmäler („Moldauklöster") und besitzt immer noch kulturelle Strahlkraft (Rumäniens zweitgrößte Universität in Iaşi). Doch ist ihre frühere, für den politischen und wirtschaftlichen Aufstieg maßgebende strategische Position an der Schnittstelle der Interessenssphären von Osmanen, Habsburgern, Polen und Russen verloren gegangen. Nach der Vereinigung der Donaufürstentümer litt die Moldau außerdem unter der Verlagerung politischer und wirtschaftlicher Zentralität in die Walachei. So hat die Moldau, die bis zum Ende des vorigen Jahrhunderts wirtschaftlich besser entwickelt und dichter besiedelt gewesen war als die Walachei, an wirtschaftlicher Bedeutung eingebüßt (REY/BRUNET 1996, S. 174).

Die *Große Walachei* oder *Muntenien* [Muntenia] ist die heutige Kernregion Rumäniens. Sie hat sowohl von der Vereinigung der Donaufürstentümer als auch von den Gebietszuwächsen im Jahr 1878 (Dobrudscha) und nach dem Ersten Weltkrieg am meisten profitiert. Sie erholte sich dadurch von osmanischer Dominanz schneller und konnte ihre Wirtschaft besser modernisieren als der Rest des „Alten Königreichs". Ihre Stärken sind die Hauptstadt Bukarest, Rumäniens Tor zur Welt und ein Innovationszentrum, sowie ihre günstige Lage im internationalen Verkehrsnetz. Die regionale Identität der Großen Walachei ist die des rumänischen Rückgrats.

---

[10] Eine kurz nach der ungarischen Landnahme (9./10. Jahrhundert) von den ungarischen Königen als Grenzwächter angesiedelte Volksgruppe ungewisser ethnischer Abstammung, die sich schon seit langem als Teil des ungarischen Volks fühlt und Ungarisch spricht.

[11] Im 12. und 13. Jahrhundert von den ungarischen Königen ins Land gerufene Moselfranken, die mit dem für Deutschsprechende landesüblichen Namen „Sachsen" benannt wurden. Sie traten im Zuge der Reformation fast geschlossen zum Luthertum über.

[12] Die griechisch-katholische oder unierte Kirche anerkennt den römischen Papst und die Dogmatik der katholischen Kirche, pflegt aber den byzantinischen Ritus der Orthodoxie. Sie wurde als westorientierte Kraft unter den Rumänen Siebenbürgens vom Wiener Hof gefördert.

Die Kleine *Walachei* oder *Oltenien* [Oltenia] gilt als die kleine Schwester der Großen Walachei, wirtschaftlich weniger entwickelt und in einer ungünstigen Verkehrslage. Sie kann weder auf eine ruhmreiche eigene politische Vergangenheit zurückblicken, noch ein außergewöhnliches kulturelles Erbe vorweisen. Auch ihre Grenzlandfunktionen sind nicht erheblich. Ihre Identität ist daher vom Image der Provinz geprägt.

Die *Dobrudscha* [Dobrogea] ist bestimmt durch ihre lange und direkte Beherrschung durch das Osmanische Reich (bis 1878), ihre früher intensive ethnische Mischung, die einige Spuren hinterlassen hat, und ihre etwas abgelegene Position „am anderen Ufer der Donau". Wegen ihrer Funktion als Rumäniens Tor zu den Meeren, als das Haupttourismusgebiet des Landes und ausgestattet mit dem Donaudelta [Delta Dunarii] als einem der wertvollsten Naturreservate Europas verfügt sie jedoch über etliche Entwicklungsperspektiven. Sie bietet so Ansatzpunkte für positive Identifikation.

4. Was hindert Rumänien an Regionalisierung und Dezentralisierung?

Berücksichtigt man die natürlichen und historischen Voraussetzungen, die starke und wieder auflebende Identifikation der Bevölkerung mit ihrer Region ohne separatistischen Hintergrund sowie den europäischen Trend zur Stärkung regionaler Strukturen, so erhebt sich die Frage, was Rumänien daran hindert, sich zu regionalisieren und zu dezentralisieren.

4.1. Rumäniens unitaristische Tradition von Anfang an

Wie schon gezeigt, war bereits die Vereinigung der beiden Donaufürstentümer von radikalem Zentralismus begleitet, der sich ohne jede Unterbrechung bis heute fortsetzte. Die jetzt gültige rumänische Verfassung vom 8. Dezember 1991 bestätigt diese Grundhaltung, indem sie Rumänien als einen „unitären, unauflöslichen Nationalstaat" bezeichnet, „über den das rumänische Volk die Souveränität ausübt".

4.2. Das „siebenbürgische Dilemma"

Als Rumänien im Jahr 1918 in den Besitz der früher österreichisch-ungarischen Gebiete innerhalb des Karpatenbogens und in der Bukowina gelangte, war es mit der Aufgabe konfrontiert, ein sehr großes, deutlich besser entwickeltes und westorientiertes Territorium einzugliedern. Auch wenn dieses Territorium eine rein rumänische Bevölkerung gehabt hätte, wäre diese Aufgabe schwer genug gewesen. Kein anderes Land Europas war in der jüngeren Geschichte imstande, einen so großen Gebietsgewinn auf Dauer zu halten.

> Wenn man nur jene Gebietszuwächse in Betracht zieht, die auch heute noch zu Rumänien gehören, wuchs Rumänien im Jahr 1918 der Fläche nach um 74% und der Bevölkerung nach um ca. 70% (PÁNDI 1995, S. 402). Berücksichtigt man auch noch die nördliche Bukowina, Bessarabien und die südliche Dobrudscha, die später wieder verloren

gingen, machten die Zugewinne sogar 213% der Fläche wie auch der Bevölkerung nach aus (PÁNDI 1995, S. 402).

Die Gebietsgewinne Rumäniens, die bis heute gehalten werden konnten, stehen nur denen Serbiens nach, wenn man die Bildung eines Staates der Serben, Kroaten und Slowenen im Jahr 1919 als eine Expansion Serbiens ansieht (Flächenzuwachs 171%, Bevölkerungszuwachs ca. 200%). Sie ähneln der Erweiterung der tschechischen Länder um die Slowakei und die Karpato-Ukraine[13] nach dem Ersten Weltkrieg der Fläche nach (79%), übertreffen diese aber der Bevölkerung nach bei weitem (32%). Sie übertreffen auch die Gebietsgewinne Polens nach dem Zweiten Weltkrieg in bezug auf sein endgültiges Territorium (60% Flächenzuwachs).

Serbien und Tschechien haben ihre „Gebietsgewinne" mittlerweile wieder verloren. Polen kolonisierte Gebiete, die von ihrer autochthonen Bevölkerung verlassen werden mußten und befand sich damit in einer von Rumänien sehr verschiedenen Position.

Andere Gebietsgewinne europäischer Staaten in jüngerer Zeit, die erfolgreich integriert werden konnten, waren wesentlich kleiner: der Anschluß der Woiwodina [Vojvodina] an Serbien bedeutete für Serbien einen Zugewinn von 33% nach Fläche und Bevölkerungszahl; durch die Wiedervereinigung der früheren DDR mit Deutschland wuchs das frühere Westdeutschland um 43% (Fläche) bzw. 23% (Bevölkerung).

Abgesehen von den reinen Größenproportionen bezog sich diese Integrationsaufgabe aber auch auf Gebiete mit einem beträchtlich höheren Niveau wirtschaftlicher und sozialer Entwicklung. Weitaus besser entwickelte Gebiete sollten sich also einem schwächeren Zentrum zu- und unterordnen.

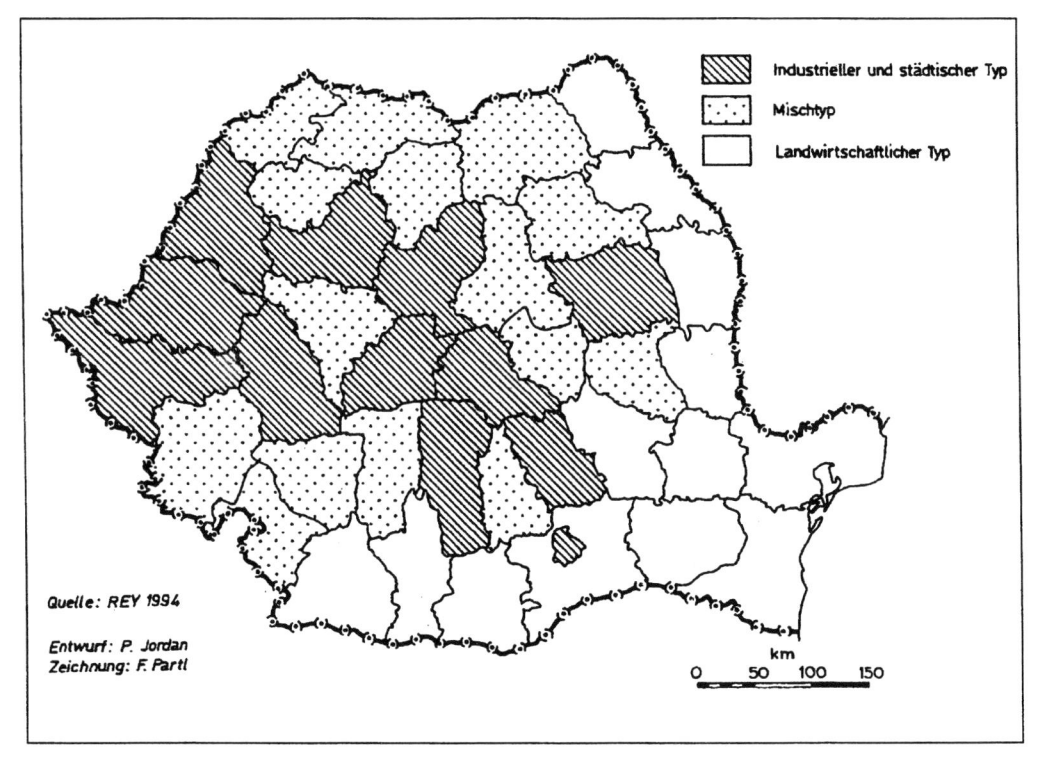

Abb. 4: Sozio-ökonomische Typisierung 1969

---

[13] Noch weniger als im Falle des immerhin von den Serben deutlich dominierten SHS-Staates kann man bei der 1919 gegründeten Tschechoslowakei aber von einer tschechischen Expansion sprechen.

Als die österreichisch-ungarischen Gebiete im Jahr 1918 von Rumänien übernommen wurden, wiesen sie im Vergleich zum rumänischen Altreich ein wesentlich dichteres Eisenbahnnetz, ein ausgebautes Städtesystem, eine soziale Schichtung mit relativ gut ausgebildetem Mittelstand[14] und eine gut entwickelte Industrie auf, obwohl sie innerhalb Österreich-Ungarns zu den rückständigsten Regionen gezählt hatten.

Diese Unterschiede wurden im Laufe der Zeit geringer, verschwanden aber nicht völlig. Violette REY zeigt in ihrer Arbeit „La question régionale dans l´espace roumain" (REY 1994), wie deutlich im Jahr 1969 die sozio-ökonomischen Unterschiede zwischen dem „Alten Königreich" und den 1918 erworbenen Gebieten immer noch waren (Abb. 4).

Die Ceauşescu-Ära mit ihren oft weit über das Ziel schießenden Bemühungen, das Land zu homogenisieren, schritt in der Beseitigung der ererbten Unterschiede tatsächlich relativ weit voran, doch blieben einige weiter bestehen. In einer von Kazimierz ZANIEWSKI entworfenen Karte mit Daten aus der Mitte der 1980er Jahre hebt sich Siebenbürgen immer noch deutlich genug vom Gebiet außerhalb des Karpatenbogens ab, obwohl auch innerhalb Siebenbürgens Unterschiede erkennbar sind (ZANIEWSKI 1992). In der Karte kommt ein „Index des sozialen Wohlstands" (Index of social well-being) zum Ausdruck, der

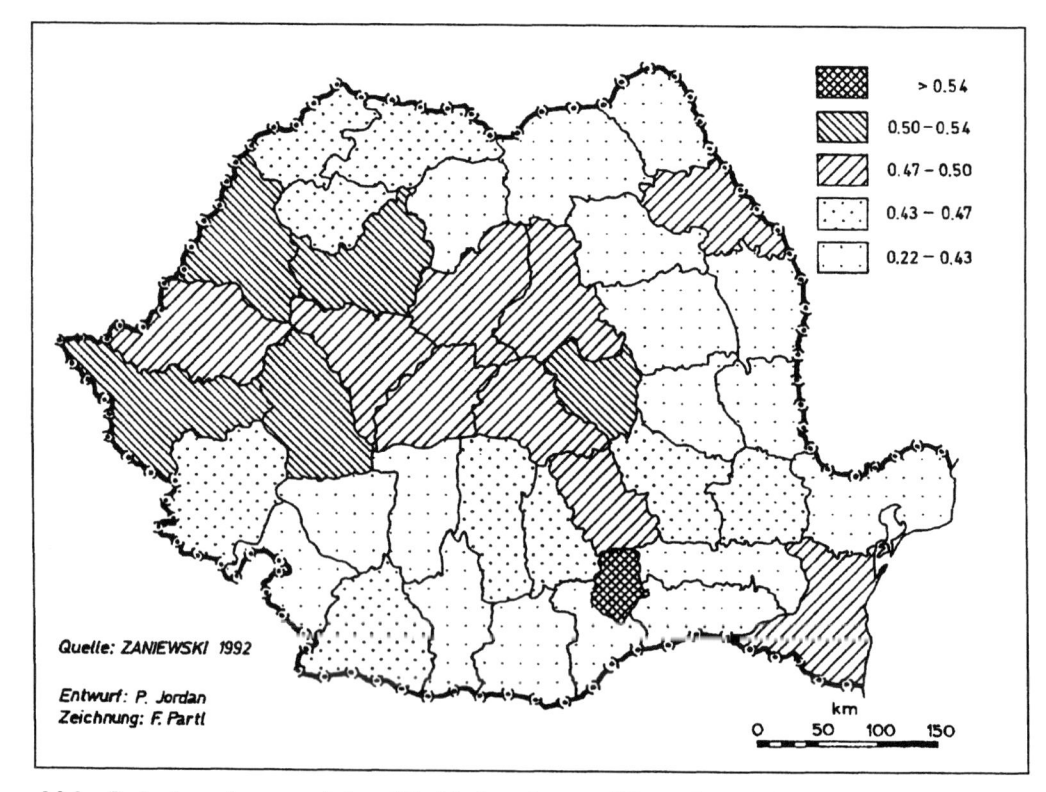

Abb. 5: Index des sozialen Wohlstands zur Mitte der 1980er Jahre

---

[14] In den gerade erst vereinigten Donaufürstentümern lebten 1859/60 nur 17,6% der Bevölkerung in Städten (CIORICEANU 1928). Es gab so gut wie keinen ethnisch-rumänischen Mittelstand (BERINDEI 1989, S. 104).

sich auf Merkmale des Gesundheitsversorgung (Kindersterblichkeit, Spitalsbetten pro Einwohner), auf die Wohnfläche pro Kopf der Bevölkerung und Merkmale der Kommunikationsinfrastruktur (Telephon- und Fernsehanschlüsse pro Kopf der Bevölkerung) stützt (Abb. 5).

Nach der Öffnung der Grenzen im Jahr 1990 und nachdem Rumänien von einem isolierten Staat zu einem Land geworden war, das die wirtschaftliche und politische Integration in Europa anstrebt, haben sich die alten Unterschiede zumindest teilweise wieder verstärkt. Das ist eine Folge der Außen- und Handelsbeziehungen, die (zumindest bisher) Regionen begünstigen, die der ungarischen Grenze näher liegen. Das ist auch eine Folge der wieder wirksam gewordenen Marktkräfte, die ökonomische Standortvorteile wieder mehr wahrnehmen als dies zu Zeiten der kommunistischen Planwirtschaft der Fall war. Einige Indikatoren, die diese Aussagen bestätigen, werden auf zwei von Violette REY entworfenen Karten gezeigt (Abb. 6, REY 1994, S. 371): Die obere stellt Typen der Transformation dar, die auf der Grundlage der Bevölkerungsentwicklung 1989–1992, der Entwicklung der Geburtenhäufigkeit 1989–1992, des Anteils privat bewirtschafteter Flächen an der gesamten landwirtschaftlichen Nutzfläche im Jahr 1992, des Anteils privater Handelsbetriebe an der Gesamtzahl der Handelsbetriebe im Jahr 1992, der Arbeitslosenrate, der Zahl von Telex- oder Fernschreiberanschlüssen pro 1000 Einwohner und des Anteils internationaler Telephongespräche an der Gesamtzahl der Telephongespräche gebildet wurden. Die untere Karte zeigt die Zahl der Telephonanschlüsse pro 10 000 Einwohner im Jahr 1992.

Man kann es verstehen, daß eine Zentralregierung, die sich vor die Aufgabe gestellt sieht, große Gebiete mit einer bis 1918 anderen historischen Entwicklung, mit einem höheren sozio-ökonomischen Niveau und einem anderen Lebensstil zu integrieren, davor zurückscheut, diesen Gebieten regionale Selbstverwaltung zu gewähren und daß sie statt dessen versucht, ein zentralistisches Verwaltungssystem beizubehalten.
Die Position der Zentralverwaltung war besonders nach 1918 prekär. Aber auch das Jahr 1989 mit seinen Folgen stellt wieder eine besondere Herausforderung dar, weil die Gebiete innerhalb des Karpatenbogens ihre traditionelle Westorientierung wieder kulturell und ökonomisch verwerten können und sich dadurch besser entwickeln.

4.3. Die ethnische Gruppe der Ungarn

Die relativ große (1930: 1 426 000, 7,9% der Gesamtbevölkerung Rumäniens; 1992: 1 620 199, 7,1% der Gesamtbevölkerung Rumäniens, 20,7% der Bevölkerung innerhalb des Karpatenbogens) ungarische Minderheit verstärkte und verstärkt das „siebenbürgische Dilemma". Die schiere Zahl wäre für Rumänien noch kein so großes Problem, wenn die ungarische Volksgruppe nicht in Siebenbürgen (innerhalb des Karpatenbogens) lokal und regional dominant in Erscheinung träte. Diese gesellschaftliche Dominanz in von Ungarn kompakter besiedelten Gebieten ist im wesentlichen auf die folgenden Faktoren zurückzuführen:

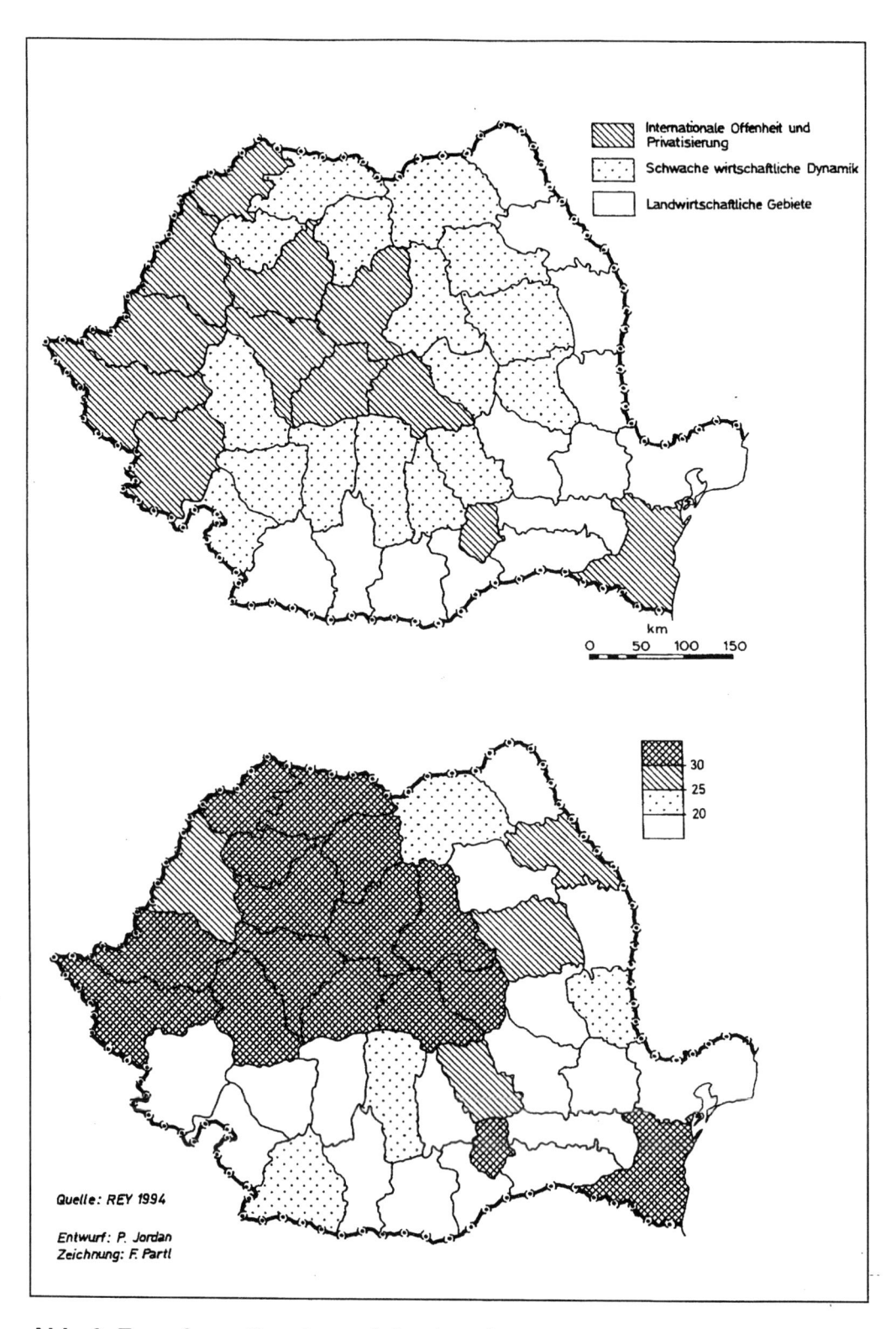

**Abb. 6: Transformationstypen (oben) und
Telex-/Fernschreiberanschlüsse pro 10 000 Einwohner (unten) 1992**

- Die ethnische Gruppe der Ungarn war bis 1918 politisch, sozial und wirtschaftlich die führende Bevölkerungsgruppe in Siebenbürgen. Der Anschluß Siebenbürgens an das „Alte Königreich" im Jahr 1918 bedeutete für die Ungarn eine vollständige Inversion der sozialen Schichtung. Sie wurden mit einem Schlag in eine politische und (durch eine Landreform) auch in eine wirtschaftliche Minderheitenposition versetzt. Eine derartige Umdrehung der Verhältnisse konnte praktisch nur durch eine zentralistische Verwaltung exekutiert werden. Im kollektiven Gedächtnis der Rumänen wie auch der Ungarn ist die frühere soziale Schichtung immer noch präsent und wirkt als eine psychologische Barriere zwischen den beiden. Viele Rumänen halten die Ungarn immer noch für fähig, unter dezentralisierten Verhältnissen regional ihre frühere sozio-ökonomische Position wieder zu erlangen.

- Die ethnische Gruppe der Ungarn verfügt über eine ausgeprägte kulturelle Identität. Sie bewahrt ihre Sprache, führt ein aktives, gut organisiertes Gemeinschaftsleben, hat ihr Bildungssystem und enge persönliche und kulturelle Kontakte mit dem benachbarten Ungarn (einschließlich des Empfangs ungarischer Fernseh- und Radioprogramme).

- Die Ungarn in Rumänien genießen hohes Kulturprestige, was sogar Angehörige anderer ethnischer Minderheiten in Rumänien (z.B. Roma, zeitweilig auch Deutsche) dazu veranlaßt, sich in ungarischen Mehrheitsgebieten bei Volkszählungen als Ungarn zu deklarieren oder Ungarisch im außerfamiliären Sprachgebrauch zu verwenden.

- Die ungarische Gruppe in Rumänien ist durch die „Demokratische Union der Ungarn Rumäniens" [UDMR, Uniunea Democată Maghiară din România / A Romaniai Magyar Demokrata Szövetség] politisch gut organisiert und vertreten. Diese ethnische Sammelpartei der Ungarn erhält bei Wahlen üblicherweise mehr Stimmen als bei Volkszählungen ethnische Ungarn gezählt werden und ist an der heute in Rumänien regierenden konservativen Koalition beteiligt. Eine Regionalisierung Rumäniens würde mit großer Wahrscheinlichkeit bedeuten, daß diese Partei zumindest in zwei der dann selbstverwalteten innerkarpatischen Regionen (Siebenbürgen, Kreischgebiet-Marmarosch) großen politischen Einfluß hätte und eventuell sogar die stärkste Einzelpartei wäre (Abb. 7).[15] Die politische Vertretung der ungarischen Minderheit agiert maßvoll, und separatistische oder irredentistische Ziele werden ihr mit Ausnahme kleiner Randgruppen sicherlich zu Unrecht unterstellt. Sie steuert jedoch ein Höchstmaß an Minderheitenrechten an und äußert sich häufig und vernehmlich zu allgemeinen politischen Problemen des Landes. Sie erweckt dadurch bei der rumänischen Mehrheitsbevölkerung oft den Eindruck, die ungarische ethnische Gruppe wäre gegenüber Problemen, die sie genauso betreffen und unter Mißständen, unter denen sie genauso zu leiden hat, übersensibel und strebe nach einem privilegierten Sonderstatus. Unter der rumänischen Mehrheitsbevölkerung ist auch die Meinung weit verbreitet, die ungarische ethnische Gruppe wäre politisch besonders gut vertreten und würde ohnehin erreichen, was sie wollte.

---

[15] Die dort derzeit stärkste Partei, die Demokratische Konvention Rumäniens [Convenția Democată din România, CDR], ist ein loses Wahlbündnis aus mehreren Einzelparteien (MANGOTT et al. 1998, S. 4ff).

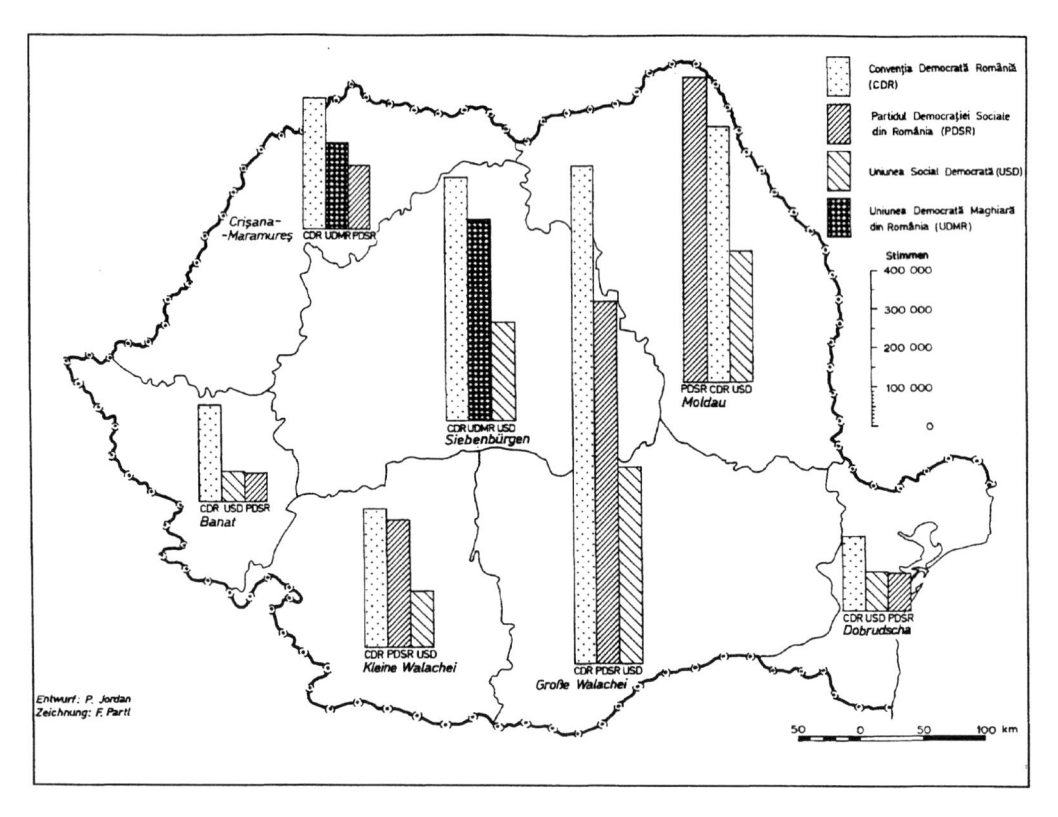

Abb. 7: Abschneiden der jeweils größten drei Parteien bei den Parlamentswahlen November 1996 (Abgeordnetenhaus)

- Die ungarische Minderheit in Rumänien wird seit 1990 von Ungarn aus zumindest auf kulturellem Gebiet unterstützt, was bei Rumänen Irredenta-Ängste nährt.

- Die Ungarn in Rumänien sind wirtschaftlich mehr als das rumänische Mehrheitsvolk und als andere ethnische Gruppen von der wieder offenen Grenze mit Ungarn, einem der Vorreiter des Reformprozesses im östlichen Europa, begünstigt. Die Vorteile entstehen v.a. durch die verwandtschaftlichen und persönlichen Beziehungen nach Ungarn, durch die gemeinsame Sprache zusätzlich zur Kenntnis des Rumänischen, durch leichteren Zugang zu Informationen und durch ungarische Investitionen in den von Ungarn bewohnten Gebieten Rumäniens (FIDRMUC 1995).

In den Augen vieler Rumänen überschattet die durch diese Faktoren bewirkte Dominanz die Tatsachen, daß die Ungarn heute in Rumänien nur im östlichen Teil Siebenbürgens (im Szeklerland) und weit entfernt von der ungarischen Staatsgrenze ein ethnisch kompaktes Gebiet bewohnen, aber ansonsten räumlich gestreut sind (siehe JORDAN 1995a) und daß ihre Bevölkerungszahl abnimmt (1977–1992: -5,5%).

5. Quellen und Literatur

Academia Română, Institutul de Geografie (1996): România. Atlas istorico-geografic. Bucureşti.
BERENTSEN, W.H. (Hg.) (1997): Contemporary Europe. A Geographic Analysis. 7. Aufl., New York, Chichester, Weinheim, Brisbane, Toronto, Singapore.
BERINDEI, D. (1989): Sozial-kulturelle Aspekte der Gesellschaft Rumäniens im Jahrzehnt vor der Erringung der Unabhängigkeit (1866-1876). In: W. LUKAN, A. GOTTSMANN (Hg.): Beiträge zur Geschichte und Kultur Südosteuropas, Wien, S. 99-112.
CIORICEANU, G. (1928): La Roumanie économique et ses rapports avec l'étranger de 1860 à 1915. Paris.
FIDRMUC, J. (1995): Ethnic Minorities and Regional Unemployment. In: The Regional Dimension of Unemployment in Transition Countries, hg. v. OECD, Paris, S. 382-395.
FOUCHER, M. (1993): Fragments d'Europe. o.Ort.
FOUCHER, M. et al. (1993): The Next Europe. An Essay on Alternatives and Strategies towards a new Vision of Europe. Hanover.
HELIN, R. (1967): The volatile administrative map of Romania. In: Annals of the Association of American Geographers, Jg. LVII, Nr. 3.
IORDAN, I.; REY, V. (1994): La carte administrative de la Romanie: probable ou impossible retour à l'etat d'avant-guerre? In: Bulletin de la Société languedocienne de géographie, Nr. 4.
JORDAN, P. (1992a): Die Regionen des mittleren Donauraums im Hinblick auf die europäische Integration. In: Geographica Slovenica, Bd. 23, S. 187-208.
JORDAN, P. (1992b): Regionale Identität in Mitteleuropa im Hinblick auf die europäische Integration. In: Mitteilungen der Österreichischen Geographischen Gesellschaft, Jg. 134, S. 177-188.
JORDAN, P. (1995a): Ethnische Struktur Südosteuropas um 1992 [1: 1,500.000]. In: Atlas Ost- und Südosteuropa, hg. v. Österreichischen Ost- u. Südosteuropa-Institut, red. v. P. JORDAN, Wien, Nr. 2.7-S1.
JORDAN, P. (1995b): Rumänien – permanente Peripherie Europas? In: Zeitschrift für den Erdkundeunterricht, Jg. 47, Nr. 2, S. 42-51.
KLEMENČIĆ, M. (1997). Atlas Europe. Zagreb.
MAGOCSI, P.R. (1993): Historical Atlas of East Central Europe. Seattle, London.
MANGOTT, G.; HEUBERGER, V.; JORDAN, P. (1998): Die Wahlen der Jahre 1994–1997 in Mittel- und Südosteuropa. Begleittext zur Karte im Atlas Ost- und Südosteuropa, hg. v. Österreichischen Ost- und Südosteuropa-Institut, red. v. P. JORDAN, Wien, Nr. 6.2-G5.
MAYER, F. (1977): Staat – Verfassung – Recht – Verwaltung. In: GROTHUSEN, K.-D. (Hg.): Rumänien. Südosteuropa-Handbuch, Bd. II, Göttingen.
PÁNDI, L. (1995): Köztes-Európa 1763-1993 (Térképgyüjtemény). Budapest.
REY, V. (1994): La question régionale dans l'espace roumain. In: L'espace géographique, Bd. 4, S. 361-376.
Romanian Government and European Commission (1997). Green Paper. Regional Development Policy in Romania. Bucureşti.
RONNÅS, P. (1984): Urbanization in Romania. Stockholm.
SLAWINSKI, I. (1989): Verwaltungsgliederung Ost- und Südosteuropas. Begleittext zur Karte im Atlas Ost- und Südosteuropa, hg. v. Österreichischen Ost- und Südosteuropa-Institut, red. v. P. JORDAN, Wien, Nr. 5.1-G1.
ZANIEWSKI, K. (1992): Regional Inequalities in Social Well-being in Central and Eastern Europe. In: Tijdschrift voor economische en sociale geografie, Jg. 83, Nr. 5, S. 342-352.

Aspekte der Urbanisierung, der Verkehrsentwicklung und der Umweltprobleme Japans [1]

Walther MANSHARD (Freiburg i. Br.)

Selected Aspects of Urbanisation, Transportation development, and Environmental problems in Japan

Abstract

The paper gives a synopsis of three main problems in contemporary Japan: the continuous growth of Tokyo and other large urban agglomerations, the phenomena of migration, commuting and transportation development, and the environmental problems and anti-pollution measures. The situation which in many ways – also with regard to the political and legal framework – differs from the European situation is characterised on account of the author's experiences.

Kurzfassung

Der Beitrag gibt einen Überblick über drei Hauptprobleme Japans: das nach wie vor anhaltende Wachstum von Tokyo und anderen großen Agglomerationen, die damit zusammenhängenden Bevölkerungsbewegungen und Verkehrsentwicklungen sowie die Probleme und Maßnahmen im Umweltbereich. Es wird die Situation in Japan, die von der europäischen in vielfacher, darunter auch rechtlicher Hinsicht abweicht, aufgrund eigener Erfahrungen charakterisiert.

Zur Jahrtausendwende wird Japan eine Bevölkerung von über 130 Mio. Menschen aufweisen, d.h. im Vergleich zu 1930 eine doppelt so hohe Einwohnerzahl – und das trotz des Zusammenschrumpfens der Fläche Japans nach dem Zweiten Weltkrieg auf 55 % des ehemaligen Areals (Flüchter 1998).

Für die Zukunft des Landes sind die Fragenkomplexe Urbanisierung, Verkehrsentwicklung und Umweltprobleme von entscheidender Bedeutung, und jeder, der einmal in Japan gewesen ist, nimmt als einen Haupteindruck die

---

[1] Dieser Beitrag zur Kultur- und Wirtschaftsgeographie Japans ist Karl Sinnhuber gewidmet, mit dem mich seit Anfang der 50er Jahre eine enge Freundschaft verbindet. Da ich den mir angetragenen Festvortrag in Wien aus Termingründen nicht übernehmen konnte, möchte ich mich auf diesem Wege an der Festschrift für den Jubilar beteiligen, zumal Karl – auch in der Tradition seines Amtsvorgängers Leopold Scheidl – mehrfach Japan bereist hat.

W. M.

Konzentration des wirtschaftlichen und sozialen Lebens auf wenige Zentren mit, denn sie ist – sogar im Vergleich zu Europa – ausgesprochen hoch. So konzentrieren sich ein großer Teil des ökonomischen Topmanagements, des Großhandels, aller Bankguthaben, der College- und Universitätsstudenten sowie der Computerindustrie allein auf Tokyo und Osaka, wo es zusammen 120 Universitäten und Hochschulen gibt, und zur "Medienlandschaft" viele Fernsehprogramme und mehrere Tageszeitungen mit Millionenauflagen gehören.

Man rechnet für die Metropolregion Tokyo für das Jahr 2015 mit etwa 35 Mio. Einwohnern, das sind fast 28 % der Gesamtbevölkerung, und zwar trotz aller Bestrebungen, diese Wachstumsprozesse zu verlangsamen und die Entwicklung zu dezentralisieren. Der Agglomerationsraum Tokyo wird also seine weltweite Spitzenposition vor New York, Mexico-City, Sao Paulo, Shanghai und Bombay behaupten können.

Um die mit der **Urbanisierung** der letzten Jahrzehnte zusammenhängenden Probleme etwas genauer zu erfassen, soll die Entwicklung im Falle Tokyos in großen Zügen umrissen werden. Unter den Weltstädten ist Tokyo keineswegs ein Neuling. Schon vor über 200 Jahren, im Jahre 1786, war es mit einer Bevölkerung von damals 1,4 Mio. die größte Stadt der Erde. Übrigens noch vor London mit einer knappen Million Einwohner.

Allerdings war Edo, wie es damals noch hieß, im 18. Jahrhundert eigentlich noch keine echte Metropole im heutigen Sinne, da es ziemlich isoliert und vom Rest der Welt abgeschnitten war. Seit dem 17. und verstärkt im 18. Jahrhundert entwickelte sich Edo zum Hauptzentrum als Sitz der Shogune. Kurz vor Mitte des 19. Jahrhunderts, also vor der Öffnung Japans durch die Amerikaner, machten die Samurai etwa ein Drittel der Bevölkerung Edos aus. Der Konsum von Luxusgegenständen durch eine große Zahl von Kriegern, Höflingen, Leibgarden usw. führte zur Ansiedlung zahlreicher Handwerker und Kaufleute. Man nutzte die billigen Arbeitskräfte der im Umland lebenden ländlichen Bevölkerung, und diese Art der Arbeitsteilung konnte nach dem Eindringen der westlichen Technologien z.T. für die industrielle Entfaltung des Landes übernommen werden. 1869 wurde das Fort Edo zur kaiserlichen Residenz; man ging also nicht ins alte Kyoto zurück. Edo wurde als östliche Hauptstadt unter dem Namen Tokyo zur Kapitale des Landes. Nach 1786 verringerte sich die Bevölkerung der Stadt allerdings zunächst und 1873 waren es noch 600.000 Einwohner. Aber bereits 1890 wurde die alte Zahl von 1,4 Mio. wieder erreicht. 1920 waren es 3,4 Mio., und auch das verheerende Erdbeben von 1923 tat der weiteren Entwicklung keinen Abbruch. Die Wohnbezirke dehnten sich weiter nach Westen aus. Die Industrie konzentrierte sich im Süden um den Hafen an der Tokyo-Bay und in Richtung auf Yokohama. Bei Kriegsausbruch 1941 wurde die Sieben-Millionen-Grenze überschritten. Im Zweiten Weltkrieg kam es – ähnlich wie bei uns – durch die Luftangriffe zu einem Rückgang der Bevölkerung. 1945 lebten etwa 3 Mio. Menschen in Tokyo, und fast 60 % aller Häuser waren zerstört.

Das starke Wachstum der Nachkriegszeit hing nicht nur mit der natürlichen Zunahme der Bevölkerung zusammen (hier lag das Maximum eher in den

20er und 30er Jahren), sondern erklärte sich einseitig aus hohen Wachstumsraten durch Zuwanderung, die in den 50er und 60er Jahren z.T. je 200.000 Personen pro Jahr und mehr betrugen. Außerdem erhöhte sich die allgemeine Lebenserwartung, die bis heute in Japan höher liegt als bei uns. Die Hauptkonzentration der Bevölkerung erfolgte räumlich gesehen in den küstennahen Flachlandgebieten, die als Kanto-Ebenen bezeichnet werden, und wo über 25 Mio. Menschen leben, also etwa 20 % der Gesamtbevölkerung Japans.

Strukturell, funktional und von den administrativen Abgrenzungen her lassen sich eine Reihe von Raumeinheiten unterscheiden, unter denen die "Tokyo Metropolitan Government Area" als der Verwaltungsraum Groß-Tokyos besonders auffällt. Es war der erste einheitliche, städtische Verwaltungsraum der Erde, in dem die 10-Mio.-Menschen-"Schallmauer" durchbrochen wurde. Darüber hinaus gibt es eine Gesamt-Agglomeration Groß-Tokyo, das Tokyo der Planer, das eine Region mit einem Radius von etwa 80 bis 100 km vom Zentrum aus umfaßt.

Nach diesem kurzen Blick auf die Entwicklung Tokyos soll die Frage der mit der Urbanisierung zusammenhängenden *Bevölkerungsbewegungen* angesprochen werden. Seit Anfang der 70er Jahre ist in fast allen Industrieländern eine gewisse Rückläufigkeit der bisherigen Bevölkerungsmigration aus den peripheren ländlichen Räumen in die großen Metropolen zu beobachten. Es handelt sich nicht um eine reine "De-Agglomeration", sondern die Bevölkerungswanderungen der jüngsten Zeit verlaufen sehr viel komplexer in verschiedenen Richtungen. Selbstverständlich werden diese Bewegungen hauptsächlich durch räumliche Veränderungen der wirtschaftlichen Möglichkeiten reguliert, und die neu entstehenden Siedlungssysteme, in denen Großstädte und Metropolen weiterhin wichtige Eckpfeiler bilden, müssen im sozio-ökonomischen Rahmen der nationalen Entwicklung Japans gesehen werden. Das Volumen der Binnenwanderung (ausgedrückt in der Zahl der umgezogenen Personen) betrug in Japan zu Anfang der 20er Jahre etwa zwei Mio. In den 50er Jahren stieg diese Zahl auf über 5 Mio., in den späten 60er Jahren dann auf über 7 Mio. an, und 1973 wurde ein Höhepunkt mit 8,5 Mio. erreicht. In den 80er und 90er Jahren hat sich diese Zahl stabilisiert. Die früher rein rural-urbane Migration, eine Art "Landflucht" von der Peripherie zum Zentrum, ist also heute eher multidirektional ausgerichtet.

Nach einem Jahrzehnte andauernden übermächtigen Einströmen der Bevölkerung in die großen Agglomerationsräume scheint sich zur Zeit eher wieder ein Vorkriegsphänomen durchzusetzen, d.h. die jungen Leute gehen in die Städte und die älteren Menschen kehren nach einer gewissen Zeit aufs Land zurück. Dieses sog. "U-Turn", d.h. Umkehrphänomen, verläuft sehr vielschichtig, denn erstens hat sich der Unterschied zwischen ländlicher und städtischer Lebensweise – ähnlich wie bei uns – sehr stark verwischt, und das rural-urbane Kontinuum ist ebenso deutlich ausgeprägt wie in Europa, und zweitens werden von dieser Migration vor allem verstärkt (bis zu 40 %) die sog. "White Collar Workers" und "Salary-men" betroffen, also Fachkräfte, die den Erfordernissen des modernen Managements entsprechend eine höhere Mobilität aufweisen.

Neben den Hauptkonzentrationsgebieten der sog. Tokaido-Megalopolis (d.h. von Tokyo bis Osaka) haben sich in den letzten Jahren vor allem vier weitere Zentren stark vergrößert:
1. Sapporo (Hokkaido)
2. Sendai (Nordhonshu)
3. Hiroshima (Westhonshu)
4. Fukuoka (Nordkyushu).

In diesen Zentren, ebenso wie entlang der Hauptachse Tokyo - Nagoya - Kyoto - Osaka, ist das starke Wachstum des tertiären Sektors auffällig.

Als zentrale Metropole wächst Tokyo auch heute noch weiter, allerdings hauptsächlich in den Vorortbereichen, über die Grenzen der benachbarten Präfekturen in die Kanto-Ebenen hinein. Osaka dagegen, lange Hauptrivale Tokyos in der zentralörtlichen Hierarchie, ist in der Einwohnerzahl nach Yokohama auf den dritten Platz abgestiegen. Allerdings gehört Yokohama funktional gesehen zu Groß-Tokyo und auch die Grenzen des Einflußbereiches von Osaka sind nach allen Seiten fließend.

Wichtig sind im Zusammenhang mit der Urbanisierung die **Verkehrsverhältnisse**. Bekanntlich ist man in Japan mit Expresszügen wie dem "Shinkansen", der im 20-Minuten-Takt die großen Zentren mit Geschwindigkeiten von über 200 km/h miteinander verbindet, sehr erfolgreich gewesen. Kein anderes Land der Erde hat ein ähnliches Hochgeschwindigkeits-Eisenbahnnetz aufgebaut, das gut funktioniert und nicht subventioniert zu werden braucht. In Europa gibt es ja erst Ansätze in dieser Richtung. Man denke an die TGV's (Train à Grand Vitesse) in Frankreich oder die ICE-Schnelltrassen in Deutschland.

Die zweite beachtliche Leistung des japanischen Schienenverkehrs sind die hervorragend ausgebauten und profitträchtigen Nahverkehrsnetze rings um die großen Zentren. Sie werden zum großen Teil von privaten Eisenbahngesellschaften getragen.

Der tägliche Pendelverkehr ist allerdings ein beachtliches Problem, das sich als Agglomerationsnachteil direkt auf die Lebensqualität auswirkt. (Die etwa 3,6 Mio. täglichen Einpendler Tokyos benötigen für eine Wegstrecke im Durchschnitt 75 Minuten; Flüchter 1997).

Auch in Japan macht sich zunehmend die Konkurrenz Schiene - Straße und vor allem Flugzeug - Schiene bemerkbar. Flugzeug und Autobus sind überall zum Massenverkehrsmittel geworden. Im Vergleich zum Schienenverkehr bietet der Autoverkehr besonders in den Agglomerationen kaum eine Alternative. Zähflüssiger Verkehr und lange Staus sind die Regel.

Vor allem die schwierigen Reliefverhältnisse mit einem Gebirgsanteil von über 70 % haben den modernen Verkehrsausbau erschwert. So kommt besonders den innerjapanischen Fluglinien eine wesentliche Bedeutung zu.

Die **Umweltproblematik** Japans soll vor allem in bezug auf die Städte betrachtet werden. Im Japanischen spricht man bei der Umweltschädigung vom sog. "Kogai"-Phänomen, was soviel heißt wie "öffentliche Störung, Schaden, Mißbrauch, Ärgernis". Ein Hauptcharakterzug Japans war und ist die außerordentliche Konzentration von Bevölkerung und Industrie auf sehr engem Raum. Über 60 % der Bevölkerung leben in Agglomerationsräumen, die zusammen nur wenige Prozent der Gesamtfläche einnehmen. Ein Resultat dieser Ballung ist der Grad der Umweltbelastung pro Quadratkilometer bewohnter Fläche, der deshalb viel höher ist als in den meisten anderen Ländern der Erde.

Diese räumliche Konstellation führte zu einer hohen Konzentration umweltbelastender Industrien (z.B. Schwerindustrie, Zementproduktion, Holz- und Papierverarbeitung, Textilindustrie, Chemische Industrie, Wärmekraftwerke usw.). Hinzu kam die schnelle Zunahme des Verkehrs, bei einem eher zögerlichen Ausbau der erforderlichen Infrastrukturen (z.B. des Straßennetzes, aber auch der Abwässerentlastung, Abfallbeseitigung usw.).

Diese Entwicklungen, vor allem das in den ersten Nachkriegsjahrzehnten fast uneingeschränkte wirtschaftliche Wachstum, führten dazu, daß Japan zeitweise eines der extremsten Beispiele für eine geradezu verheerende Umweltverschmutzung war. Damals machte das böse Wort vom "ökologischen Harakiri" die Runde (Gunnarson 1974).

In diesem kurzen Überblick sollen nun einige wichtige Punkte erwähnt werden:

1. Die Luftverunreinigung: Sie wird hauptsächlich durch industrielle Abgase, Wärmekraftwerke und den KFZ-Verkehr verursacht. Daneben spielen zunehmend auch sekundär eingeleitete photochemische Prozesse eine Rolle. Während man einige Verunreinigungen (SO_2, Schwermetallbelastung durch Kadmium, Blei) durch schnell greifende Maßnahmen wie Katalysatoren einigermaßen in den Griff bekommen hat – früher jedenfalls als bei uns -, sieht die Situation im photochemischen Bereich nicht so günstig aus.

2. Das Wasser, d.h. sowohl Süß- als auch Meerwasser: In und um die großen Agglomerationen ist die Belastung sehr hoch. Man braucht sich nur einmal die Abwasserkanäle oder die kanalisierten Flußrinnen in Tokyo oder Osaka anzusehen. Starke Grundwasserentnahme und die Bodenversiegelung führten zum Sinken des Grundwasserspiegels.
Auch die küstennahen Gewässer sind stark belastet. Die Schwermetallverunreinigung (z.B. durch Kadmium, Quecksilber, Blei, Arsen) ist zwar etwas vermindert worden. Ein wichtiges Problem war lange die unzureichende Entsorgung der privaten Haushalte.

3. Der Boden: Ähnlich wie in Deutschland weisen auch die Böden Japans in den Ballungsgebieten sehr hohe Konzentrationen toxischer Bestandteile auf (z.B. Kadmium, Kupfer, Blei, Arsen, PCB). Ähnlich wie bei uns drohen von alten und neuen Abfalldeponien, den sog. "Altlasten", Gefahren, die noch längst nicht alle erkannt und erfaßt sind.

Schließlich sollte noch ein weiterer Faktor erwähnt werden, der gerade in Japan auffälliger ist als bei uns:

4. Die Lärmbelästigung: Aufgrund der Leichtbauweise und der sehr engräumigen Anlage der Häuser ist der Verkehrslärm, ebenso wie andere Lärmquel-

len (Fabriken, Baustellen) ein Ärgernis, das man noch kaum in den Griff bekommen hat.

Im Gegensatz zu einigen Präfekturen, wo lokale und regionale Maßnahmen für den Umweltschutz schon früher ergriffen wurden, begann die Umweltpolitik der Zentralregierung erst Ende der 60er Jahre aktiver zu werden. 1967 wurden die ersten grundlegenden Umweltgesetze verabschiedet. Bis dahin waren diese Fragen weitgehend ignoriert worden. Erst nachdem die Öffentlichkeit durch zahlreiche Erkrankungen und Todesfälle immer mehr aufgeschreckt wurde, sah sich die Regierung zu Maßnahmen veranlaßt, und zwar in einem auch für unsere Verhältnisse sehr weitgehenden und positiven Ausmaß, von dem auch wir lernen könnten.

Seit Anfang der 70er Jahre wurde das japanische Parlament aktiv. Damals wurden sehr scharfe Maßnahmen eingeleitet und anschließend von den Gerichten durchgesetzt. Kompensationszahlungen für die Opfer wurden beschlossen. Das bei uns im allgemeinen übliche, lückenlose und beweisende, mehr oder minder kausale Verursacherprinzip wurde abgelöst und durch Regelungen ersetzt, die es erlaubten, schon eine gewisse räumliche Häufung von Umwelterkrankungen für die Verurteilung der Verursacher als ausreichend anzusehen. Es wurden also die amtlichen Zahlen der registrierten Umweltopfer, der Erkrankten wie auch ggf. der Todesfälle für die betroffenen Gebiete berücksichtigt. Diese Regelungen wurden nach einem für die Betroffenen relativ freundlichen, regulativen Prinzip durchgeführt, d.h. mit Schadensersatzzahlungen bei Verdienstausfällen oder Invalidität durch Umwelterkrankungen und mit hohen Entschädigungen für die Angehörigen bei Todesfällen (Weidner 1984). Etwa 40 % der 100.000 amtlich registrierten Umweltverschmutzungsopfer leben im Großraum Tokyo (Flüchter 1997).

Weitere Maßnahmen, Gesetze und Verordnungen erstreckten sich auf fast alle Gebiete des Umweltschutzes. Mit einigen Technologien, wie z.B. neuen Entschwefelungsmethoden, wurde man geradezu zum internationalen Schrittmacher, und viele Experten, auch aus der Bundesrepublik, besuchten Japan, um von den dort gemachten Fortschritten zu lernen. In anderen Bereichen (z.B. der Wasserentsorgung und -aufbereitung) mußten die Japaner von uns lernen, da sie für ihre Siedlungen erst die erforderliche Infrastruktur schaffen mußten.

Bei der **Verknüpfung der Umwelt- und Urbanisierungsproblematik** muß auch die Frage nach der Erhaltung und Erneuerung der städtischen Zentren im Vordergrund stehen. Dabei ist unter Erhaltung nicht nur die Konservierung historischer oder künstlerischer Relikte zu verstehen. Abgesehen von einigen Tempeln und Schlössern gibt es in Japan nur sehr wenig alte Gebäude, und die Mehrzahl dieser Bauten ist oft erst in den letzten Jahrzehnten wieder neu aufgebaut und renoviert worden. Erdbeben, Taifune, Feuer und Kriege haben die traditionelle japanische Bausubstanz in weit stärkerem Maße verändert und vernichtet als das bei uns der Fall war. Wichtig ist jedoch als allgemeiner Trend der Übergang von der leichten traditionellen Holzbauweise zu modernen

Konstruktionen, d.h. einmal in Richtung Hochhaus und zum anderen, viel mehr als bei uns, in den Untergrund hinein (Schöller 1980).

Für Handels- und Dienstleistungszentren kam es in allen Großstädten zum Ausbau großer unterirdischer Geschäftsstraßen und Shopping-Passagen. Diese Form der räumlichen "Entlastung", ergibt sich aus der sehr heterogenen städtebaulichen Situation an der Oberfläche. Das unmittelbare Nebeneinander von einem alten Tempel und einer modernen Fabrik oder Tankstelle, von einem Wolkenkratzer und einem kleinen Holzhaus ist sehr typisch und geht – auch das ist eine Art Paradoxon in Japan – auf die fast völlige Abwesenheit baupolizeilicher Vorschriften zurück, mit Ausnahme der Erdbeben- und Feuersicherung. Erst in den letzen Jahren wurde hier eingegriffen. Seit 1975 gibt es Restriktionen zur Ausweitung der Untergrundzentren aus Gründen des Katastrophenschutzes oder die vielzitierten Schatten ("Shasen")-Schräglinien-Vorschriften, nach denen ein neues Gebäude den Nachbarn nicht zu viel Sonne wegnehmen darf. Typisch bleibt weiterhin ein ausgeprägter Zug zu einer meist sehr häßlichen Kommerzialisierung. Selbst in den Mittelzentren wird flächenhaft abgerissen und nach rein kommerziellen Erwägungen neu aufgebaut. Fragen der Verkehrsberuhigung – etwa in Fußgängerzonen – und des Umweltschutzes bleiben bei dieser Art der Sanierung im allgemeinen auf der Strecke. Erst in allerjüngster Zeit lassen sich, z.T. unter Druck von Bürgerinitiativen, Ansätze zu einer etwas behutsameren städtischen Sanierungspolitik beobachten.

Zusammenfassend kann man sagen, daß in Japan heute versucht wird, die Umweltbelastung auf einem Niveau zu halten, auf dem sie für die menschliche Gesundheit noch einigermaßen erträglich ist. Darüber hinaus plant man zunächst nicht zu gehen. Es gibt z.B. keine offizielle Politik, um in den belasteten Gebieten die verlorengegangenen Landschafts- oder Naturschönheiten wiederherzustellen. Auch das Mitspracherecht von Bürgerinitiativen, etwa bei der Lokalisierung neuer Industriegebiete, ist begrenzt. Wie überhaupt die umweltorientierten Bürgerbewegungen ("Antipollution Movements") insgesamt einen geringeren politischen Stellenwert haben als bei uns.

Ein wichtiger Trend ist auch in Japan die Abkehr von der nachträglichen Kompensation für erlittene Umweltschäden und die Hinwendung zu einer eher vorbeugenden Umweltpolitik. Diese Strategie hat schon Erfolge erzielt, besonders in der Luftreinhaltung. Als Hauptproblem bleibt jedoch die Verknüpfung des Umweltschutzes mit der Regional- und Landesplanung, d.h. z.B. der Planung der Industriegebiete um und in den großen Zentren. Ein politisch ziemlich zentralistisch organisiertes Regierungssystem, noch dazu auf einer Insel, hat natürlich im Vergleich zu Mitteleuropa den großen Vorteil, daß man nicht so weitgehend auf den Konsens und die Zusammenarbeit mit benachbarten Ländern angewiesen ist. Es gibt kein hochentwickeltes urbanes System auf der Erde, in dem Maßnahmen des Umweltschutzes in Verbindung mit einer sinnvollen Regionalplanung der städtischen Zentren und ihrer Verkehrsbeziehungen so vordringlich sind wie in Japan.

Literatur:

FLÜCHTER, W. (1990): Japan. Die Landesentwicklung im Spannungsfeld zwischen Zentralisierung und Dezentralisierung. - In: Geographische Rundschau, 42, S. 182-195.
FLÜCHTER, W. (1997): Megastadt Tokyo. - In: Geographie und Schule, 110, S. 30-38.
FLÜCHTER, W. (1998): Japan. Weltwirtschaftsmacht mit Raum- und Ressourcenproblemen. - In: Geographie heute, 158, S. 3-7.
FOLJANTY-JOST, G., H. WEIDNER (1981): Environmental Disruption, Government Policy and the Anti-Pollution Movement in Japan. - In: IIUG Paper, 81/14, Wissenschaftszentrum Berlin.
GUNNARSON, B. (1974): Japans ökologisches Harakiri oder das tödliche Ende des Wachstums. - Hamburg.
KIUCHI, S. (1967): Recent Regional Development and Planning. - In: Festschrift für L. Scheidl. Wien, S. 67-73.
MANSHARD, W. (1987): Urbanisierung und Umweltprobleme Japans. - In: MARTIN, B. (Hrsg.): Japans Weg in die Moderne. Frankfurt-New York, S. 139-152.
MARTIN, B. (Hrsg.) (1987): Japans Weg in die Moderne. - Frankfurt-New York, 195 S.
SCHÖLLER, P. (1980): Umweltschutz und Stadterhaltung. - Paderborn.
WEIDNER, H. (1984): Japan - Erfolge und Grenzen technokratischer Umweltpolitik. - In: IIUG Paper, 84/3, Wissenschaftszentrum Berlin.

ROCK´N´ROLL-AKROBATIK-DIENSTLEISTUNGEN
Eine unternehmensgeographische Analyse [1]

Robert POMBERGER und Christian STAUDACHER (Wien)

Kurzfassung

Auf Basis wirtschafts- und besonders dienstleistungsgeographischer Konzepte werden in systematischer Form die Besonderheiten von Rock´n´Roll-Akrobatik-Dienstleistungen und die daraus resultierenden organisatorischen und räumlichen Konsequenzen für Rock´n´Roll-Akrobatik-Dienstleistungsunternehmen diskutiert: gestufter Produktionsprozeß, Integration des externen Faktors, räumlich-zeitlich synchroner Kontakt, multiple Standortorganisation, Vernetzungsstruktur, etc. Im Anschluß daran wird am Beispiel eines modellhaft konstruierten, internationalisierungswilligen europäischen Rock´n´Roll-Akrobatik-Unternehmens das Internationalisierungsproblem für Dienstleistungsunternehmen diskutiert und eine räumliche Segmentierung des Auslandsmarktes USA durchgeführt. Es sollen mögliche Problemlösungen der räumlichen Organisation solcher spezieller Dienstleistungsunternehmen veranschaulicht werden: Konzept der Standortfaktoren / Standortpotentialanalyse; Dienstleistungsmarketing, branchenspezifische Standortanforderungen, internationale Netzbildung.

Abstract

The special characteristics of rock 'n' roll acrobatics cause organisational and spatial consequences for service vendors in the rock 'n' roll acrobatics' business: stepwise production process, integration of the external factor, spatio-temporal synchronous contact, multiple location-organisation, network structure, etc All these keywords are examined more closely on the basis of theory in the field of geography of services. The problems of internationalisation of service vendors are discussed on an European rock 'n' roll acrobatics vendor's model as well as the spatial segmentation of the U.S. market. This article shows possible solutions of the spatial organisation's problems faced by specialised service vendors: factors of location/analysis of potential locations; service-marketing: special trade requests of locations, development of an international network.

---

[1] Dieser Beitrag basiert auf der von R. Pomberger an der Abteilung Praxisorientierte Wirtschaftsgeographie und Räumliche Integrationsforschung der WU Wien 1995 verfaßten Dissertation „Internationalisierung von Dienstleistungsunternehmen – US-Markteintrittsmodell für die „Rock´n´Roll-Akrobatik Sparte", die mit dem L.Scheidl-Preis 1995 der Österr. Gesellschaft für Wirtschaftsraumforschung ausgezeichnet wurde.

Die Dienstleistungsgeographie ist in ihren Forschungsansätzen noch sehr jung, verfügt allerdings in der Zwischenzeit über eine Fülle von Forschungsergebnissen und Erkenntnissen (DANIELS 1986, STAUDACHER 1992, u.v.a.). Die Überprüfung dieser Ergebnisse und Hypothesen ist besonders fruchtbar, wenn „ausgefallene" Branchen unter den Scheinwerfer dieser Ergebnisse gestellt werden. In diesem Beitrag sollen – als Auszug der wesentlichen Ergebnisse einer Dissertation (POMBERGER 1995) – die Rock´n´Roll-Akrobatik-Sparte und die Rock´n´Roll-Akrobatik-Unternehmer als ein solches Beispiel verwendet werden. Es wird damit angestrebt, grundlegende Erkenntnisse der Dienstleistungstheorie zu bestätigen, die Konzepte auf die Praxisrelevanz zu prüfen und ein Unternehmens- und Internationalisierungskonzept für ein Modellunternehmen zu entwickeln.

1. ROCK´N´ROLL-AKROBATIK ALS SPEZIELLE DIENSTLEISTUNG

Zunächst sollen einige wesentliche Aussagen der Dienstleistungstheorie auf die Rock´n´Roll-Akrobatik angewendet bzw. übertragen werden, wobei folgende Definitionen als Grundlage verwendet werden (vgl. dazu GUTENBERG 1983, SCHIERENBECK 1993, WÖHE 1990, MALERI 1973, BEREKOVEN 1974, KAUFMANN 1977, SCHEUCH 1982, CORSTEN 1988, HUBER 1992, STAUDACHER 1991, 1994):

- „*Dienstleistungen* sind der Bedarfsdeckung dienende Prozesse, die durch materielle und/oder persönliche Leistungsträger im Rahmen eines räumlich und zeitlich synchronen Kontaktes mit einem notwendigerweise zu integrierenden externen Faktor ausgeführt werden, mit dem Ziel, im Moment der Verrichtung eine Veränderung oder Bewahrung eines Zustandes der Person des Leistungsnehmers bzw. dessen Verfügungsobjektes unter Erhaltung deren Identität zu bewirken" (HUBER 1992: 24).

- Das *Dienstleistungsunternehmen* ist ein spezieller Unternehmenstyp, der

    – *markttheoretisch* auf Basis der konstitutiven Grundsätze der Autonomie, der Erwerbswirtschaftlichkeit oder Prinzipien des öffentlichen Interesses und des privaten oder öffentlichen Eigentums als oberstes Formalziel den profit- bzw. effizienzorientierten Absatz von Dienstleistungen zum Ziel hat.

    – *Produktionstheoretisch* hat er als dominantes Sachziel die Produktion von Dienstleistungen und/oder von Dienstleistungspotentialen, die nur im Rahmen eines räumlich-zeitlich synchronen Kontaktes mit einem notwendigerweise zu integrierenden externen Faktor möglich ist.

    – Die *Produktionsart* des Dienstleistungsunternehmens ist durch einen prozessualen, stark personenbezogenen *Verrichtungscharakter* gekennzeichnet, welcher sich organisatorisch in einer hierarchischen Zweiebenenstruktur manifestiert, die aus der Potentialproduktion (Leistungsbereitschaft) und der Endkombination (Leistungserstellung) besteht.

    – Das grundlegende *Muster der Standortorganisation* und des Standortverhaltens von Dienstleistungsunternehmen ergibt sich als Folge der Zwei-

Ebenen- und der (häufig vorkommenden) Prozeßphasenstruktur der Organisation der Dienstleistungsproduktion. Für die räumliche Organisation von Dienstleistungsproduktion entstehen bemerkenswerte Potentiale zur Ausbildung einer multiplen Standortorganisation (multiple Netzbildung) bzw. in weiterer Folge von Mehrbetrieblichkeit und Plurilokalität (plurilokale Netzbildung) bzw. zur Ausbildung flexibler Netze (vgl. unten Kap. 3).

Vergleicht man die Rock´n´Roll-Akrobatik mit anderen Dienstleistungen, so ist einsichtig, daß es sich dabei um eine sehr spezielle Dienstleistung handelt, die sehr typische Erscheinungs- und Organisationsformen ausbildet. Es gibt *fünf Ausprägungsformen* von Dienstleistungsprozessen: Trainieren von Paaren und Formationen, Ausbilden zum Trainer, Ausbilden zum Wertungsrichter, Durchführen von Shows, Ausrichten von Turnieren. Diese Ausprägungsformen und Funktionen treten nicht nur als Leistungen für den Endverbraucher auf (z.B. Ausbildung zum Trainer), sondern auch in vielfältiger Vernetzung als Leistung zur Potentialerstellung (z.B. Ausbildung zum „eigenen" Trainer) und führen so zu vielgestaltigen formellen und informellen Unternehmensnetzwerken.

BEISPIEL: ANFÄNGERTRAINING

Das zeigt sich bereits im Bereich des Anfängertrainings. Die Tanzschüler mit durchschnittlicher Begabung erlernen den Neuner-Grundschritt, den wichtigsten Tanzschritt der Rock'n'Roll Akrobatik, parallel zu anderen Grundkenntnissen in drei bis sechs Trainingseinheiten (bei jeweils einstündigem Umfang). Die richtige Ausführung des Neuner-Grundschrittes bedingt eine Vielzahl an Informationen, die der Trainer den Anfängern nicht auf einmal geben kann, sondern aufgrund der Rückmeldungen (korrekte und falsche Bewegungen, Takt-, Rhythmus-, Stilfehler, Grad der Ermüdung, usw.) nach und nach mitteilt. Die anspruchsvolle Grundtechnik wird methodisch in Teile zerlegt geübt und in einem konstruktivem Vorgang gemeinsam mit den Schülern Stück für Stück zusammengesetzt; z.B. nach der folgenden sehr grob wiedergegebenen methodischen Übungsreihe (Erlacher 1993):

1. Erlernen der ‚hop' Bewegung,
2. Erlernen der ‚kick' Bewegung ohne ‚hops',
3. Verbinden der ‚kicks' und ‚hops',
4. Erlernen der ‚kick ball change' Bewegung und
5. Verbinden aller Teile zum Neuner-Grundschritt.

Wird das Musiktempo allmählich gesteigert (von 40 auf 48 – 52 Vierviertaktake pro Minute), treten im allgemeinen beim Grundschritt zu alten Schwächen neue Fehler hinzu, die der Trainer nur in einem geduldigen, andauernden Unterrichtsprozeß beseitigen kann.

Es zeigt sich also klar, daß es sich um einen phasenhaft gegliederten Dienstleistungsprozeß handelt, bei dem eine klare Trennung zwischen Potentialproduktion und Endkombination feststellbar ist und daß auch die Standortorganisation eine ganz besondere ist: Trennung von Büro und Turnsaal.

In diesem Beitrag wird nur die *Ausprägungsform Trainieren* als Beispiel genauer behandelt (für die anderen Ausprägungsformen vgl. POMBERGER 1995). Unter dem Begriff „Training" ist ein „komplexer Handlungsprozeß mit dem Ziel der planmäßigen Einwirkung auf die sportliche Leistungsentwicklung" (JOST 1990: 1) der ganzen Person zu verstehen. Das „Leistungsgesamt" (BEREKOVEN 1974: 34) des Trainierens bzw. Ausbildens weist eindeutig einen verrichtungsartigen, prozessualen Charakter auf, weil diese Dienstleistung nur in Form eines Lehrvorganges und Lernprozesses durch den Sportlehrer produziert bzw. vom Sportschüler konsumiert werden kann. Das Training bzw. die Ausbildung dienen der (bei entsprechend kleinen Lerngruppen individuellen) Bedarfsdeckung der Sportler bzw. der Kandidaten zur Trainerausbildung. Die Nachfrage resultiert aus qualitativen oder quantitativen Nachteilen einer Selbstverrichtung oder aus dem Ergebnis wirtschaftlichen Abwägens von Eigen- oder Fremdfertigung.

Die für Dienstleistungen typischen „*bedarfsauslösenden Zwecke*" (SCHEUCH 1982: 75) treten sowohl separat als auch kumuliert auf:

- Bei *Konsumenten als Endverbraucher:* Die speziellen Fähigkeiten und Fertigkeiten (Know-how, Erfahrung, Professionalität, Charme, ...) der Dienstleistungsanbieter führen den Nachfragern vor Augen, daß ihnen die Selbstverrichtung in gleicher Güte nicht möglich ist, daß geringe Fähigkeit zur Selbstanalyse und keine ausreichende Problemlösungskompetenz der Paare und Formationen besteht und daß Lerndefizite zu Qualitätsnachteilen führen (z.B. mangelnde Ausführung von Grundtechnikfiguren, fehlende Sicherung der Rock´n´Roll Akrobatinnen, ...).

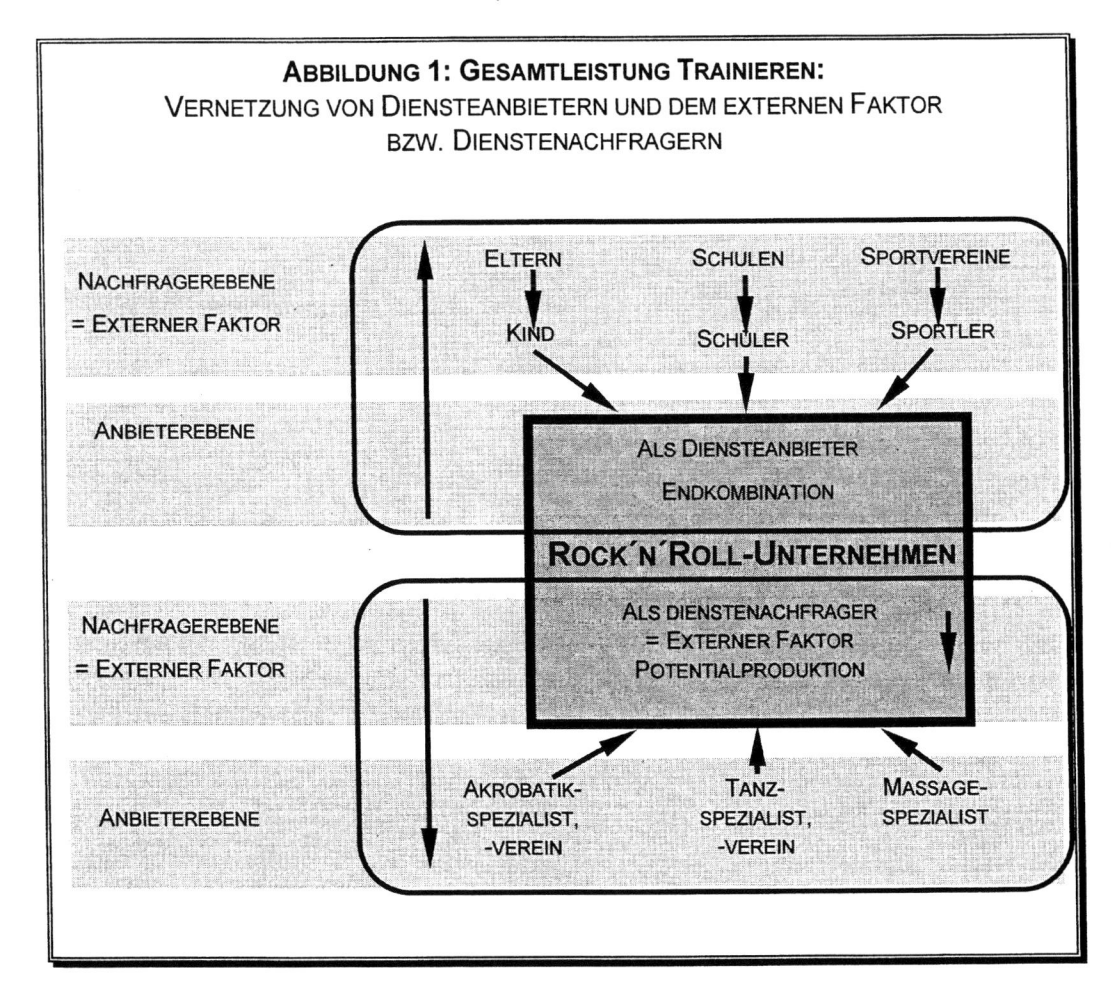

ABBILDUNG 1: GESAMTLEISTUNG TRAINIEREN:
VERNETZUNG VON DIENSTEANBIETERN UND DEM EXTERNEN FAKTOR BZW. DIENSTENACHFRAGERN

NACHFRAGEREBENE
= EXTERNER FAKTOR

ELTERN   SCHULEN   SPORTVEREINE
KIND   SCHÜLER   SPORTLER

ANBIETEREBENE

ALS DIENSTEANBIETER
ENDKOMBINATION

ROCK´N´ROLL-UNTERNEHMEN

ALS DIENSTENACHFRAGER
= EXTERNER FAKTOR
POTENTIALPRODUKTION

NACHFRAGEREBENE
= EXTERNER FAKTOR

ANBIETEREBENE

AKROBATIK-SPEZIALIST, -VEREIN   TANZ-SPEZIALIST, -VEREIN   MASSAGE-SPEZIALIST

- Bei *R´n´R-Unternehmen als intermediäre Nachfrager:* Eine Auslagerung von Dienste- und Teilverrichtungen kann z.B. auf folgende „bedarfsauslösende Zwecke" zurückgeführt werden:
  - Bei unerwarteten, kurzfristig auftretenden *Kapazitätsproblemen* beim Diensteanbieter wird dieser zum Nachfrager und der auftretende Bedarf wird dadurch befriedigt, daß die für die Problemlösung erforderlichen Prozesse ausgegliedert werden, weil eine Selbstverrichtung angesichts zu hoher Bereitschaftskosten bei langfristig zu geringer Kapazitätsauslastung ökonomisch nicht sinnvoll wäre (z.B. unerwarteter Ansturm von Anfängern im Kindertraining).
  - Bei *unzureichender Ausrüstung* kann ein überraschender Verrichtungsbedarf beim Nachfrager auftreten, der in der Form der Fremdverrichtung ökonomisch sinnvoll durchgeführt werden kann (z.B. schadhafte Verankerung der Deckenlonge).
  - *Geplante und dauernde Auslagerung* tritt dort auf, wo die Selbstverrichtung ökonomisch nicht sinnvoll erscheint, vor allem wegen mangelnder Spezialisierung oder fehlenden Know-hows; besonders günstig erweisen sich dabei verschiedene Formen der Kooperation und des Aufbaus von Netzwerken.

TABELLE 1: ROCK´N´ROLL-AKROBATIK – TRAINIEREN:
VERNETZUNG VON DIENSTEANBIETERN, EXTERNEN FAKTOREN BZW. DIENSTENACHFRAGERN

	Anbieter	externer Faktor	Nachfrager
Beteiligte	Rock´n´Roll-Akrobatik Unternehmen	Sportler: Paare, Formationen SchülerInnen, Kinder	Schulen, Eltern
Ziel / Dienstleistungsnutzen	**Produktion und Absatz der Dienstleistung**: Trainieren der Athleten: Paare, Formationen (= Sachziel) Unternehmensgewinn (= Formalziel)	**Sportler, SchülerInnen, Kinder**: Vorbereitung auf Shows und (inter)nationale Turniere, Verbesserung oder Erhaltung des Trainingszustandes; Selbstverrichtung nicht möglich	**Schulen:** Erweiterung des Angebotes Selbstverrichtung nicht möglich **Eltern:** fachspezifisches Kindertraining, stundenweise Übernahme der Kinderbetreuung
Produktionsfaktoren der Leistungsbereitschaft	**Arbeit:** Trainer, Manager **Betriebsmittel:** Studio, Büro, Musik-, Videoanlage, Tanzspiegel, Matten, Deckenlonge, ... Werkstoffe: keine **Potentialfaktoren:** Trainingsplan, Tanzprogramm, Werbemittel		
Produktionsfaktoren der Leistungserstellung, Verrichtung	**derivate Produktionsfaktoren:** dienstefähige Trainer, Trainingsplan, Tanzprogramm, Sporthalle, Studio, ... **Werkstoff:** Magnesium	**EXTERNER FAKTOR** = SportlerInnen, SchülerInnen (direkt), = Eltern, Schule („Überlasser") sportspezifische Merkmale und Fähigkeiten, Bereitschaft zum Trainieren, sportspezifische Ausrüstung	
räumlich u. zeitlich synchroner Kontakt	**Kontaktort**: (gemietete) Sporthalle, Studio, Sportplatz im Freien, gemeinsame Trainingszeiten		

Die R´n´R-Akrobatik – hier dargestellt am Leistungsbereich Trainieren – läßt sich durch folgende weitere typische Merkmale als Dienstleistung beschreiben (vgl. auch Abb. 1 und Tab. 1):

- *Anbieter* sind *Rock´n´Roll-Akrobatik-Unternehmen*, die über die Produktion und den Absatz von Trainingsleistungen unter Einsatz ihrer speziellen Produktionsfaktoren und unter Mithilfe, -wirkung des „externen Faktors" ihr Formalziel zu erreichen versuchen. Wie bei allen Wirtschaftsunternehmen stellt das Management (bei Kleinbetrieben oft ident mit dem Trainer) den entscheidenden Faktor dar.

- Die relevanten *Produktionsfaktoren* der Leistungsbereitschaft bestehen aus leistungsfähigen und leistungsbereiten *Trainern*, die den für die Dienstleistung Rock´n´Roll-Akrobatik-Training erforderlichen persönlichen Leistungsträger verkörpern. Die materiellen Hilfsmittel wie Musik-, Videoanlage, Tanzspiegel, Matten, Deckenlonge, Federtuch, Magnesium, etc. repräsentieren die für fast alle Dienstleistungen typische materielle Seite. Das Magnesium muß nicht zwingend bei der Dienstleistungsproduktion „Training" verwendet werden; der Werkstoff hat sich in letzter Zeit bei jenen Aktiven der obersten Turnierklasse eingebürgert, die häufig mit Sportakrobaten trainieren. Bei der Endkombination sind die derivaten Produktionsfaktoren wie die eingesetzten *Trainer* und die *Trainingspläne*, Tanzprogramme usw. sowie die *Merkmale und Fähigkeiten der Sportler* entscheidende Produktionsfaktoren.

- Auf der *Nachfragerseite* müssen externer Faktor und Nachfrager nicht notwendigerweise ident sein. Häufig interessieren sich zunächst *Eltern* oder *Turnlehrer* für Rock´n´Roll-Akrobatik. Die Begeisterung der Eltern und Lehrer fällt bei den *Kindern* und Schülern nicht selten auf fruchtbaren Boden, weil das Bedürfnis dieser Altersgruppe nach Ausleben ihres natürlichen Bewegungsdrangs latent vorhanden ist. Da Rock´n´Roll-Akrobatik normalerweise von Erwachsenen über 30 Jahre nicht mehr ausgeübt werden kann, bietet es außerdem den nach Autonomie strebenden 11- bis 15-jährigen Schülern die Möglichkeit, sich von der Generation ihrer Eltern und Lehrer sichtbar zu unterscheiden und sich gleichzeitig vor ihren gleichaltrigen Mitschülern, deren Meinung ihnen in der puberalen Phase besonders wichtig ist, zu profilieren (JOST 1990, NEUBAUER 1994). Viele weitere Motive können dazu führen, daß die Rock´n´Roll-Schüler nicht nur externe Faktoren im Dienstleistungsvorgang bleiben, sondern auch zu aktiven Nachfragern werden.

- Hinter dem abstrakten Fachbegriff *externer Faktor*, der für die Leistungserstellung per definitionem unerläßlich ist (HUBER 1992), verbirgt sich hier der Sportler (Paar, Formation). Der externe Faktor kann frei entscheiden, ob er das Dienstleistungsangebot Training annimmt oder nicht (z.B.: Ein gegen seinen Willen von den Eltern in das Training geschickte Kind als Verfügungssubjekt der nachfragenden Erziehungsberechtigten wird die Mitarbeit trotzig verweigern; es entzieht sich der autonomen Disponierbarkeit durch den Trainer als derivatem Faktor). Darin drückt sich auch der stark personenbezogene (BEREKOVEN 1974) Verrichtungscharakter des Rock´n´Roll-Akrobatik-Trainings aus.

- Das *konstitutive Dienstleistungsmerkmal „räumlich und zeitlich synchroner Kontakt"* spielt eine wesentliche Rolle in der Frage der Standortwahl. Trainer und Schüler „müssen ... im Rahmen eines räumlich und zeitlich synchronen Kontaktes ..." (HUBER 1992: 24) miteinander in Beziehung treten. Die Dienstleistung Trainieren von Tanzschülern wird üblicherweise in Turnsälen oder ersatzweise angemieteten Räumlichkeiten als kooperativ beschafften *Kontakt- und Verrichtungsorten* zu vereinbarten *Trainingszeiten* verrichtet. Es liegt auf der Hand, daß Rock´n´Roll-Akrobatik nur dann erlernt werden kann, wenn die diversen Bewegungen in richtiger Ausführung vorgezeigt werden und die begangenen Fehler der Aktiven durch die Trainer unmittelbar (zeitlich-räumlich synchron) korrigiert werden. Dienstleistungstheoretisch ist zwar ein Fernunterricht etwa durch eine (teure!) Videokonferenzschaltung denkbar, aber in der Trainingspraxis wäre trotz aller Videotechnik ein Assistent vor Ort notwendig, um beispielsweise das Paar vor Stürzen, die nur Erfahrene im Ansatz schon erkennen, zu sichern. Im Schul- und Berufsalltag bedeutet das, daß die Zusammenarbeit von Sportlern und Trainern im allgemeinen nur an Werktagsabenden in freien Schulturnsälen möglich ist.

- Das Training wird verrichtet, um „... eine *Veränderung oder Bewahrung eines Zustandes der Person des Leistungsnehmers ...* unter Erhaltung deren Identität zu bewirken" (HUBER 1992: 24). Das Ziel des Trainers ist es also, auf den Trainingszustand der Rock´n´Roll-Akrobaten mittels sportwissenschaftlicher und praktischer Erkenntnisse formverbessernd, formerhaltend oder fehlerpotentialvernichtend – so individuell wie nur möglich – einzuwirken (FRECH 1993), daß die Paare und Formationen in der Lage sind, erfolgreich an Schauauftritten und Wettkämpfen teilzunehmen.

Insgesamt zeigt sich damit, daß die Rock´n´Roll-Akrobatik zwar eine spezielle Dienstleistung ist, daß aber auch in diesem außergewöhnlichen Fall die Grundkonzepte der Dienstleistungstheorie zu einer Klärung der Produktions- und Absatzbedingungen beitragen und als brauchbares Analyseinstrumentarium eingesetzt werden können.

2. ROCK´N´ROLL-AKROBATIK-UNTERNEHMEN ALS DIENSTLEISTUNGSUNTERNEHMEN

2.1. Trends und Strukturen im Rock´n´Roll-Akrobatik Markt

Aufgrund des in den letzten fünf Jahren stark angestiegenen Niveaus der Rock´n´Roll-Akrobatik-Wettkämpfe und der damit verbundenen anspruchsvollen Nachfrage nach geeigneten Trainern, Trainingsmitteln und -hallen haben sich die Tanzschulen weitgehend vom Rock´n´Roll-Turniersport zurückgezogen. Der Markt wird nun von *Spezialisten* versorgt:

- *Vereine*, die sich der Förderung des Rock´n´Roll-Akrobatik-Sports verschrieben haben, sind zwar gemeinnützig ausgerichtet haben aber auch bedarfswirtschaftlichen Zwecke (HASITSCHKA/HRUSCHKA 1982).

- *Freiberufliche Rock´n´Roll-Akrobatik-Dienstleistungsunternehmer* wickeln ihre Geschäfte nach dem Prinzip der Erwerbswirtschaftlichkeit, der Autonomie und des Privateigentums ab (GUTENBERG 1983, SCHIERENBECK 1993, WÖHE 1990).

Die erwerbswirtschaftlich agierenden Spezialisten treten in der Regel als *Einzelunternehmer* auf, müssen sich aber häufig des Vehikels eines eigenen, selbstgegründeten *Sportvereins* bedienen, damit ihre Sportschüler an den Rock´n´Roll-Akrobatik-Turnieren teilnehmen dürfen. Sie zollen damit der Tatsache Tribut, daß in Europa traditionellerweise der organisierte Sport von ‚not for profit'-Vereinen und -Verbänden getragen wird (BOHUS 1986, RICHTER 1985). Da die Unternehmer über den formalen Umweg Verein aktiv sein müssen (um z.B. auch zu günstigen Preisen Turnhallen mieten zu können), wird es erklärlich, warum sie im allgemeinen im Rock´n´Roll-Sport nicht als Freiberufliche, sondern als Funktionäre bekannt sind; dadurch entsteht z.T. der Eindruck, daß es überhaupt keine Profis gibt. Der Großteil der *Profipaare* ist nur im Showgeschäft tätig und/oder verdient als Aktive der höchsten Wettkampfklasse bei entsprechender Plazierung bei international prominent besetzten Masters-Turnieren Preisgelder, die derzeit noch bescheiden sind.

Eine kleinere Gruppe von Profipaaren bietet freiberuflich erfolgreich ein Dienstleistungssortiment an, das sich vom Trainieren der Tanzschüler (Hobbytänzer/Anfänger, top ten Wettkampfsportler) über die Trainerausbildung und das Durchführen von Shows bis zum Veranstalten bzw. Ausrichten von Turnieren erstreckt. Es gibt also tatsächlich einige wenige *Rock´n´Roll-Akrobatik-Unternehmen*, die ein vollständiges Dienstleistungsprogramm haben. Das Problem der geringen Größe dieser Unternehmen führt häufig dazu, daß sie nur über äußerst bescheidene finanzielle und personelle Ressourcen verfügen und sich damit das Nachfragepotential in ausländischen Märkten nicht einmal ansatzweise zunutze machen können. Die Zeit für die Gründung von ein bis drei europäischen (Groß-)Unternehmen mit dem Ziel der Eroberung sehr attraktiver außereuropäischer Beschaffungs-, Show- und Sportmärkte (z.B. USA) für die Rock´n´Roll-Akrobatik-Sparte ist reif: Das zusätzliche Wachstum auf den bisher bearbeiteten nationalen Märkten ist nämlich beschränkt und ein vielversprechendes Wachstum kann im wesentlichen nur durch die Erschließung neuer Märkte außerhalb Europas realisiert werden.

2.2. Ein fiktives „Modellunternehmen"

Da derzeit kein Rock´n´Roll-Akrobatik-Dienstleistungsunternehmen bekannt ist, das ein Auslandsengagement auf außereuropäischen Märkten eingegangen ist oder anstrebt, muß hier ein fiktives „*Modellunternehmen*" konstruiert werden. An diesem Beispiel sollen dann die speziellen organisatorischen Ausprägungen, die Standortorganisation und die Internationalisierungsfrage diskutiert werden.

Dieses Modellunternehmen soll folgende Charakteristiken aufweisen (vgl. Kasten).

> ### ROCK´N´ROLL-AKROBATIK – MODELLUNTERNEHMEN
>
> Dieses fiktive europäische Unternehmen sollte die Rechtsform einer Gesellschaft mit beschränkter Haftung haben, deren geschäftsführende Gesellschafter *Rock'n'Roll-Akrobatik-Unternehmer(paare)* sind und deren *Partner* (Sportartikelproduzenten, Tanzschulen, Versicherungen, Banken) die Vorfinanzierung (OBERHUBER 1987) übernehmen. Die bereits jetzt existierenden Rock'n'Roll Akrobatik Kleinstunternehmungen dieser Gesellschafter sollten als Einlage in das Vermögen des europäischen Unternehmens eingebracht werden und deren *Betriebe als nationale Filialen*, die mit großer Autonomie ausgestattet sein müssen, ihre bisherigen Stammärkte in Europa weiterhin bedienen. Dieses Rock'n'Roll-Akrobatik-Unternehmen fungiert als *finanzwirtschaftliche und juristische Einheit*, die einen *organisatorischen Gesamtrahmen* bildet, um die Aufgaben der organisatorisch-technischen, örtlich getrennten Produktionseinheiten (STAUDACHER 1991) in Europa lose und die Aktivitäten des europäischen Unternehmens in Übersee zu koordinieren. Das europäische Rock'n'Roll-Akrobatik-Unternehmen hat die Vorteile der Flexibilität (durch die kleinbetriebliche Struktur) mit den Vorteilen erhöhter finanzieller (gemeinsames Basisvermögen: Stammkapital und aufgenommenes Fremdkapital) und personeller (Geschäftsführerteam, Trainerpool, Administratoren, weites Kontaktnetz zu unternehmensexternen Spezialisten) Ressourcen verknüpft. Das *lean management* eines solchen europäischen Unternehmens wäre in der Praxis vermutlich von Personen entweder aus den romanischsprachigen Euroregionen (unter der Führung Frankreichs vor allem Italien und Teile von Belgien bzw. der Schweiz) oder aus den germanischsprachigen Regionen Europas (hauptsächlich Deutschland, Schweiz, Österreich, Niederlande, Norwegen, Schweden, Dänemark) zu bilden und das Trainerteam wäre sehr multikulturell zusammengesetzt.

2.3. Organisationsstrukturen

Das *dominante Sachziel*, die Produktion und der Absatz von Dienstleistungen, ist ein konstitutives Merkmal von Dienstleistungsunternehmen (MALERI 1973, BEREKOVEN 1974) und manifestiert sich bei Rock´n´Roll-Akrobatik-Unternehmen in einem Produktionsprogramm, das vom „Trainieren der Rock´n´Roll-Athleten", „Ausbilden zum Rock´n´Roll-Trainer", „Ausbilden zum Rock´n´Roll-Wertungsrichter", „Durchführen von Rock´n´Roll-Akrobatik-Shows" bis zum „Ausrichten von Rock´n´Roll-Turnieren" reichen kann. Die für Dienstleistungsunternehmen *typische Produktionsweise* ist durch einen prozessualen (BEREKOVEN 1974) und dominant personenbezogenen Verrichtungscharakter (SCHEUCH 1982) gekennzeichnet. Der *Verrichtungscharakter* erfordert aus organisatorischer Sicht eine hierarchische Zweiebenenstruktur der Produktion: die Potentialproduktion und die Endkombination (CORSTEN 1988).

a) **Potentialproduktion:**

Auf dieser Ebene werden innerbetrieblich die charakteristischen Produktionsfaktoren Arbeit (hohe Intensität), Werkstoffe (wenig oder gar kein Bedarf) und Betriebsmittel (Sachanlagen) zu derivaten Potentialfaktoren, die die Leistungsbereitschaft repräsentieren, autonom – also vom Externen Faktor unabhängig – kombiniert. Hält man sich die Inhalte der Leistungsbereitschaft für das

„Trainieren von Rock´n´Roll-Akrobaten" beispielsweise vor Augen (siehe Tab. 1), so fällt auf, daß eine ganze Reihe von Faktoren für ein konkurrenzfähiges Diensteangebot notwendig ist:

- Die *Entwicklung und der Aufbau eines Personalpotentials*, das sich einerseits aus staatlich geprüften Trainern für Rock´n´Roll (und verwandte Sportsparten) und andererseits aus Administratoren (Manager, Sekretärin) mit einer entsprechenden Qualifikation und Leistungsbereitschaft zusammensetzen muß. Das bedeutet aber nicht unbedingt, daß das Personal mit Angestelltendienstverträgen an das Unternehmen gebunden werden muß (MOHAB 1992); es genügen leistungsorientierte Verträge und eine wettbewerbsfreundliche Unternehmenskultur.

- *Betriebsmittel*, die in Immobilien (Turnsaal, Studio, Sportplatz im Freien, Garderoben, Massageraum, Sauna, Büro, ...) und mobile Betriebsmittel (Musikanlage, Tonträger, Musiktitel, Videoanlage, Tanzspiegel, Matten, Deckenlonge, Büromaterial, ...) eingeteilt werden können, die zur richtigen Zeit am richtigen Ort zur Verfügung stehen müssen (Eigentum, Leasing, Pacht, Anmietung, etc.).

- Die Trainer erstellen mit Hilfe der Betriebsmittel ziegruppengerechte, sofort anwendbare *Trainingspläne, Tanzprogramme*, Spiele, usw. als derivate Potentialfaktoren. Für das Durchführen solcher Vorarbeiten benötigt man keine Sportler, die ja erst bei der Endkombination aktiv werden.

Da die Nachfrage nach der Dienstleistung „Trainieren" durch viele Umstände variabel ist, ist die *Leistungsbereitschaft* in qualitativer, intensitätsmäßiger, quantitativer, zeitlicher und räumlicher Hinsicht – nach Möglichkeit – *flexibel* zu gestalten (CORSTEN 1988, STAUDACHER 1991):

- Die *qualitative Anpassung* der Arbeitskräfte ist dann am elastischsten, wenn das Unternehmen Trainer beschäftigt, die hochqualifiziert und niedrigspezialisiert sind, und daher für alle Sportlerzielgruppen (Kinder, Jugendliche, Erwachsene, Hobbysportler und Turniertänzer aller Klassen und Niveaus) einsetzbar sind (= Rollenflexibilität, Arbeitsbündelung). In der Praxis wird die Unternehmung gut beraten sein, neben den ausgezeichnet ausgebildeten Generalisten auch hochqualifizierte Spezialisten, die beispielsweise im Bereich von risikoreichen Akrobatikkombinationen für Innovationen sorgen sollen, zu beschäftigen. Das Trainerteam der Unternehmung kann durch ehemalige Turniertänzer der Anfängerklasse (niedrige Qualifikation), deren Rock´n´Roll Begeisterung und überdurchschnittliche Kontaktfreudigkeit branchenbekannt sind, komplettiert werden: Sie werden im allgemeinen mit der Betreuung des Hobbytrainings des eigenen Fanklubs, der Akquisition neuer Trainingskunden und Public Relations Aufgaben (Spezialisierungen) betraut.

- Eine *intensitätsmäßige Anpassung* der Leistungsbereitschaft findet vor allem seinen Niederschlag im veränderbarem Arbeitstempo der Betreuer. Erfahrene Trainer sind in der Lage, die durch eine größer gewordene Schülergruppe gesteigerte Nachfrage nach individueller Betreuung mit einer erhöhten Unterrichtsgeschwindigkeit zu befriedigen. In der Praxis bedeutet das, daß sich die Trainer bei einer neu vorzustellenden Figur auf die Vermittlung der wesentlichen Bewegungsinformationen beschränken oder sich bei der Akrobatikanalyse auf das Beseitigen der gravierenden Fehler konzentrieren. Das gesteigerte Lehrtempo kann Betreuungsdefizite sozialer Natur hervorrufen, die sich auf die Motivation und die Leistung psychisch instabiler oder unselbständiger Wettkampfsportler oder nach verbaler Anerkennung heischender Hobbytänzer negativ auswirken. Wird die hohe Intensität für einen längeren Zeitraum beibehalten, so könnte der Unternehmenserfolg durch den Verlust einiger Kunden und negative Mundpropaganda beeinträchtigt werden.

- Die *quantitative Anpassung* kann durch die Variation der Zahl der Trainer und Übungsleiter, eine Filialisierung oder Zentralisierung, Veränderung der Trainingsräume (Gliederung des Turnsaals in funktionale Bereiche (für Tanz, Akrobatik) verschiedener Größe, Benützung unterschiedlich dimensionierter Turnhallen) u.v.m. erreicht werden.

- Die *zeitliche Anpassung* sollte sich theoretisch an den flexiblen Leistungszeitwünschen der Nachfrager orientieren. Da fast alle Unternehmungen ihren Raumbedarf ausschließlich durch die Mitbenützung von Schulturnhallen oder Gemeindeturnsälen decken können, ist das zeitliche Variationspotential sehr klein. In der Realität können die fremdbestimmten (Schulwartegewerkschaft, Schulleitung, Gemeindevertreter, etc.) Turnhallenzeiten lediglich in ein zuerst angesetztes Kindertraining und ein nachfolgendes Jugend- und Erwachsenentraining eingeteilt und die Unterrichtsdauer der Kindergruppe zu Gunsten oder zu Lasten der zweiten Altersgruppe verändert werden.

- *Die räumliche Anpassung* (vgl. Kap. 3) kann aufgrund der immobilen Betriebsmittel (Turnhalle, Studio) nur durch eine vorausschauende, die Erfordernisse des Leistungsprogramms „Trainieren von Rock´n´Roll Akrobaten" berücksichtigende Standortentscheidung bzw. Filialisierung einigermaßen flexibel gestaltet werden. Die räumliche Gestaltungsmöglichkeit der Leistungsbereitschaft wird in der Praxis darauf beschränkt sein, jene Schul- und Gemeindeturnhallen für ein weiteres Jahr zur stundenweisen Mitbenützung zugesprochen zu bekommen, die hinsichtlich ihrer Standort- und Lagefaktoren den Wunschvorstellungen der Unternehmung am nächsten kommen. Eine hohe räumliche Mobilität liegt hingegen bei Teilaspekten des Dienstepotentials „Trainieren" vor: Beispielsweise kann der Trainer ein observatives Training – es handelt sich hierbei um ein „planmäßiges, wiederholtes und gezieltes Beobachten der Bewegungen anderer Sportler" (JOST 1990: 18) – mit seinen Sportlern mittels Videoanlage (mobiles Betriebsmittel) auch in kleinen Räumen durchführen. Die Möglichkeiten der Wahl der Produktionsorte vervielfachen sich, wenn eine akkumulatorbetriebene oder an die Autobatterie angeschlossene Videoanlage eingesetzt wird und Trainer bzw. Schüler (externer Faktor) zur Mobilität bereit sind.

Die oben aufgezählten Maßnahmen zur Gestaltung der Leistungsbereitschaft sind so zu setzen, daß sich das Dienstepotential einerseits nach der variablen Nachfrage richtet und andererseits sach- und formalzielgerechte Produktionssysteme ermöglicht (STAUDACHER 1991).

b) Endkombination/Leistungserstellung:

Auf dieser Stufe erfolgt die *Kombination der derivaten Produktionsfaktoren der ersten Ebene mit dem externen Faktor,* der für den Dienstleistungsproduzenten nicht autonom disponibel ist. Der externe Faktor muß dabei an einem bestimmten Ort zu einem bestimmten Zeitpunkt mit dem Leistungsanbieter in Verbindung sein (HUBER 1992). Die Art und Weise der Organisation des Kontaktes zwischen dem Rock´n´Roll-Akrobatik-Unternehmen (Produzent) und den Sportlern (Konsumenten) wird klarerweise neben der bereits beschriebenen Gestaltung des Dienstepotentials auch von der Art und dem Grad der Aktivität der Tanzschüler abhängen. Die Aktivität des externen Faktors kann mit Hilfe nachfolgender Systematik bestimmt werden (CORSTEN 1988, STAUDACHER 1991):

* *Qualität der Aktivität:* Ob und wie die Leistungskapazität der Sportler im Trainingsprozeß beeinflußt werden kann, hängt von ihrer Bereitschaft zum Trainieren, der Leistungsbereitschaft, und von ihren sportartrelevanten Fähigkeiten, der Leistungsfähigkeit, gleichermaßen ab (JOST 1990).

* *Intensität der Aktivität:* Der Leistungseinsatz äußert sich im Grad des aktiven Mittrainierens („Anstrengung" (JOST 1990: 28), aufmerksamen Zuhörens bei Bekanntgabe von Informationen, im genauen Beobachten von vorgezeigten Figuren und manchmal in der nicht uneigennützigen Überlassung der neuesten, mitgebrachten Musikhits zum Zweck des Abspielens für das gemeinsame Aufwärmen.

* Unter *Quantität der Aktivität* ist hier die Anzahl der Rock´n´Roll-Tänzer zu verstehen, die natürlich auch über die Häufigkeit und die Dauer des Einsatzes variiert werden kann.

* Die *zeitlichen Aspekte* der Aktivität können anhand der Trainingshäufigkeit (= Anzahl der Trainingseinheiten pro Woche) und des Reizumfangs (= Summe der Arbeit pro Zeitabschnitt) gesteuert werden. Die Dienstenachfrage tritt aber insbesondere im Hobbybereich *unregelmäßig* auf, und zwar sowohl im Tages- als auch im Wochen- und Jahresablauf (Saisonalität).

* *Räumliche Aktivität:* Im allgemeinen akzeptieren die Sportler, daß sie den praktischen Unterricht nur in einer Turnhalle – und nicht zu Hause – erhalten. Die räumliche Mobilität der Rock´n´Roll-Tänzer kann quantifiziert werden. Erfahrungsgemäß beträgt in Großstädten die durchschnittliche Anfahrtszeit mit öffentlichen Nahverkehrsmitteln zum regelmäßigen Training für Kinder im Alter von 6 – 12 Jahren bis zu 20 Minuten, für Jugendliche und Erwachsene bis zu 30 Minuten.

In der kompositorischen Sportsparte Rock´n´Roll-Akrobatik (ZAUNER 1993) erfolgt die Dienstleistungserstellung „Trainieren" eigentlich fast immer in einem *mehrstufigen Kontaktvorgang* mit den Dienstleistungsnachfragern (Athleten), um ein präzises Abstimmen von Nachfrage und Angebot zu ermöglichen. Daraus resultiert ein mehrmaliger Wechsel von Phasen der Potentialproduktion, Teilverrichtung und Endkombination (STAUDACHER 1991). Diese zeitliche Strukturierung der Dienstleistungsproduktion wird als *Prozeßphasenstruktur* bezeichnet (KAUFMANN 1977). Am einfachsten läßt sich der mehrstufige Kontaktvorgang – stark vereinfacht – am Beispiel der Erstellung eines neuen, individuellen Tanzprogramms für den Wettkampfsport illustrieren (vgl. Kasten).

PROZESSPHASENSTRUKTUR DER ERSTELLUNG EINES TANZPROGRAMMES

- Das nach einem konkurrenzfähigen Programm nachfragende Tanzpaar teilt dem Trainer in der Turnhalle (1. Kontaktort) mit, daß es zuwenig Einfälle für die neue Choreographie hat (= Nachfragesituation).
- Der Diensteanbieter prüft die Figurenvorschläge des Paares auf ihre Umsetzbarkeit und nimmt eine erste Einteilung bzw. Reihung vor (= Problemanalyse bzw. erste Konkretisierung).
- Im Studio (2. Kontaktort) stellt der Betreuer gemeinsam mit dem Paar beim Videostudium (= Teilverrichtung) fest, welche Akrobatikfiguren von den konkurrierenden Paaren am häufigsten gezeigt werden. Das Ergebnis einer intensiven Diskussion ist die Zustimmung, neben den drei bisher fixen Akrobatikfiguren vier alternative Akrobatiken in das Programm aufzunehmen.
- Der Trainer baut selbständig (= Potentialproduktion) um die sieben Akrobatikfiguren ein komplettes Tanzprogramm (= Bearbeitung).
- Im Turnsaal (1. Kontaktort) präsentiert der Diensteanbieter seinen Dienstenachfragern das neuerstellte Tanzprogramm. Dem Paar sagt das Akrobatikprogramm zu. Bei der praktischen Umsetzung (= Teilverrichtung) tritt allerdings nach einigen Trainingseinheiten das Problem immer deutlicher auf, daß das Paar an mehreren Stellen der Choreographie die Figurenübergänge nicht hinreichend gut ausführen kann (qualitative Aspekte der Aktivität des externen Faktors!).
- Der Betreuer löst das Problem, indem er die störenden Elemente aus dem Programm herausnimmt und durch andere Figuren, die von alten Choreographien (= Austausch von internen derivaten Produktionsfaktoren) stammen, ersetzt (Potentialproduktion).
- Diese exemplarisch beschriebenen Vorgänge setzen sich in ähnlicher Art und Weise über viele Wochen fort (Prozeßphasenstruktur), bis der Dienstleistungsprozeß (Erstellung und Umsetzung eines konkurrenzfähigen Akrobatikprogramms) abgeschlossen wird und das Paar mit dem Leistungsergebnis "wettbewerbswürdiges Programm" beim Turnier auftreten kann.

---

3. STANDORTORGANISATION UND INTERNATIONALISIERUNG

Eine wesentliche Kernerkenntnis der Dienstleistungsgeographie besteht in der Tatsache, daß aufgrund der besonderen Produktionsbedingungen – insbesondere aufgrund der Einbeziehung des externen Faktors in den Produktionsprozeß und der daraus ableitbaren Aufgabe des Aufbaus einer entsprechenden räumlichen Kontaktorganisation – *besondere räumliche Organisationsformen* möglich/notwendig werden, die mit dem Begriff der *multiplen Standortorganisation* bezeichnet werden. Daraus leitet sich auch eine besondere Situation für die Internationalisierung solcher Unternehmungen ab, da ein Direktexport nur sehr bedingt möglich ist (ausländische Nachfrager, die im Inland Ausbildung konsumieren, Tätigkeit von Trainern im Ausland). Eine Internationalisierung erfordert also aktives Auslandsengagement in der Form von Direktinvestitionen oder von Kooperationen und ähnlichen „Neuen Formen".

3.1. Die multiple Standortorganisation von Rock´n´Roll-Akrobatik-Unternehmen

Die besonderen Produktionsbedingungen bei Dienstleistungen – bei der Rock´n´Roll-Akrobatik-Dienstleistung "Trainieren" ist es die notwendige Einbindung der Schüler und Jugendlichen in einen räumlich und zeitlich synchronen Phasenprozeß, der sich über längere Zeit erstreckt und nur bei entsprechender räumlicher Nähe realisiert werden kann – können in der Realität zu einer oder mehreren der folgenden *Grundvarianten der multiplen Standortorganisation* (STAUDACHER 1991) führen:

1. Die Integration von Potentialproduktion und Endkombination am Ort des Anbieters kann durch ein **Abholsystem** gekennzeichnet sein, wo der Dienstleistungsbetrieb einen fixen Standort hat, ohne daß zusätzlich mobile derivate Potentialfaktoren (etwa Vertreter) zur Verfügung stehen, und der mobile, externe Faktor nur mit Hilfe eines Abholsystems an der Diensteverrichtung teilnehmen kann (z.B. klassischer Einkauf beim Einzelhandelsgeschäft).

2. Die Integration am Ort des Nachfragers kann durch ein **Liefersystem** bewerkstelligt werden. Hier erfolgt die räumliche Integration der Produktion auf erster und zweiter Ebene dadurch, daß ein vollständig mobiler Dienstleistungsbetrieb agiert, der zum Standort des externen Faktors kommt und dort produziert (z.B. ständig mobile Wanderhändler).

3. *Vertretersysteme:* Ist einerseits die Potentialproduktion örtlich fixiert und andererseits der externe Faktor immobil, so werden im allgemeinen derivate Potentialfaktoren (Vertreter), die mobil sind, produziert, die nun das erforderliche Leistungspotential zum externen Faktor liefern und dort die nachgefragte Dienstleistungserstellung erbringen (z.B. Reinigen eines Gebäudekomplexes durch Reinigungspersonal = Vertreter).

4. *Kombinierte Standortsysteme:* Die Standorte der Endkombination können variabel bzw. alternativ gewählt werden, weil bei fixem Dienstleistungs-Betriebsstandort sowohl derivate Potentialfaktoren als auch der externe Faktor (oder sein Vertreter) mobil sind (z.B. Versandhandel, Führen einer Bergtour) (STAUDACHER 1994: 14).

5. *Medienkontakt:* Eine simultane Dienstleistungsverrichtung bei Vorlage von gespaltenen Produktionsaktionsplätzen in einem „virtuellen Raum" kann mit Hilfe medialer Kontakte erbracht werden (z.B. Datenbankdienste über Telefonleitungen).

Für die Rock´n´Roll-Akrobatik-Dienstleistungen läßt sich diese räumliche Organisationsform am Beispiel „Training" recht anschaulich darstellen (vgl. Abb. 2):

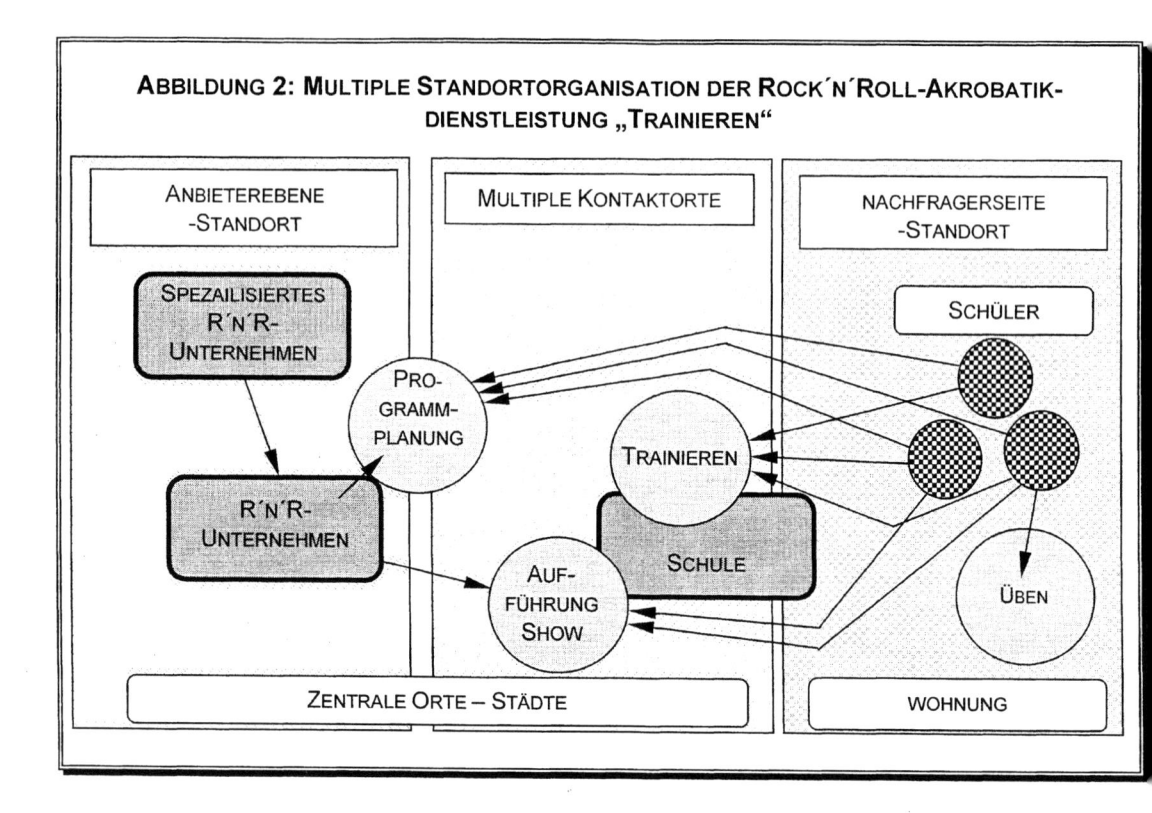

ABBILDUNG 2: MULTIPLE STANDORTORGANISATION DER ROCK´N´ROLL-AKROBATIK-DIENSTLEISTUNG „TRAINIEREN"

ANBIETEREBENE -STANDORT	MULTIPLE KONTAKTORTE	NACHFRAGERSEITE -STANDORT
SPEZAILISIERTES R´N´R- UNTERNEHMEN	PROGRAMMPLANUNG	SCHÜLER
R´N´R- UNTERNEHMEN	TRAINIEREN SCHULE AUFFÜHRUNG SHOW	ÜBEN
ZENTRALE ORTE – STÄDTE		WOHNUNG

- Das Training findet i.d.R. weder im *Büro* des Unternehmens noch in der Wohnung des Schülers, sondern in einem stundenweise angemieteten Turnsaal (= 1. Kontaktort) statt; d.h., daß zum einen

- die Trainer zur *Turnhalle* fahren und ihre technischen Hilfsmittel wie Musik- und Videoanlage mitnehmen müssen. Damit also die Dienstleistung Trainieren in der Turnhalle erstellt werden kann, hat das Dienstleistungsunternehmen einen *Teil des Dienstepotentials* (Trainer, Hilfsmittel) zu *mobilisieren* (die Turnhalle selbst ist klarerweise immobil).

- Die *Kontaktherstellung* zur Vereinbarung von Terminen erfolgt durch *Telefonate* (mediale Dienstleistungsproduktion).

- Der *externe Faktor* muß ebenfalls *mobil* sein, zum Training in die Turnhalle kommen, wobei recht beschränkte räumliche Reichweiten bestehen.

- Es gibt aber durchaus den Fall, daß die Beteiligten im *Büro des Unternehmens* (2. Kontaktort bei mobilem externen Faktor) sich zu Besprechungen über Tanzprogramme oder zum theoretischen Unterricht treffen.

- Das *Üben* von Trainingsteilen kann aber auch durch observatives Training per Videostudium ergänzt und in der *Wohnung* des Aktiven (3. Kontaktort bei mobilem Dienstepotential) durchgeführt werden.

- Aufführungen und Shows finden in *Veranstaltungshallen* oder anderen *Präsentationsorten* statt, an denen sich dann Schüler, Trainer usw. zusammenfinden.

Betrachtet man alle in der Realität vorkommenden Facetten des Trainings (Hauptkontaktort Turnhalle, zusätzlicher Kontaktort beim Anbieter bzw. externen Faktor), so liegt hier eindeutig die *multiple Standortorganisation* der kombinierten Standortsysteme vor. Bei Rock'n'Roll-Akrobatik-Unternehmen besteht wie bei sehr vielen Dienstleistungsunternehmen ein latenter Bedarf, das multiple Standortnetz durch die *Bildung eines plurilokalen Netzes* zu ergänzen oder zu ersetzen. Hält man sich allerdings den Umfang der Investitionen in die dauerhaften Knoten eines größeren Filialnetzes (z.B. Trainingshalle, Tanz-, Tontechnik-, Videotechnikstudio, Massageraum, Sauna, Hörsaal, Turnierveranstaltungshalle, ...) vor Augen, so wird rasch klar, daß das Vorhaben für Kleinunternehmen nicht realisierbar ist; derzeit gibt es auch keine solches Unternehmen.

Das Rock'n'Roll-Akrobatik-Unternehmen kann aber die Vorteile verschiedener Standorte (Marktnähe bzw. Kontaktvorteile) durch den Aufbau eines *flexiblen Standortnetzes* lukrieren, indem es Kooperationsformen ohne Kapitalbeteiligung (z.B. Schulungs- und Managementverträge) und Kooperationsformen mit Kapitalbeteiligung (z.B. Joint Venture mit Minderheitsbeteiligung) mit anderen Unternehmen eingeht bzw. auf Kooperationen setzt, die auf persönlichen Bindungen oder Abhängigkeiten von gesellschaftlichen oder politischen Elitegruppen (BRÖSSE 1993) oder diversen Berufs- und Freizeitvereinigungen basieren. Ruft man sich die bei den verschiedenen Dienstleistungen aufgetretenen Vernetzungen der Rock'n'Roll-Akrobatik-Unternehmung mit den übrigen Beteiligten (externer Faktor, andere Diensteanbieter, ...) in Erinnerung, dann kann man sich leicht vorstellen, daß die Netzknoten (Kontaktplätze, Betriebe, etc.) dieses dichten flexiblen Standortnetzes in Agglomerationsräumen liegen. Denn gerade diese zeichnen sich durch optimale räumliche Voraussetzungen für Versorgungssysteme (z.B. sportmedizinische Versorgung), eine räumliche Ballungen von Betrieben gleicher Branche (z.B. Konkurrenz von Rock'n'Roll-Anbietern) bzw. durch Betriebe mit funktionaler Komplementarität (z.B. Sportartikelhandel, Tontechnikstudio, Rechtsanwaltskanzlei) oder durch die Agglomerationsvorteile einer räumlichen Funktionsspezialisierung aus (z.B. Showstadt, Wettkampfstadt mit „Olympiahalle") (CHRISTALLER 1968, ISARD 1956, LÖSCH 1962, BÖKEMANN 1982, SCHÄTZL 1978, STAUDACHER 1984; u.a.).

3.2. Internationalisierung von Dienstleistungsunternehmen – Der US-Markt für Rock'n'Roll-Akrobatik-Unternehmungen

Die Frage der *Internationalisierung von Dienstleistungsunternehmen* wird hier am Beispiel eines fiktiven Modellunternehmens (vgl. oben) diskutiert. Die Standortwahl zählt neben der Länderwahl und der Kundensegmentierung zu den bedeutendsten Entscheidungen einer internationalisierungswilligen Rock'n'Roll-Akrobatik-Unternehmung, weil die Standortwahl mit einem großen Ressourceneinsatz verbunden ist. Während die Investitionen in das Humankapital (Trainer) in der ersten Phase der Internationalisierung im Vordergrund stehen, spielen Investitionen in Kooperationsformen mit Kapitalbeteiligung bzw. in örtlich fixierte Betriebe erst in späteren Phasen eine Rolle und werden hier daher nur am Rande erwähnt.

Die Standortentscheidung wird i.d.R. auf Basis einer Bewertung der erwarteten Erfolge und des Risikopotentials getroffen werden. Je höher das Gewinnpotential und je niedriger die mit der Geschäftätigkeit einhergehenden Risiken eines betrachteten Standortes sind, desto größer ist die Attraktivität desselben. Das Gewinnpotential bzw. die Risiken werden allerdings von mehreren Faktoren, die nicht vollständig im Entscheidungsprozeß berücksichtigt werden können, beeinflußt. Es können daher nur jene Faktoren Berücksichtigung finden, die aus der Sicht des konkreten Unternehmens relevant bzw. bedeutungsvoll sind (SCHÖLLHAMMER 1989).

3.2.1. Regionale Standortfaktoren und –anforderungen zur räumlichen Segmentierung der USA

Da bisher kein *Katalog von Standortfaktoren* für die Rock´n´Roll-Akrobatik-Sparte vorliegt, muß an dieser Stelle eine eigene Liste von regionalen Standortfaktoren und entwickelt werden. Die Liste berücksichtigt betriebliche *Struktur- und Strategievariable* genauso wie *dimensionale Aspekte*.

Zur Erstellung dieser Liste bietet sich als erster Schritt der *nachfrageseitige Ansatz* an: Zum Dienstleistungsabsatz ist bekanntlich die Integration des externen Faktors notwendig, d.h. es muß die (zunächst makro-räumliche) *Nähe zum externen Faktor* gesucht werden. Der externe Faktor muß bestimmte Merkmale und Fähigkeiten aufweisen, die durch die Sachzielorientierung des Unternehmens bestimmt werden. Im Fall des Sachziels Trainieren von Rock´n´Roll-Akrobatik Sportlern konnten bereits *soziale, demographische, sportliche und psychographische Merkmale* herausgearbeitet werden, die das relevante Kundensegment abgrenzen (5- bis 18-jährige Schülerinnen und Schüler, sportlich befähigt oder begabt, an neuen Sportarten bzw. koedukativer Teambildung in Paaren, Formationen interessiert). Aus der Perspektive des Formalziels Gewinnerwirtschaftung muß der Nachfrager zusätzlich ökonomischen Anforderungen genügen (Kunde gehört der gutverdienenden Mittelschicht an und besucht eine Privatschule) bzw. eine hohe regionale Dichte von Kunden mit den erforderlichen Merkmalen gegeben sein.

Aufgrund der oben angestellten Überlegungen kann man bereits ein *erstes räumliches Segmentierungskriterium* erkennen. Die für den sachlichen und ökonomischen Erfolg zwingend notwendige Existenz eines großen *Kundenpotentials* (mit den angeführten Merkmalen) ist nur in bevölkerungsreichen Regionen der USA, also z.B. in Kalifornien mit 30 Mio. oder New York mit 18 Mio. Einwohnern vorzufinden. Da aber die Privatschulen, deren Besuch ein Abgrenzungskriterium darstellt und die daher eine räumliche Orientierung ermöglichen, auch auf schuleigenen Campusgrundstücken in dispersen Räumen situiert sein können, muß erst überprüft werden, ob dies häufig der Fall ist. Vergleicht man die Einwohnerzahlen der Bundesstaaten mit der Anzahl der führenden Privatschulen (und deren angegebenen Schülerzahlen) für den jeweiligen Bundesstaat, so kann man feststellen, daß die Bevölkerungsdichte des Bundesstaates mit der Häufigkeit der Privatschulen positiv korreliert (Baratta et al. 1993, PORTER 1991).

Zum Erreichen des Sachziels Trainieren (und des Formalziels Gewinnerwirtschaftung) müssen weitere Umsatzträger eingesetzt werden: *Durchführen von Rock´n´Roll-Akrobatik Shows*, Ausrichten von Turnieren, Ausbilden von Trainern und Wertungsrichtern. Es ist für die Tanzschüler von eminenter Bedeutung, daß sie in Shows und bei publikumswirksamen Wettkämpfen auftreten. Das Durchführen von Shows soll aber nicht nur die Tanzschüler in ihrer sportlichen Entwicklung unterstützen, sondern auch die Nachfrage nach dem gesamten Dienstleistungssortiment des Rock´n´Roll-Akrobatik-Unternehmens multiplizieren. Daher wird sowohl das Erreichen eines maximal großen Zuschauerkreises als auch das Gewinnen der Aufmerksamkeit von „Schlüsselzusehern" (Showagenten, Manager großer Veranstaltungen, Tanzstudiobesitzer, Opinion Leaders, etc.) anzustreben sein. Die zweite, strategisch entscheidende Zuschauergruppe kann mit großer Wahrscheinlichkeit dort erreicht werden, wo sich ein regelrechter *Show-Markt* entwickelt hat. Im Sinne einer Unternehmenspolitik, die die nationale Erschließung des großen Inlandsmarktes USA ebenso wie die Eroberung asiatischer und lateinamerikanischer Märkte verfolgt, sind jene Regionen von strategischem Interesse, die ein Showzentrum mit internationaler und nationaler Bedeutung besitzen und daher auch eine tragende Nachfrage nach neuen Showangeboten haben.

Es sollten deswegen jene Regionen bevorzugt werden, wo eine *Agglomeration von internationalen und nationalen Showplattformen* existiert. Klarerweise sollte es sich um Showzentren handeln, die sich auf Tanz- und Akrobatikdienste spezialisiert haben. Die Shownachfrage kann grundsätzlich auch via Nutzung optischer Medien befriedigt werden, es werden jedoch zur Kontaktherstellung Agenten (SOENCKSEN 1992, LYNCH 1992)<D> gebraucht, die wiederum erst am regionalen Showmarkt persönlich kontaktiert bzw. von der Qualität der Showdienstleistung überzeugt werden müssen.

Neben der makroräumlichen Nähe zu den Nachfragern nach Training und Shows bzw. zu den Showdienstevermittlern ist die *Nähe zu Informationen* aus dem Showbereich (Informationen erhält man eher im persönlichen Vieraugengespräch als beim Telefonieren) genauso wichtig wie zu den *Teilmärkten der qualifizierten Trainer*. Die wegen des Tanzlehrerüberangebotes überwiegend nur teilzeitbeschäftigten Tanztrainer sind einerseits als Nachfrager der Dienstleistungen „Ausbilden zum Trainer bzw. zum Wertungsrichter" und andererseits als Dienstepotential (Assistenztrainer, Choreographen, Spezialisten einzelner Sparten, zukünftig leitende Trainer für Auslandsfilialen) für das Trainieren von Rock´n´Roll-Akrobatik-Sportschülern interessant (SOENCKSEN 1992). Es liegt auf der Hand, daß die Agglomeration von bereits ausgebildeten Trainern verwandter Sportarten in den relevanten *‚high skill'-Regionen*, die sich mit den Showmärkten räumlich überschneiden oder decken, gegeben ist.

Weiters ist die makroräumliche *Nähe zu den Kooperationspartnern* wie Tanzstudios und Privatschulen zu suchen, die über verrichtungsrelevante Potentialfaktoren wie Branchenwissen, Kontaktnetze, immobile Studioräume bzw. Turnhallen und Trainer- bzw. Lehrerpersonal verfügen. Zur Absicherung mehrerer Kooperationsalternativen wird das international tätige Rock´n´Roll-Akrobatik-Unternehmen gut daran tun, Regionen mit einer Agglomeration von Tanzstudios und Privatschulen zu wählen.

Ein sehr gutes *Image eines Bundesstaates* ist zwar einerseits für die Dienstleistungsproduktion nicht zwingend notwendig, wirkt sich aber andererseits auch nicht gerade geschäftsschädigend aus. Sollten zwei oder mehrere Regionen als gleich attraktiv bewertet werden, so gewinnt der Standortfaktor mit der geographisch geringeren *Entfernung zu Europa* in einer langfristigen Betrachtung zunehmend an Bedeutung: Transfer/Export/Reexport von Showtänzern, Wettkampfsportlern, Summercamp-Teilnehmern, Trainern, Wertungsrichtern, etc.

Strebt die europäische Rock´n´Roll-Akrobatik Unternehmung eine intensive Zusammenarbeit mit US Produktunternehmen (etwa der Sport- und Musikindustrie), die für die gegenständliche Sparte brauchbare Artikel produzieren und/oder verkaufen, an, so ist der Vorschlag der regionalen *Nähe zu potentiellen Sponsoren* jedenfalls diskussionswürdig.

Die oben formulierten *regionalen Standortfaktoren* sind nun zusammengefaßt dargestellt folgende:

- *hohe Dichte junger Privatschüler*, hohe Bevölkerungsdichte (vor allem Ost- und Westküste),

- *Showzentren von internationaler und nationaler Bedeutung* (international: Los Angeles, Kalifornien; New York, eher national: Orlando, Florida; Chicago, Illinois; Atlanta, Georgia),

- *Tanzzentren* (weltweite Bedeutung: New York),

- *Agglomeration von ausgebildeten Trainern* verwandter Sportarten (um Show- und Tanzzentren entstandene high skill Region: z.B. New York, Kalifornien),

- *Konzentration von Tanzstudios* (um Show- und Tanzzentren),

- *Agglomeration von führenden Privatschulen* (in wirtschaftlich starken, bevölkerungsreichen Bundesstaaten: z.B. Kalifornien, New York), sehr gutes Image (z.B. Washington State, Oregon, Kalifornien, Hawaii bzw. Massachusetts, Connecticut, New York; aufstrebend: Georgia, Arizona) (MATHIASON 1993),

- geographisch *geringe Entfernung zu Europa* (Ostküste) – eventuell Nähe zu Sponsoren der Sportartikel- und Musikindustrie (Westküste, Ostküste).

Überprüft man mit Hilfe der erarbeiteten Standortfaktoren die einzelnen Regionen, so erweisen sich die **Bundesstaaten New York und Kalifornien** als die vielversprechendsten Regionen, mit mittelfristig realisierbaren Marktentwicklungsmöglichkeiten in den benachbarten Bundesstaaten Connecticut, Massachusetts und Oregon, Washington State, Arizona bzw. Bedienung des Showmarktes in Las Vegas, Nevada. Weitere Inlandswachstumschancen können langfristig durch den mittelfristigen Aufbau von „Brückenköpfen" unter Ausnutzung der Zentren- und Hierarchiewirkungen von Chicago, IL und Detroit, MI zur Erschließung des nördlichen Teils des Mittleren Westens und Atlanta, GA zur Bearbeitung des südlichen Teils der Ostküste und des Südens der Vereinigten Staaten von Amerika geschaffen werden. Das Argument, daß in den Bundesstaaten New York und Kalifornien große und tüchtige Show- und Tanzkonkurrenz ansässig ist, soll nicht einfach mit dem Ausspruch „no risk no fun" vom Tisch gewischt, sondern dadurch entkräftet werden, daß die Rock´n´Roll-Akrobatik als ‚crazy' neue Show (FINN 1992) bestimmt nachgefragt wird und sie sich aufgrund der Vorbildwirkung durchsetzen wird (ZIERING 1992, LOVE 1992, ZEITVOGEL 1993, POMBERGER 1995).

3.2.2. Meso- und mikroräumliche Standortfaktoren und -anforderungen

Für die *Dienstleistung Trainieren* sind in der Praxis im wesentlichen folgende mehr oder weniger fix vorgegebene interne Infrastrukturen (permanent oder stundenweise angemietete Betriebe, selten im Eigentum) *für die Potentialproduktion* relevant: Büro, Endkombination: Turnhalle/Wiese einer Freisportanlage, Tanzstudioraum, Büro als Unterrichts-/Videostudioraum.

- Das *Büro für Management und Verwaltung* (mit Nebenräumen) muß eine hinreichende Flächengröße für das Erstellen von Tanzprogrammen oder das Zwischenlagern von transportablen Stereoanlagen, Videoanlagen und mobilen Tanzspiegeln aufweisen und könnte unter Umständen zunächst ein in einer Wohnung eingerichteter Büroraum sein. Das Büro sollte mit Telefon, Anrufbeantworter, Faxgerät, PC, Drucker, Fernsehapparat und den entsprechenden Anschlüssen ausgestattet sein. Trotz des hohen Mechanisierungsgrades in den USA ist darauf zu achten, daß Telefon und Faxgerät an einem Netz einer long distance Telefongesellschaft angeschlossen sind, über das auch mit dem Ausland Kontakt aufgenommen werden kann (Private lokale und regionale Netzwerksbetreiber haben nämlich nicht immer Verträge mit den Erhaltern von Ferngesprächsnetzen abgeschlossen!).

- Die erforderlichen physischen Gegebenheiten des *Turnsaals* können hier stichwortartig zusammengefaßt werden:
  - Hallenhöhe: lichte Höhe 6 – 8 Meter! Die Hallen, die diesen zwingenden Standortfaktor erfüllen, sind zu 95 % Schulsportsäle (MUELLER 1993), Federtuchspringen: 10 m; keine tiefhängenden Beleuchtungskörper, Rohre, etc.;
  - Saalfläche: pro Paar 5 x 5 m, (Sparvariante 3 x 3 m.) zum Vergleich: ein Basketballfeld hat mind. 24 x 13 m. und max. 28 x 15 m;
  - Art des Bodens: schwingender, federnder Untergrund z.B. Parkettboden, Tanzteppich, Gummi, (Wiese für Training im Freien):

- Art der Decke: geeignet für Befestigung von Deckenlongehalterungen (nur für obere Leistungsklassen), künstliche Beleuchtung:
- Ausstattung: Mindestanforderung: Matten (können dazugekauft werden) ideal: Federtuch:
- Zusatzräume: Mindestanforderung: Geräteraum, Garderoben, WC, Duschen; ideal: Massageräume, Sauna;
- Versorgungsanschlüsse: elektrischer Strom.

Aus den Produktionszielen, den notwendigen Produktionsfaktoren bzw. den Ansprüchen der Leistungserstellung lassen sich folgende *meso- und mikroräumlichen Standortbedingungen* ableiten:

- Neben der physischen Ausstattung sollten Büro und Trainingshalle an die **Infrastruktur des öffentlichen und individualen Verkehrs** gut angeschlossen sein, um einerseits rasch zu den in der Umgebung liegenden Standorten der Endkombination (Turnhallen, Tanzstudioräume, Showbühnen, etc.) zu gelangen und andererseits eine günstige Erreichbarkeit für die Tanzschüler zu gewährleisten (relative Kundennähe). Die Suche nach geeigneter Auftrittsmusik oder die langwierige Durchsicht von Videoaufnahmen kann nämlich aus praktisch-organisatorischen und aus Kostengründen nur im Büro durchgeführt werden. Die relative Bewertung des Standortpotentials des Büros drückt sich im Mietpreis aus, welcher als bestimmender Standortfaktor genau quantifizierbar ist und nach Maßgabe des Budgets der Rock´n´Roll-Akrobatik Unternehmung eine mehr oder weniger große Rolle spielt.

- Ob das **Büro** und der Tanzstudioraum eine **Zentren- oder Randlage** in der Hauptstadt eines attraktiven Bundesstaates haben, ist bei einer guten Anbindung an den Verkehr sekundär; primär ist die **Lage in oder in der relativen Nähe eines Showtanzkünstlerwohn- oder Showtanz-Bühnenviertels** interessant, um die Vorteile einer hohen Kontakthäufigkeit und Informationsdichte zu lukrieren, die Tanztrainerarbeitsmarktlage zu beobachten und eine Marktpräsenz zu signalisieren. Das Büro sollte eine Stadtlage haben, deren Adresse für den Kundenstock der Schüler führender Privatschulen akzeptabel, deren Image einigermaßen positiv und deren Kriminalitätsrate im US-weiten Vergleich niedrig ist.

- Neben den externen Ersparnissen, die sich aus den Lagevorteilen zur gesamten Tanzbranche als von ‚location economies' ergeben (z.B. Austausch von Akrobatik Know-how gegen Insiderinformation, Kooperation beim Produktionsengpaß Trainingshalle), werden auch **Vorteile aus der räumlichen Nähe zu komplementären Einrichtungen** gezogen (‚urbanization economies'): Dienstevielfalt (Kopierdienste, medizinische Versorgung, rechtliche Beratung für Versicherung, Verbands- und Unternehmensgündung, Berichterstattung der Medien, Friseur), Infrastrukturdichte der Stadt (Restaurants für Geschäftsessen, Wäscherei, Autoreparaturwerkstätte, Bank, Versicherung), Verbundproduktion (Tontechnikstudio, Schneiderei, Porträtfotograf).

- Angesichts der überschaubaren Anzahl an interessanten **Privatschulen** und der relativen Knappheit an Sporthallen (nicht jede Schule besitzt einen Turnsaal (ROSS/PATE 1987, SOENCKSEN 1992) muß das Rock´n´Roll-Akrobatik-Unternehmen besonders vorsichtig bei der Festlegung der bestimmenden Lagefaktoren und deren Überprüfung vorgehen.

- Damit es zur notwendigen **Integration des externen Faktors** (Sportschüler, Show-zuschauer) kommt, muß die Erreichbarkeit durch eine **günstige Verkehrslage** möglich gemacht werden. Die starke Zersiedelung und das nicht besonders gut organisierte öffentliche Verkehrswesen führte dazu, daß engmaschige Straßennetze für den Individualverkehr gebaut wurden. Als unmittelbare Folge ergibt sich für die Dienstleistungswirtschaft mit ihren Liefer- und/oder Abholsystem, daß die Standortorganisation ein entsprechend großes Kundenversorgungsgebiet sichern muß. Sofern es sich nicht um Internatsschüler handelt, werden die ‚students' der ‚primary' und ‚secondary schools' vorwiegend von den Eltern mit dem Privatauto zur Schule gebracht, mit dem Schulbus transportiert oder sie fahren selbst mit dem Auto (ab 16 Jahre), dem Motorrad und selten mit dem Fahrrad.

- Während die Sportschüler eine durchschnittliche **Anfahrtszeit** von bis zu einer halben Stunde zum Training akzeptieren, müssen die Trainer aufgrund der Größe des Einzugsgebietes für Trainer (50 km – 100 km Luftlinie vom Büro; SOENCKSEN 1992) mit einer Fahrzeit von einer Viertelstunde (Stadtzentrumslage der Schule) bis zu eineinhalb Stunden (Stadtrandlage, suburbane, periphere Lage, Campus am Land) rechnen. Show- und Turnierdienstepotentiallieferungen sind mit drei (Kinder) bzw. fünf (Jugendliche) Reisestunden in einer Richtung räumlich mehr (Auto) oder weniger (Flugzeug) limitiert.

- Neben dem Lagevorteil der **Agglomeration von Lehrern** vor Ort ist die positive **„Ausstrahlung" der Schule in die Umgebung** genauso relevant wie diverse Fernwirkungen aus meso- und makroräumlich entfernten Gebieten. Einerseits könnten Freizeit- und Unterhaltungsindustrien die jungen Kunden anziehen, ablenken bzw. binden, andererseits könnten diverse konkurrierende Anbieter geselliger Freizeitdienste (Konkurrenzschulen, Tanzstudios, Gemeindezentren, boy/girl scouts, ...) mit ihren Programmen der vergangenen Jahre die Bereitschaft zur aktiven geselligen Gestaltung der Freizeit der Kinder und Jugendlichen erhöht und damit den Boden für Rock´n´Roll-Akrobatik Dienste aufbereitet haben. Weitere bestimmende Lagefaktoren sind: positive Meinung zum Sport – nicht nur unter den Schülern, sondern auch in vielen anderen Gesellschaftsgruppen – und ein gutes Image des Tanzes und/oder der akrobatikverwandten Sportausübung; zumindest sollten diese Aktivitäten wohlwollend kommentiert werden.

5. ZUSAMMENFASSUNG – ERGEBNISSE

Für die *Dienstleistungswirtschaft* gibt es inzwischen einige wesentliche *wirtschaftsgeographische Grundkonzepte* (vgl. STAUDACHER 1991 ff), die als Grundlage von konkreten Untersuchungen des *Standortverhaltens* und der *Standortwirkungen* von Dienstleistungsunternehmen herangezogen werden können: gestufter Produktionsprozeß, Integration des externen Faktors, räumlich-zeitlich synchroner Kontakt, multiple Standortorganisation, Vernetzungsstruktur, etc. Auf dieser Basis wurde versucht, unter Einbeziehung praktischer Beispiele die Besonderheiten der *Rock´n´Roll-Akrobatik-Dienstleistungen* und die organisatorischen und räumlichen Konsequenzen für Rock´n´Roll-Akrobatik-Dienstleistungsunternehmen zu diskutieren.

Dabei ergibt sich eine klare *Bestätigung der Tragfähigkeit der bestehenden dienstleistungstheoretischen Grundkonzepte*. Am Beispiel eines modellhaft konstruierten, internationalisierungswilligen europäischen Rock´n´Roll-Akrobatik-Dienstleistungsunternehmens wurde dann das *Internationalisierungsproblem für Dienstleistungsunternehmen* diskutiert und eine räumliche Segmentierung des Auslandsmarktes USA durchgeführt. Es werden mögliche Problemlösungen der räumlichen Organisation solcher spezieller Dienstleistungsunternehmen herausgearbeitet: Konzept der Standortfaktoren / Standortpotentialanalyse; Dienstleistungsmarketing, branchenspezifische Standortanforderungen, internationale Netzbildung.

Literatur- und Quellenverzeichnis

BARATTA M. v. (Hrsg.): Der Fischer Weltalmanach 1994, Fischer Taschenbuch Verlag, Frankfurt am Main 1993.
BEREKOVEN L.: Der Dienstleistungsbetrieb. Wesen, Struktur, Bedeutung, Gabler Verlag, Wiesbaden 1974.
BOHUS J.: Sportgeschichte. Gesellschaft und Sport von Mykene bis heute, BLV Verlagsgesellschaft, München 1986.
BÖKEMANN D.: Theorie der Raumplanung, Regionalwissenschaftliche Grundlagen für die Stadt-, Regional- und Landesplanung, Wien 1982.
BRÖSSE U.: Netze, Netzwerke und Milieus in der Euregion Maas-Rhein, Aufsatz, Aachen 1993.
CHRISTALLER W.: Zentrale Orte in Süddeutschland. Eine ökonomische Untersuchung über die Gesetzmäßigkeiten der Verbreitung und Entwicklung der Siedlungen mit städtischen Funktionen, Darmstadt 1993, Nachdruck 1968.
CORSTEN H.: Betriebswirtschaftslehre der Dienstleistungsunternehmungen. Einführung, R. Oldenbourg Verlag, München/Wien 1988.
DICHTER E.: Neues Denken bringt neue Märkte: Analyse der unbewußten Faktoren, Umsetzung ins Marketing, Anregungen und Beispiele, Verlag Carl Ueberreuter, Wien 1991.
GUTENBERG E.: Grundlagen der Betriebswirtschaftslehre, Band 1: Die Produktion, 24. Auflage, Berlin 1983.
HASITSCHKA W./HRUSCHKA H.: Nonprofit-Marketing, Verlag Franz Vahlen GmbH, München 1982.
HASLINGER J.: Das Elend Amerikas. 11 Versuche über ein gelobtes Land, Fischer Taschenbuch Verlag, Frankfurt am Main 1992.
HUBER R.J.: Die Nachfrage nach Dienstleistungen, Verlag Dr. Kovac, Hamburg 1992.

ISARD W.: Location and Space Economy. A General Theory Relating to Industrial Location, Market Areas, Land Use, Trade and Urban Structure, New York 1956.

JOST J.: Allgemeine Trainingslehre, Skriptum, o.V., Weiz 1990.

KAUFMANN E.J.: Marketing für Produktivdienstleistungen, Thun Verlag, Frankfurt am Main 1977.

LÖSCH A.: Die räumliche Ordnung der Wirtschaft, Stuttgart 1962 (1944).

OBERHUBER R.: Staatliche Exportförderung im Dienstleistungsbereich. Grundlagen und Anwendungspraxis", Diplomarbeit, Wirtschaftsuniversität Wien 1987.

ÖRRV (Österreichischer Rock´n´Roll Verband): Turnierordnung des Österreichischen Rock´n´Roll Verbandes (ÖRRV), Fassung vom 16. Oktober 1993.

POMBERGER R.: Internationalisierung von Dienstleistungsunternehmen – US Markteintrittsmodell für die Rock´n´Roll-Akrobatik Sparte", Dissertation, Wirtschaftsuniversität Wien 1995.

PORTER SARGENT PUBLISHERS, INC: The Handbook of Private Schools. An Annual Descriptive Survey of Independent Education; seventy-second edition, Boston, Massachusetts, 1991.

RICHTER R.: Soziokulturelle Dimension freiwilliger Vereinigungen. USA, BRD und Österreich im Vergleich. In: VOIGT R. (Hrsg.): Beiträge zur Kommunalwissenschaft, Bd. 19, Minerva Publikationen, München 1985.

ROSS J.G./PATE R.R.: The National Children and Youth Fitness Study II. In: Journal of Physical Education, Recreation and Dance, Vol.58, 1987, No.9, p.51-56.

SCHÄTZL L.: Wirtschaftsgeographie 1, Theorie, 4. Auflage, Verlag Ferdinand Schöningh, Paderborn 1992.

SCHEUCH F.: Dienstleistungsmarketing, Verlag Franz Vahlen GmbH, München 1982.

SCHIERENBECK H.: Grundzüge der Betriebswirtschaftslehre, 11. Auflage, R. Oldenburg Verlag GmbH, München 1993.

SCHÖLLHAMMER H.: Internationale Standortwahl. In: MACHARZINA K./WELGE M.K. (Hrsg): Enzyklopädie der Betriebswirtschaftslehre, Bd. 12 Handwörterbuch Export und Internationale Unternehmung, Poeschel Verlag, Stuttgart 1989.

STAUDACHER C.: Dienstleistungsgeographie. Räumliche Polarisation und räumliche Integration in der Dienstleistungsgesellschaft, Service-Fachverlag WU, Wien 1991.

STAUDACHER C.: „Fremdenverkehrs-/Freizeit-Dienstleistungen". Ansätze zu einer Geographie der Tourismus- und Freizeit-Unternehmungen. In: Wirtschaftsgeographische Studien H.19/20, 1994, S.1-23.

STAUDACHER C.: Zentralörtliche Muster in alpinen Räumen. In: Wiener Geographische Schriften Bd. 59/60, 1984, S.122-132.

WÖHE G.: Einführung in die Allgemeine Betriebswirtschaftslehre, 17. Auflage, Verlag Franz Vahlen GmbH, München 1990.

Liste der Gesprächspartner

EDWARD FINN, teacher of gymnastics, partner of Satellite Gymnastics, Inc., New York, NY, 15.7. und 12.8.1992.

UTE FINN, teacher of gymnastics, partner of Satellite Gymnastics, Inc., New York, NY, 15.7. und 12.8. 1992.

STEVE LOVE, teacher, Lezly Dance & Skate School, New York, NY, 28.9.1992

RACHEL LYNCH, student at Sandra Cameron Dance Center, featured on ABC & NBC TV, New York, NY, 18.9.1992.

DR. JOHN R. MATHIASON, Deputy Director, Division for the Advancement of Women, UNO, New York, NY, 31.1.1993 und 27.6.1993.

ULI MUELLER, partner, Dreams of Florida, Fort Myers, Florida, 5.5.1993.

BENJAMIN SOENCKSEN, teacher, Stepping Out – Ballroom & Latin Dance Studios, New York, NY, 26.9.1992.

OLIVER ZEITVOGEL, Turniertänzer, Fellbach, Deutschland, 16.4.1993.

LEZLY ZIERING, teacher, director of Lezly Dance & Skate School, New York, NY, 29.9.1992.

Sonstige Quellen

MAG. UDO ERLACHER, staatlich geprüfter Lehrwart für Rock´n´Roll, Turniertänzer, Referat vom 12.12.1993 an der Bundesanstalt für Leibeserziehung Graz, Österreich.

FRANZ FRECH, Sportlehrer, Referat vom 23.10.1993 an der Bundesanstalt für Leibeserziehung Graz, Österreich.

MAG. MANFRED MOHAB, Sekretär der World Rock´n´Roll Confederation, Referat vom 9.9.1992 an der Bundesanstalt für Leibeserziehung Graz, Österreich.

DR. NEUBAUER, Psychologe, Referat vom 12.5.1994 an der Bundesanstalt für Leibeserziehung Graz, Österreich.

DR. SCHNEEWEIS, Richter, Referat vom 27.5.1994 an der Bundesanstalt für Leibeserziehung Graz, Österreich.

MAG. KARIN ZAUNER, staatlich geprüfte Lehrwartin für Rock´n´Roll, Turniertänzerin, Referat vom 4.3.1993 an der Bundesanstalt für Leibeserziehung Graz, Österreich.

ÖSTERREICHISCHE GESELLSCHAFT FÜR WIRTSCHAFTSRAUMFORSCHUNG

GESELLSCHAFTSNACHRICHTEN

Zusammenfassender Tätigkeitsbericht über die Jahre 1993/94 – 1998/99

(Fortsetzung der zuletzt im Heft Nr. 19/20 dieser Reihe erschienenen Tätigkeitsberichte)

1. Rahmenbedingungen der Gesellschaft

Seit September 1991 hatte die Gesellschaft in der Peter Jordan-Straße 6, 1190 Wien, in den Räumlichkeiten der Abteilung Praxisorientierte Wirtschaftsgeographie und räumliche Integrationsforschung („AWI") des Instituts für Wirtschafts- und Sozialgeographie der WU Wien, ihren Sitz. Die personelle und institutionelle Nähe zur genannten Abteilung hat sich im Berichtszeitraum bestens bewährt.

Die alljährlich gegen Ende Juni stattfindende „Gartenparty" in der Peter Jordan-Straße hat sich zum inoffiziellen „Jour fixe" vor allem der jüngeren ÖGW-Mitglieder entwickelt.

Ende September 1999 ist nun die erwähnte Abteilung in ein von der Wirtschaftsuniversität neu angemietetes Haus in der Roßauer Lände 23, 1090 Wien, übersiedelt. Dort wird auch die Geschäftsstelle der ÖGW ihren Sitz haben. Es ist zu hoffen, daß sich auch am neuen Standort die Aktivitäten weiter entfalten.

Zur Verbesserung der internen Kommunikation unter den Mitgliedern wird seit März 1996 das Mitteilungsblatt „ÖGW – AKTUELL" herausgegeben. Diese Publikation wird vom Generalsekretär Hofrat Dr. Fritz Benesch praktisch im Alleingang hergestellt und hat es bisher auf acht Folgen gebracht.

2. Forschungsprojekte, Exkursionen und andere wissenschaftliche Aktivitäten

Forschungsprojekte

Die im vorangehenden Band dieser Reihe (*Nr. 23, „5 Jahre AWI – ein Arbeits- und Leistungsbericht"*) angeführten anwendungsbezogenen Forschungsprojekte wurden weitergeführt. Neu hinzu kamen folgende Projekte:
- „Sanfte Mobilität" in Wiener Neustadt
- Dorfgasthaus und Dorfkaufmann in Niederösterreich
- Chancen des Tourismus in der Region Mödling
- Geographische Faktoren des Überschwemmungsrisikos
- Grundlagenforschung für das Stadtmarketing in Niederösterreich.

Exkursionen

- **USA – „Frontierland today"**, Doz. Dr. F. Jülg, Juni/Juli 1994

- **China–Exkursion**, Doz. Dr. K. Arnold, Oktober 1994
- **Baltische Staaten und St. Petersburg**, Doz. Dr. K. Arnold, Mai 1995
- **Israel–Jordanien–Exkursion**, Doz. Dr. K. Arnold, November 1995
- **Mexiko–Exkursion**, Doz. Dr. K. Arnold, März/April 1996
- **Sardinien–Exkursion**, Doz. Dr. Ch. Staudacher gemeinsam mit Prof. Dr. F. Rainer, Institut für Romanische Sprachen der WU, Mai 1996
- **Südafrika-Exkursion**, Doz. Dr. K. Arnold, Februar/März 1997
- **Slowakei–Exkursion**, Doz. Dr. Ch. Staudacher, Ass. Dr. A. Hofmayer, April/Mai 1997
- **Polen–Ostdeutschland–Exkursion**, Doz. Dr. F. Jülg, April/Mai 1998.

Wissenschaftliche Veröffentlichungen

Im Berichtszeitraum hat die ÖGW mehrere Bände der „Wirtschaftsgeographischen Studien" und Band 65 der „Wiener Geographischen Schriften" (Hofmayer, Räumliche vs. nichträumliche Strukturmerkmale als Einflußgrößen des Versorgungsverhaltens, 1997) veröffentlicht.

Die wissenschaftlichen Publikationen jener ÖGW-Mitglieder, die am Institut für Wirtschafts- und Sozialgeographie der WU tätig sind, werden alljährlich im „Geographischen Jahresbericht aus Österreich" angeführt, so daß auf eine Nennung an dieser Stelle verzichtet wird (bezüglich der Publikationen im Zeitraum 1991 bis 1996 vgl. das Verzeichnis in Band 23 dieser Reihe).

Über die wissenschaftlichen Veröffentlichungen der übrigen ÖGW-Mitglieder liegen leider keine systematischen Meldungen vor. Als ein Beispiel – unter wahrscheinlich vielen – sei angeführt, daß im Rahmen der WU-Jahrestagung 1998 Herr Mag. Harald Friedrich ein vielbeachtetes Referat über seine laufenden Untersuchungen zur Standortverlagerung der Wiener Industrie gehalten hat, das auch im Tagungsband publiziert wurde.

Sonstige wissenschaftliche Aktivitäten, Kooperationen

Dissertantenseminare: Mit Unterstützung der ÖGW finden seit 1995 speziell für die Dissertant/inn/en der Abteilung AWI mindestens einmal pro Jahr Wochenendseminare statt. Sie werden als Lehrveranstaltung „Oberseminar für Dissertanten aus Wirtschaftsgeographie (mit methodischen und wissenschaftstheoretischen Grundlagen)" von allen Dozenten der Abteilung gemeinsam abgehalten, meist unter Beteiligung ausländischer Wissenschaftler, und bieten den Doktoranden eine intensive individuelle Beratung in entspannter Atmosphäre. Bisher fanden die Seminare an folgenden Orten statt: Litschau (Feriendorf Königsleiten, 1995), Bad Loipersdorf (1996), Zeillern (Seminarzentrum im Schloß, 1997 und 1999), Badgastein (Sporthotel Sonngastein, 1998).

Kooperationen mit wissenschaftlichen Gesellschaften: Neben dem Schriftentausch, der Betreuung von Gästen aus dem In- und Ausland und ähnlichen Kontakttätigkeiten, die weiter gepflegt wurden, hat die ÖGW im Berichtszeitraum mit einigen wissenschaftlichen Gesellschaften bzw. Initiativen regelmäßige Kooperationen aufgebaut:

ATG (Arbeitsgemeinschaft Tourismus und Geographie): Beteiligung an den gesamtösterreichischen Diplomandenseminaren zur Fremdenverkehrsgeographie (Prof. Jülg, Prof. Staudacher);

VÖWA (Verband österr. Wirtschaftsakademiker): Kooperation im Bereich Veranstaltungen (Prof. Arnold);

Club Tourismus: Kooperation im Bereich Veranstaltungen (Prof. Arnold).

3. Vortragsveranstaltungen der ÖGW

Die Vortragsreihe „Kolloquium Raum und Wirtschaft" wurde weitergeführt; dazu gab es fallweise Symposien zu speziellen Themen (vgl. Studienjahr 1998/99).

„Kolloquium Raum und Wirtschaft", Studienjahr 1993/94

12.10.93 Bundesministerin Maria Rauch-Kallat: Das Spannungsfeld Ökologie – Ökonomie, Österreich als Vorreiter *(gemeinsam mit der Österr. Geogr. Gesellschaft)*

27.10.93 Mag. Metka Speš (Laibach): Umweltsituation in Slowenien

15.12.93 *Referate der L.Scheidl-Preisträger 1992/93 (vgl. Band 19/20)*

26.01.94 Mag. Stefan Sellschopp: Markteintrittsstrategien ausländischer Unternehmen in den chinesischen Markt

18.05.94 *Referate von L.Scheidl-Preisträgern*

Studienjahr 1994/95

30.11.94 Dr. Richard Plitzka (ECO-PLUS): Kulturtourismus in Niederösterreich

13.12.94 Dr. Walter Petrowitz: Panamakanal 1994, eigene Beobachtungen
(gemeinsam mit der Österr. Geogr. Gesellschaft)

11.01.95 Diavorträge über die großen Auslandsexkursionen 1994:
Die westlichen USA, ein Land voller Gegensätze (Doz. Dr. F. Jülg);
China – ein Gigant erwacht (Doz. Dr. K. Arnold)

05.04.95 Mag. Peter Christian Huber: Ladakh und Zanskar – ein traditioneller Lebens- und Wirtschaftsraum

03.05.95 Mag. Harald Friedrich: Wirtschaftliche Analyse von Golfsportanlagen an unterschiedlichen Standorten *(L.Scheidl-Preis 1994)*

17.05.95 Doz. Dr. Klaus Arnold: Osteuropa im Umbruch – eine Exkursion auf den Spuren der österreich-ungarischen Monarchie

21.06.95 Doz. Dr. Thomas Reichart (Nürnberg): Die räumliche Nische als innovatorischer Spielraum – Zur Genese von zwei Fremdenverkehrsformationen

Studienjahr 1995/96

08.11.95 Dr. Wolfgang Schwarz (NÖ Landesregierung):
Die Regionalpolitik der Europäischen Union und ihre Umsetzung in Österreich

22.11.95 Dipl.-Ing. Gerhard Fülöp (Österr. Bundesinst. f. Gesundheitswesen):
Österreichischer Krankenanstaltenplan 1994 (ÖKAP 1994)

06.12.95 Univ.Doz. Dr. Gerhard Palme (WIFO Wien):
Die Wettbewerbsfähigkeit der österreichischen Regionen

22.05.96 Hofrat DDr. Hans Lentner:
Die Stellung der ÖBB im Rahmen der EU

29.05.96 Mag. Erich Pifer (Casinos Austria AG):
Die Casinos Austria AG und ihre Unternehmenspolitik

12.06.96 Dr. Cem Kinay: Gulet Touristik, ein innovatives Unternehmen der österreichischen Reiseveranstalter-Branche

19.06.96 Univ.Doz. Dr. Lothar Beckel (Fa. GEOSPACE):
Wirtschaftsgeographische Informationen durch Satelliten-Erdbeobachtung

Studienjahr 1996/97

16.10.96 Prof. Mag. Werner Jungwirth: Das Regionale Innovationszentrum in Wiener Neustadt: ein Beispiel für Initiativen zur regionalen Entwicklung

23.10.96 *Referate der L.Scheidl-Preisträger 1995:*
Mag. Dr. Roland J. Schachl: Das internationale Kooperations-, Forschungs- und Innovationspotential der Wiener Wirtschaft;
Mag. Dr. Robert Pomberger: Die Internationalisierung von Dienstleistungen am Beispiel von Rock'n'Roll-Akrobatik

06.10.96 Doz. Dr. Klaus Arnold und Diplomanden: Südafrika – Wirtschaftsraum der Zukunft?

22.11.96 Oberrat Dr. Peter Fritz (WU): Wienerwald ade? Ein stadtnahes Landschaftsschutzgebiet im Spannungsfeld ökonomischer Interessen

15.01.97 Hofrat Dr. Fritz Benesch: Die Raab-Ödenburg-Ebenfurther Eisenbahn und die Badner Bahn: Beispiele erfolgreicher Betriebsführung

21.05.97 *Referate von zwei L.Scheidl-Preisträgerinnen 1996:*
Mag. Nina Pichler: Ökologische Probleme der Lagune von Venedig;

Mag. Angelika Saul: Lebensqualität in städtischen Randlagen: eine empirische Untersuchung von Stammersdorf (Wien)

Studienjahr 1997/98

15.10.97 Univ.Prof. Dr. Wigand Ritter (Univ. Nürnberg):
Umbrüche im Welthandel und Geographie der Globalisierung

29.10.97 Abg. z. NR Peter Marizzi / AOProf. Dr. Klaus Arnold:
Restrukturierung der Alten Industrieregion Niederösterreich-Süd

05.11.97 Bürgermeister Ing. Heinrich Eder (Katzelsdorf): Dorferneuerung in Österreich am Beispiel der Gemeinde Katzelsdorf

12.11.97 Staatssekretär Dr. Peter Wittmann: Kulturpolitik in Österreich

03.12.97 Dr. Fritz Wehdorn (VÖI Wien - Niederösterreich):Wirtschaftsstandort Niederösterreich

21.01.98 Renate Moser (Rheintalflug AG): Regionalflugmarkt in Europa – 'Star Alliance' mit Lufthansa

13.05.98 Ing. Hans Stefan Augustin: Indochina, eine Region im Umbruch (Reisebericht)

03.06.98 Prof. Dr. Thomas Reichart (Univ. Regensburg / Nürnberg):
Andorra – Bedrohtes Wirtschaftswunder in den Pyrenäen

10.06.98 *Referate von zwei L.Scheidl-Preisträgern 1996 und 1997:*
Mag. Dr. Ingrid Binder: Standort, Produkt- und Branchenlebenszyklus als Faktoren des Unternehmenserfolges;
Mag. Martin Paulik: Das zyklische Phänomen im Fremdenverkehr am Beispiel des Ötscherlandes

17.06.98 AOProf. Dr. K. Arnold, Mag. Alexander Rief, Mag. Andrea Schröttner, Mag. Thomas Wiedner: Die baltischen Staaten im Aufbruch: ein wirtschaftsgeographischer Länderbericht

Studienjahr 1998/99

11.11.98 Mag. Dr. Josef H. Behofsics: Globalisierungstendenzen intermediärer Dienstleistungen *(L.Scheidl-Preis 1997)*

09.12.98 Univ.Prof. Dr. Wolfgang Kromp (Universität Wien):
Aspekte der Risikoforschung von Atomreaktoren

20.01.99 AOProf. Dr. Klaus Arnold, Dr. Albert Hofmayer (beide WU):
Einkaufsverhalten in Niederösterreich 1998 – Regionale Fallstudien

27.01.99 Birgit Hauke, Frank Reichelt (Frankona Rückversicherung München):
Risikomanagement von Naturgefahren am Beispiel von Stürmen in Europa

24.03.99 Univ.Prof. Dr. Helga Kromp-Kolb (Inst. f. Meteorologie, BOKU Wien):
Das Risiko von Kernkraftunfällen und ihre Schadensausbreitung

26.05.99 Bürgermeister Kurt Lentsch (Neusiedl a. S.):
Neusiedl am See – der Strukturwandel einer burgenländischen Stadt

28.05.99 **ÖGW-Symposium „Innovativer Tourismus",** *mit Referaten von*
Dr. Cem Kinay: GTT, der innovative Weg bei den österreichischen Reiseveranstaltern;
Mag. Helmut Peter (Hotelier): Destinationsmanagement in Österreich;
Mag. Rudolf Mertl (ÖW): Zukunftsstrategien im österreichischen Tourismus;
Mag. Ludwig Morasch: Infotainment-Centers – die neue Welt des Tourismus

02.06.99 Ing. Hans Stefan Augustin: Patagonien und Feuerland (Reisebericht)

4. Nachrichten aus dem Vorstand und den Hauptversammlungen

4.1. Neubesetzungen wichtiger Funktionen und personelle Veränderungen im Vorstand

In den letzten Jahren hat sich der Vorstand der Gesellschaft verjüngt, indem nach Ablauf von Funktionen junge Absolventen bzw. Dissertanten der Abteilung in den Vorstand kooptiert bzw. gewählt wurden. Derzeit sind folgende Personen im Vorstand mit konkreten Aufgaben vertreten:

AOProf. Dr. Klaus Arnold (Präsident); Hofrat Dr. Friedrich Benesch (Generalsekretär); Mag. Harald Friedrich; Dr. Albert Hofmayer; AOProf. Dkfm. Dr. Felix Jülg (Vizepräsident); Hofrat DDr. Hans Lentner; Dkfm. Maria Praxl; Mag. Martin Schwarz; Dkfm. Dr. Stefan Skowronek; AOProf. Dr. Christian Staudacher (Vizepräsident); Mag. Klaus Wilhelmer; Dkfm. Dr. Dieter Wintersberger.

Der Vergabemodus des Leopold-Scheidl-Preises wurde 1999 durch einen Vorstandsbeschluß neu geregelt. Unter den neu bestellten Juroren sind sowohl Vertreter der Wissenschaft wie auch der Wirtschaftspraxis aus dem In- und Ausland.

4.2. Mitgliederstand

Von rund 70 Mitgliedern im Jahre 1994 ist, dank aktiver Werbemaßnahmen und steigendem Interesse der Absolventen des Instituts, der Mitgliederstand auf derzeit (September 1999) rund 170 gestiegen. Diese erfreuliche Erhöhung bedeutet natürlich auch einen vermehrten Verwaltungsaufwand.

4.3. Finanzielles

Ehrenpräsident Prof. Sinnhuber hat der Gesellschaft aus Anlaß seines 80. Geburtstags eine Spende von ATS 50.000,-- zukommen lassen, welche zur Gänze zur Aufstockung der Mittel für den Leopold-Scheidl-Preis bestimmt ist. Seine Großzügigkeit möge Nachahmer finden!

Gegenwärtig laufen Bemühungen um die Anerkennung der Steuerabzugsfähigkeit von Spenden zugunsten der wissenschaftlichen Aktivitäten der ÖGW.

4.4. Personalia / Vorstandsaktivitäten

Auf Einladung von Hofrat DDr. Hans Lentner, Direktor der ÖBB-Direktion Villach, unternahm der Vorstand am 1./2. Juni 1996 eine äußerst gelungene Exkursion nach Slowenien und zum Zentralen Verschiebebahnhof Villach-Süd.

Eine ähnliche Exkursion, ebenfalls von Herrn DDr. Lentner gefördert, gab es im Mai 1997 nach Innsbruck, wo an der Universität die Überreichung des Goldenen Doktordiploms an Ehrenpräsident Prof. Sinnhuber (Promotion 1947) gefeiert wurde.

Erst ‚post festum' wurde der Redaktion bekannt, daß am 17. Dezember 1996 Herr Dkfm. Dr. Stefan Skowronek sein 60. Lebensjahr vollendet hat. Ähnlich überraschend kam der 60. Geburtstag des Generalsekretärs Hofrat Dr. Fritz Benesch im Juli 1997. Die Gesellschaft gratuliert beiden Vorstandsmitgliedern im nachhinein sehr herzlich und dankt ihnen namens aller Mitglieder für ihren unermüdlichen Einsatz.

Mit 1. Mai 1998 tritt AOProf. Dkfm. Dr. Felix Jülg als Universitätsbediensteter in den Ruhestand (er erlebte diesen Tag – wie könnte es bei ihm anders sein? – im aufreibenden Einsatz als Leiter einer Exkursion in Polen). Er bleibt jedoch dem Institut als Lehrbeauftragter und der ÖGW als Vorstandsmitglied erhalten. Die Gesellschaft ist dankbar, weiterhin auf seine große Erfahrung zurückgreifen zu können.

Am 10. Jänner 1999 vollendet Ehrenpräsident Prof. Sinnhuber in voller Frische sein 80. Lebensjahr. Bei der Feier im engeren Kreise in seiner Wahlheimat Gschwandt überbringt Prof. Staudacher die Glückwünsche der ÖGW. In akademischem Rahmen wird Sinnhubers Geburtstag durch das Festkolloquium am 15. Oktober 1999 begangen.

5. Bericht über den Leopold-Scheidl-Preis für die Jahre 1993 bis 1997[1]

Folgende Arbeiten wurden mit dem L. Scheidl-Preis der ÖGW ausgezeichnet (DA = Diplomarbeit, Diss = Dissertation):

---

[1] Die Entscheidung über den L.Scheidl-Preis 1998 stand zu Redaktionsschluß noch aus.

1993 **Silberbauer**, Horst: Das Projekt eines grenzüberschreitenden Technologie- und Innovationszentrums Österreich-CSFR: Voraussetzungen und Entwicklungsperspektiven ... (DA).
Schuscha, Barbara: Der Einzelhandel mit Bekleidung in Klagenfurt – Eine wirtschaftsgeographische Analyse des Angebotes und des Einkaufsverhaltens der Kunden (DA).
Török, Ilona M.: Wien und Budapest als „konkurrierende" Weltstädte in Mitteleuropa – Attraktivität und Bewertung als Standort internationaler Unternehmen (DA).

1994 **Friedrich**, Harald: Eine wirtschaftliche Analyse von Golfanlagen in peripheren Räumen, sowie deren Entwicklungschancen und regionale Auswirkungen unter Berücksichtigung des Nachfrageverhaltens der Golfspieler (DA).
Rath, Christine: Mögliche Restriktionen land- und forstwirtschaftlicher Nutzung in einem künftigen Nationalpark Donauauen (DA).
Schwarz, Martin: Die Fußgängerzone als Planungsinstrument und deren Auswirkungen auf Kernbereiche einer Stadt unter besonderer Berücksichtigung des Dienstleistungssektors – Fallstudie Dornbirn (DA).
Wittmann, Eva: Möglichkeiten und Chancen einer Grenzregion zwischen Österreich und der Slowakei (DA).

1995 **Pomberger**, Robert: Internationalisierung von Dienstleistungsunternehmen – US-Markteintrittsmodell für die Rock`n`Roll-Akrobatik-Sparte (Diss).
Schachl, Roland J.: Das internationale Kooperations-, Forschungs- und Innovationspotential der Wiener Wirtschaft und seine Veränderung im Zuge der EU-Integrationsbestrebungen Österreichs am Beispiel von Wiener Industrie-, Gewerbe- und Dienstleistungsunternehmungen (Diss).

1996 **Binder**, Ingrid: Externe und interne Faktoren zur Bestimmung des Unternehmenserfolges mit Untersuchungsschwerpunkt auf standortbezogene Qualitätsmerkmale (Diss).
Kaspar, Robert: Die Entwicklung von Wintersportgroßveranstaltungen in Zielrichtung Umwelt (Diss).
Pichler, Nina: Die ökologischen Probleme der Lagune von Venedig (DA).
Saul, Angelika: Lebensqualität in städtischen Randlagen: Eine empirische Untersuchung von Stammersdorf (Wien) (DA).

1997 **Behofsics**, Josef H.: Internationalisierung von Wirtschaftsdiensten [...] (Diss). [2]
Paulik, Martin: Das zyklische Phänomen im Fremdenverkehr, am Beispiel des Ötscherlandes (DA).
Wachter, Heribert: Nutzungsintensitäten von Leichtathletiksportanlagen (DA).

---

[2] Diese Dissertation wurde inzwischen in Buchform vom Gabler-Wirtschaftsverlag publiziert.

Verzeichnis der Autoren und Mitarbeiter dieses Bandes

AoProf. Doz. Dr. Klaus Arnold, Abteilung Angewandte Regional- und Wirtschaftsgeographie, Wirtschaftsuniversität, Rossauer Lände 23, A-1090 Wien; E-Mail: arnold@wu-wien.ac.at

Emer. Prof. Dr. Alois Brusatti, Alt-Rektor der Wirtschaftsuniversität Wien, Mariengasse 3, A-2500 Baden.

Prof. Dr. Dr. Francis W. Carter, School of Slavonic and East European Studies, University of London, Senate House, Malet Street, London, WC1E 7HU; E-Mail: cartom@clara.co.uk

Docent Dr. Bolesław Domański, Institute of Geography, Jagiellonian University, Grodzka 64, PL 31-044 Kraków; E-Mail: bdoman@arsenal.geo.uj.edu.pl

Maynard Weston Dow, 44 Towne Road, Bristol, NH, USA 03222; E-Mail: MWD@mail.plymouth.edu; Website: http://oz.plymouth.edu/~mwd.

Dr. Albert Hofmayer, Abteilung Angewandte Regional- und Wirtschaftsgeographie, Wirtschaftsuniversität, Rossauer Lände 23, A-1090 Wien; E-Mail: hofmayer@wu-wien.ac.at

Univ.-Doz. Dr. Peter Jordan, Österreichisches Ost- und Südosteuropa-Institut, Josefsplatz 6, A-1010 Wien. E-Mail: peter.jordan@rs6000.univie.ac.at

Dr. Elke Knappe, Institut für Länderkunde, Schongauer Straße 9, D-04329 Leipzig, Deutschland; E-mail: knappe@ifl.uni-leipzig.de

Emer. Prof. Dr. Dr. h.c. Walter Manshard, p. Adr. Institut für Kulturgeographie der Universität, Werderring 4, D-79085 Freiburg im Breisgau.

Mag. Dr. Robert Pomberger, Anzengrubergasse 13, 1050 Wien.

Emer. Prof. Dkfm. Dr. Wigand Ritter, p. Adr. Lehrstuhl für Wirtschafts- und Sozialgeographie der Universität, Lange Gasse 20, D-90403 Nürnberg.

Emer. Prof. Mag. Dr. Karl A. Sinnhuber, Maierhof 13, A-4816 Gschwandt bei Gmunden, Österreich.

Prof. William Stanley, Department of Geography, University of South Carolina, Columbia, SC, USA 29208; E-mail: stanleyb@garnet.cla.sc.edu

AoProf. Doz. Dr. Christian Staudacher, Abteilung Angewandte Regional- und Wirtschaftsgeographie, Wirtschaftsuniversität, Rossauer Lände 23, A-1090 Wien; E-Mail: staudach@wu-wien.ac.at